The Welsh Highland Railway
(Light Railway) Co NWNG Section

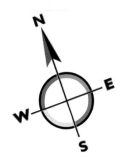

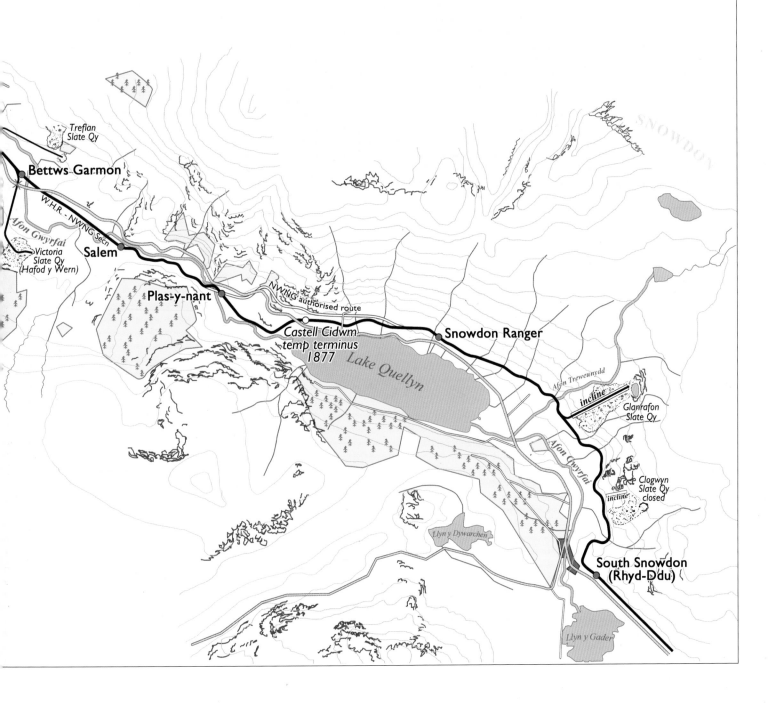

Treflan
Slate Qy

Bettws Garmon

W.H.R. - NWNG Secn

Afon Gwyrfai

Victoria
Slate Qy
(Hafod y Wern)

Salem

Plas-y-nant

NWNG authorised route

Castell Cidwm
temp terminus
1877

Lake Quellyn

Snowdon Ranger

Afon Treweunydd

incline

Glanrafon
Slate Qy

Afon Gwyrfai

old
incline

Clogwyn
Slate Qy
closed

Llyn y Dywarchen

South Snowdon
(Rhyd-Ddu)

Llyn y Gader

SNOWDON

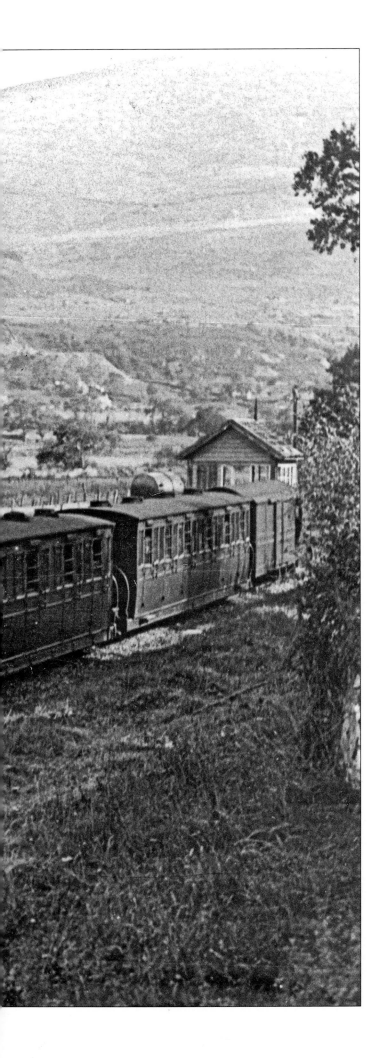

An Illustrated History of the

Welsh Highland Railway

2nd Edition

Peter Johnson

An imprint of
Ian Allan Publishing

First published 2002
Reprinted 2004 and 2006
Revised second edition first published 2009

ISBN 978 0 86093 626 8

© Peter Johnson 2007/2009

Published by Oxford Publishing Co

an imprint of Ian Allan Publishing Ltd, Hersham, Surrey KT12 4RG.
Printed in England by Ian Allan Printing Ltd, Hersham, Surrey
KT12 4RG.

Code: 0904B/

Visit the Ian Allan Publishing website at www.ianallanpublishing.com

Front cover: **The Festiniog Railway's England 0-4-0ST *Palmerston*
with a train of FR stock on test on the newly completed Welsh
Highland Railway in 1923.** *Author's collection*

Back cover, top: **Seen from the ramparts of Caernarfon Castle the
site of the WHR's 1997 terminus can be seen in standard gauge
days.** *Tuck /Author's collection*

Back cover, bottom: **Carnarvonshire location map, 1840.**
R. Creighton, *Lewis's Topographical Dictionary*, extract/
Author's collection

Endpapers: **The course of the Welsh Highland Railway and
associated branches.**

Above: **The Armco bridges at Portreuddyn, OB216 and 217 in
construction speak, will be distinctive features on the restored
WHR. With Porthmadog in the background OB217 was seen on
30 June 2008.**

Half title page: **Rhyd Ddu is the location of this view of *Gowrie* and
its train, c1910. The box of Mr Tate's cubed sugar was presumably
in transit.** *Author's collection*

Title page: **In 1923 a sequence of publicity photographs was taken
of *Palmerston* with a train of FR stock on the NWNGR section of
the Welsh Highland Railway, as seen here at Waenfawr.** *Author's
collection*

Below: **Under moody skies, *Prince* was photographed heading
towards Beddgelert at Cae'r Gors during a photographic charter
on 26 October. The train has just crossed the watershed, where the
descent to Beddgelert and Porthmadog starts.**

Contents

Introduction 6

Acknowledgements 6

Miscellanea 8

Chapter 1   **Development of the Route – 1863-1914** 9

Chapter 2   **The Creation of the Welsh Highland Railway – 1914-22** 44

Chapter 3   **Completing the Portmadoc–Dinas Railway – 1922-23** 53

Chapter 4   **The Welsh Highland Railway – 1923-37** 63

Chapter 5   **The Liquidation and Revival Proposals – 1937-90** 88

Chapter 6   **Rebuilding the Welsh Highland Railway – 1991-2009** 103

Chapter 7   **Locomotives, Rolling Stock and Infrastructure** 121

Appendix 1   **NWNGR Tonnages 1883-84** 136

Appendix 2   **NWNGR Revenue 1877-1918** 136

Appendix 3   **NWNGR Traffic 1877-1915** 137

Appendix 4   **CPR Traffic and Receipts 1904-19** 138

Appendix 5   **WHR Traffic and Receipts 1922-33** 139

Bibliography 142

Index 143

his page: **The WHR's new line across Porthmadog was used for the first time on 12 March 2009. At 05.37, in light rain, the FR's Funkey** *Vale of Ffestiniog* **hauled a train comprising the new Pullman observation carriage, the Romanian carriage and brake driving trailer No 111 across the Britannia bridge (below, left). Later that morning the loco was photographed on the Network Rail crossing, with engineers keeping a close eye on the wheel/rail interface.**

Introduction

For more than 100 years railway promoters have dreamed of linking the historic market town of Caernarfon with the slate port of Porthmadog by narrow gauge railway, but it is only with the completion of the restoration of the Welsh Highland Railway in 2009 that their dream is fulfilled. The remarkable route through the centre of the Snowdonia National Park and the scale of the enterprise has caught the imagination of public and railway enthusiasts alike. The link to the Festiniog Railway, with trains crossing the Network Rail line to Pwllheli on the level and then the main road at Porthmadog, adds to the interest.

The Welsh Highland Railway was a child of the 1920s but its origins go back to the earliest days of railways in Wales, and the desire to preserve and restore trains to it has existed for more than 40 years.

Historically, the route was an amalgamation incorporating the North Wales Narrow Gauge Railways and the Portmadoc, Beddgelert & South Snowdon Railway. The former comprised a main line from Dinas, three miles from Caernarfon, to Rhyd Ddu, with a branch to Bryngwyn serving quarries in the Nantlle Valley. In 1920 the 12 miles of railway were moribund. The latter comprised part of the horse-worked Croesor Tramway from Porthmadog and some partially constructed sections of railway around Beddgelert which had been abandoned since 1906.

The WHR promoters took control of these railways and obtained loans from the government and local authorities to complete the unfinished works and unite them as a job-creation scheme. They also took over the Festiniog and Snowdon Mountain Railways with the idea of creating an independent railway group – this was the time of the main line railway grouping. Like its predecessors, the WHR did not have a happy existence and proved to be a triumph of optimism over reality. It was taken over on a lease by the FR in 1934 and was not reopened after the 1936 season.

Embroiled in a legal quagmire, the movable assets were requisitioned in 1941, the track was lifted, the locomotives and rolling stock sold and, mostly, scrapped.

A proposal that the railway should be taken over by enthusiasts was first made before the Second World War. Despite continuous effort since the 1960s, and in the face of controversy and opposition from many sources, it was only in 2000 that the first trains ran on part of the WHR trackbed. In reversals of history, the Festiniog Railway had taken over the WHR revival and financed the works with grants from public funds and gifts from generous benefactors and supporters.

In reviving the railway, the former standard gauge trackbed between Dinas and Caernarfon, part of the Carnarvonshire Railway, itself incorporating part of the route of the Nantlle Railway, another horse-worked narrow gauge line, was added, fulfilling the ambition to extend the narrow gauge into Caernarfon, under the lee of the famous castle.

There are many strands in the WHR's story, rarely straightforward and with a constant sense of déjà vu. It is a fascinating railway with a charismatic and complicated history that captures the imagination. Although its reconstruction has been a saga of intrigue, disputes, court cases and public inquiries, it has also been a great achievement in fund-raising and construction terms. In stark contrast to the inter-war years, the WHR has made, and is making, a positive contribution to the economy of Gwynedd too. Let us hope that this time the Welsh Highland Railway fulfils all the ambitions of its promoters and supporters.

Acknowledgements

My serious interest in the WHR started in 1995, when I was asked to draft what became the 1999 WHR Transport & Works Order, that vital legal document that sanctioned the reconstruction between Dinas and Porthmadog. The commissioning of *A Portrait of the Welsh Highland Railway*, published in 1999 and reprinted in 2000, focused my attention on the WHR's history. The first edition of this book, published in 2002 and reprinted twice, took me to the Gwynedd Archives at Caernarfon and the Public Record Office, now the National Archives, at Kew. At the former I found much material concerning the former Caernarvonshire County Council's dealings with the WHR. At the latter I made use of Treasury, Treasury Solicitor's, Board of Trade, Ministry of Transport, Ministry of Town & Country Planning, Ministry of Housing & Local Government and Welsh Office files, with material dating back to the 19th century shedding light on many aspects of the WHR's development and its demise.

The Insolvency Service (IS), formerly the Official Receiver, gave access to material relating to the post-1941 receivership.

In the first edition I remarked that 'some answers are still out there waiting to be discovered' which has proved to be the case. Shortly after publication the IS found some very useful historical material, but not the WHR company minute book which was in the service's possession in 1993 and which has apparently been mislaid. Before it was deposited in the Gwynedd archives at Caernarfon some of this material was copied by the WHR Heritage Group and John Keylock provided copies.

John also loaned me photocopies of the North Wales Power & Traction Company minutes, a document that explains that company's involvement with the Portmadoc, Beddgelert & South Snowdon Railway and which, with the aid of a key document contained in the IS collection, explains how the North Wales Narrow Gauge Railways came to acquire the Hunslet locomotive *Russell*.

The collection of the solicitors T. D. Jones is held at the National Library of Wales, Aberystwyth; with a practice in London's Fleet Street and its founder born in Llanuwchllyn, the firm was well placed for attracting Welsh clients, including Carnarvonshire County Council, accumulating six boxes of material relating to the WHR, mostly covering the period from the 1920s until 1956, but including copies of some older material not seen elsewhere. Of particular interest was correspondence with the GWR concerning the use of the crossing at Portmadoc.

Returning to the National Archives, I found several files not previously catalogued. These included material dealing with the WHR's funding, construction and opening, including links to Wales' most famous politician, David Lloyd George, and copies of the construction certificates. Freedom of Information Act requests produced more files dealing with the receivership and one dealing with Trackbed Consolidation Ltd's attempt to bring the WHR company out of receivership.

At the House of Lords Records Office I saw plans and estimates deposited with the submission of Parliamentary bills and the transcripts of several opposed private bill committee cross-examinations. It was a real journey of discovery, reading the words spoken by James Chomeley Russell about his involvement with the North Wales Narrow Gauge Railways, by Hugh Beaver Roberts explaining his reason for building the Croesor Tramway, and by the engineer LeFevre explaining the origins of the Beddgelert Railway and Thomas Savin's involvement in it.

The FR Company minute books and the Boston Lodge repair books tell the story of *Palmerston's* use on the NWNGR construction contract. The minutes also contain material that helps to fill out the WHR story during the 1920s and 1930s.

The archives of the *London Gazette*, the *Scotsman*, the *Guardian* and *The Times*, available on the internet, were also useful. A small number of newspapers were viewed at the Newspaper Library at Colindale.

Additional insight into some of the correspondence seen at Gwynedd Archives in 2001 was obtained from the Carnarvonshire County Council minutes, also available at Caernarfon.

This new material has enabled me to revise text throughout the book and to correct a few misconceptions that had been perpetuated or perpetrated. The more I look at archive material the more I realise that it is unwise to impose 21st century, or even late 20th century, values on earlier times. I hope that I have avoided that pitfall and remain responsible for any errors of fact or misinterpretation. There are still some answers out there waiting to be discovered, but not as many as there were.

The paucity of relevant historical photographs means that some of the photographs used here are old friends, although it has been possible to find some new illustrations for this edition. I am particularly grateful in this respect to Adrian Gray, the FR's Archivist, and John Keylock, of the Welsh Highland Railway Heritage Group, for once again providing access to the photographic collections in their care and for the help and support they give me.

In the first edition I also acknowledged help and support received from: W. John Brown; Jonathan Clay; Tony Harden; Wyn Hobson; John Hopkins; Peter Jarvis and his wife Sue; David Allan of the Welsh Highland Railway Heritage Group; the late Roger Kidner, the founder of the Oakwood Press; Derek Lystor; David Perrin; John Sreeves; and Welsh Highland Railway Ltd.

To this list I now add Pat Ward for the provision of material from the FR archives; Sir William 'Bill' McAlpine Bt, for providing material from his family archive; Michael Bishop, who tracked down the NWPTC minutes and other PBSSR material; Sandy Ross, who made available copies of Welsh Highland Railway Society documents of the 1960s; Howard and Rosemary Wilson, who gave access to the Boston Lodge activities record for 1936 that they had found in the late Norman Pearce's collection, and my 'financial adviser', Peter 'Fuzz' Jordan, for his valiant attempts to explain the intricacies of railway company accountancy over the phone.

Gordon Rushton has once again done me proud in providing the splendid endpapers. Although the WHR crest is a figment of his imagination it is the sort of thing the old railway would have had if there had been money to pay for transfers.

I am grateful to the directors and officers of the Festiniog Railway Company and the trustees of the Festiniog Railway Trust for their interest and support over the years; any opinions expressed are mine and not theirs. Since the reconstruction started in 1997, I have received a warm welcome from personnel at the Dinas office and on site, whether employed, volunteer and contracting, and I thank them for it.

In the case of recent events, it may be too soon to determine what will be considered significant with the passage of time, but I hope that I have been able to strike a reasonable balance.

Peter Johnson
Leicester, March 2009

Unattributed photographs post-1970 taken by the author

To mark the completion of track laying and the efforts made by the volunteer track layers a 'golden bolt' ceremony was held close the connection of the WHR with the FR on 28 February 2009. Afterwards, before an admiring crowd Garratt No 87 became the first locomotive to steam from the FR to the WHR since 1936.

Miscellanea

Welsh place names

During most of the period covered by this book many Welsh place names were Anglicised. Over the last 40 years or so the Welsh forms have been restored. The archaic forms are used here where most appropriate. For clarification the places concerned are:

Bettws Garmon = Betws Garmon
Bettws y Coed = Betws y Coed
Carnarvon/Caernarvon = Caernarfon
Portmadoc = Porthmadog
Quellyn = Cwellyn
Waenfawr = Waunfawr
Rhyd Ddu is used when referring to the station throughout, regardless of its railway nomenclature.

Abbreviations

BoT	Board of Trade
BR	Beddgelert Railway
FR	Festiniog/Ffestiniog Railway
GWR	Great Western Railway
LNWR	London & North Western Railway
LRC	Light Railway Commission/Light Railway Commissioners
LRO	Light Railway Order
LMSR	London, Midland & Scottish Railway
The ministry	Ministry of Transport
MMR	Manchester & Milford Railway
MTRS	Moel Tryfan Rolling Stock Company Ltd
NA	National Archives
NWNGR	North Wales Narrow Gauge Railways
NWPTC	North Wales Power & Traction Company
PBSLR	Portmadoc, Beddgelert & Snowdon Light Railway
PBSSR	Portmadoc, Beddgelert & South Snowdon Railway
PCBTR	Portmadoc, Croesor & Beddgelert Tram Railway Co
SBLR	Snowdon & Bettws Light Railway
TWO	Transport & Works Order
WHR	Welsh Highland Railway
WHR(1964)	Welsh Highland Railway (1964) Company Ltd/Welsh Highland Railway Ltd

Currency and units of weight

£1 = 240d (pence) = 20s (shillings);
1s = 12d;
£1 guinea = £1 1s.
1 ton = 20 hundredweight (cwt);
1cwt = 4 quarters (qtr);
1qtr = 2 stone (st);
1st = 14 pounds (lb);
1lb = 16 ounces (oz)

The value of money

Equivalent value of £1 in 2008

1860	£43.16
1870	£45.70
1880	£48.31
1890	£49.89
1900	£57.06
1905	£57.35
1910	£57.06
1915	£43.06
1920	£21.21
1925	£29.97
1930	£33.42
1935	£36.98
1940	£28.72
1945	£25.95
1950	£22.78

Data extracted from the currency converter on the National Archives website: **www.nationalarchives.gov.uk/currency/**

In 1990 the FR decided that the revived WHR should tap into the existing tourist market in Caernarfon and take advantage of the former standard gauge formation between that town and Dinas. In 1828, the Nantlle Railway had been the first to use the route, seen here in the 1830s. *D. Cox & W. Radcliffe/Author's collection*

1

Development of the Route
1863-1914

The hinterland between Caernarfon and Porthmadog is mainly mountainous, forming a part of the Snowdon range. Amongst the rocks are veins of slate and some metalliferous ores of varying quality and usually of insufficient quantity to justify commercial extraction although there have been many attempts. The area has some low-level agriculture, mostly grazing sheep; in the vicinity of Porthmadog and Caernarfon the land supports some cattle. From Caernarfon, the Gwyrfai Valley provides a passage for road and railway before reaching the watershed, close to Pitt's Head, in the vicinity of the halfway point, and at 650ft above sea level it is not dissimilar to the altitude achieved by the Festiniog Railway over a similar distance between Portmadoc and Blaenau Ffestiniog. From the watershed the route follows the Afon Colwyn before joining the Glaslyn near Beddgelert. In 1871 the population of Carnarvonshire was 80,102, the towns mentioned being the largest centres; along the route only Waunfawr and Beddgelert had populations exceeding 1,200. Rhos Tryfan, served by the Bryngwyn branch, had a population of 2,000 in 1881.

Slightly beyond this area, the slate quarries in the Nantlle Valley, 10 miles from Carnarvon via Penygroes, had been rail-served since 1828 by the 3ft 6in gauge Nantlle Railway. This horse tramway was taken over by the Carnarvonshire Railway in 1867 and, between Carnarvon and Penygroes, incorporated into that company's route to Afon Wen. Close to the Nantlle quarries, on the north side of Moel Tryfan, was a small but significant cluster of quarries beyond the reach of the tramway.

There was considerable interest in expanding the area served by railways during the 1860s. In 1862 the Carnarvonshire Railway proposed a branch from Dinas to serve the Garreg Fawr quarry at Waenfawr. The Carnarvon, Beddgelert & Port Madoc & Carnarvon, Pen y Groes and Pwllheli & Nantlle Direct Railways was proposed to serve the places mentioned in 1864. Nothing came of the first, and the bill deposited for the second, with which the railway contractor and promoter, Thomas Savin, was involved, failed to pass Parliamentary standing orders.

In 1865, the Carnarvon & Llanberis Railway obtained powers to build a branch to Cae Gloddfa, Beddgelert, via Bettws Garmon. Its gauge could have been either 2ft 6in or standard. This scheme was formally abandoned by the LNWR in 1869.

The Nantlle Railway between Dinas and Caernarfon becomes of direct relevance to the WHR story only with its revival. Otherwise the oldest component of the Portmadoc–Carnarvon dream is the Croesor Tramway, a 4½-mile 2ft gauge horse-worked line that connected the quarries in the Croesor Valley with Portmadoc. It was built privately in 1863/4. The valley lies north of and parallel to the Vale of Ffestiniog and its quarries were close to those in the Tanygrisiau area served by the Festiniog Railway; in 1825 James Spooner had surveyed the Croesor valley for a railway to Portmadoc that was not built. The lie of the land was to prevent rail links being established with the FR because it would have required raising the loads several hundred feet. The tramway's proprietor was Hugh Beaver Roberts, originally a solicitor practising in Bangor. He was Lord Penrhyn's agent and had interests in several North Wales slate quarries, including Croesor Fawr, which he owned, and Braich (Moel Tryfan), which he leased.

Charles Easton Spooner, the FR's secretary and engineer, surveyed the tramway's route in 1863. A sale advertisement for Portreuddyn Castle, a house which overlooks the line near Prenteg, published in The Times on 11 April 1863 referred to 'railways' to Portmadoc harbour being in the course of

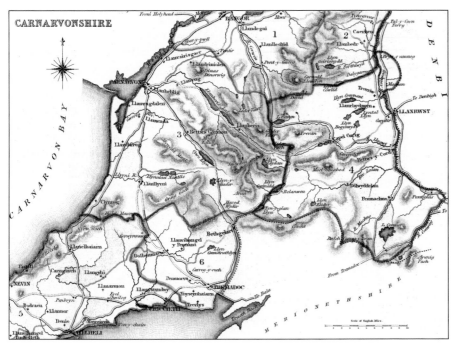

Carnarvonshire location map, 1840.
R. Creighton, Lewis's Topographical Dictionary, extract/Author's collection

Right: **To the left of Portmadoc flour mill, slightly left of centre, the Croesor Tramway can be seen crossing the Cambrian Railways line to Pwllheli on the outskirts of Portmadoc, c1900. The rock called Ynyscerrigduon referred to in the Croesor & Portmadoc Railway 1865 Act of Parliament is on the centre-right of the photograph, an enlargement from a picture postcard.** *Misch & Stock/Author's Collection*

Below: **The route of the Croesor & Portmadoc Railway as deposited in Parliament in 1864.** *HLRO*

construction. This is too early for the either the Aberystwyth & Welsh Coast Railway (AWCR)'s harbour branch or the Beddgelert Railway so the plural must be an error, but the advertisement does indicate that construction of the tramway was started earlier in 1863. Roberts was to say, in Parliament in 1872, that he built the tramway at the request of his lessees, who had determined that they could not make a success of their quarry without improved transport. Seeing the considerable expansion carried out by the Festiniog quarries since the FR had opened in 1836 was perhaps the incentive for their demands.

His lessees could not talk to the landowners, Roberts said, but he knew them and obtained wayleaves for the tramway, sure that his property was worthless without it. One of the landowners, although willing to deal with Roberts, could not offer him adequate title so, in December 1864, he deposited a Parliamentary bill in the name of the Croesor & Portmadoc Railway (CPR). The Act made on 5 July 1865 incorporated a company to maintain the existing line that 'commences at or near the rock called Carrig Hylldrem ... and terminates at or

near Ynyscerrigduon at Portmadoc ...' and to make an extension from Portmadoc to Borth y Gest. The company was allowed to use locomotives and to carry passengers. The authorised capital was £25,000; Spooner signed the £14,960 estimate for the new works.

It seems to have been assumed that the tramway in 1864 adopted the route to the harbour without amendment, but the plan deposited by the Aberystwyth & Welsh Coast Railway for its proposed 'Portmadoc public wharf branch' in December 1864 shows the tramway terminated near the Britannia bridge, at right angles to the 3ft gauge Gorseddau Tramway's wharf some half-mile from Ynyscerrigduon. The CPR's own plan, produced at the same time, shows only the proposed route and an empty formation where the AWCR plan showed the tramway. When asked, in 1872, what works had been made following the act, Roberts was to say: 'I extended it from the then terminus into Portmadoc'; there it connected with the FR sidings near the latter's zero point. It could be that the problematic land was at the level crossings of Madoc Street and London Road, later High Street, the latter at least being claimed by the Tremadoc Estate and both being sanctioned with the extension.

Roberts was also to say that in making a 'portion of the extension' he 'laid down rails for locomotives'. If this was the case, perhaps it was just the Portmadoc section that was so treated to give FR locomotives access to what became known as the Beddgelert siding, the interchange with the Cambrian Railways.

The remaining 2½ miles of the tramway, including two inclines, that lay in the Croesor valley were not covered by the act and remained under Roberts's control. The five nominated directors, including Hugh Unsworth McKie of Tremadoc, held all the issued share capital; in practice this probably meant that four had qualifying holdings only and Roberts held the rest. In 1869 an attempt to sell the CPR to the FR failed on 18 October, when the FR board refused to entertain the idea. Another £8,000 was to be raised by mortgage in 1870.

The AWCR's contractor, Thomas Savin, also worked on an independent standard gauge railway, the Beddgelert Railway (BR). This nine-mile long line between Llyn Dinas, to the east of Beddgelert, and Portmadoc harbour was intended to serve the Hafod y Llan (Snowdon) Slate Company's quarry. By the time an act of Parliament was obtained in August 1865 Savin probably already had work well in hand for the land required was already in the possession of the promoters. He became

bankrupt in February 1866 and work on the BR ceased with about 3½ miles of formation either complete or nearly complete and track laid for about a mile. By the time an act to modify the route and to extend it to Llyn Gwynant had been obtained, on 16 July 1866, the railway was over.

Afterwards, it was said that the BR's engineers, Ordish & LeFevre, obtained a default judgement against Savin and removed the rails and other materials. It was also claimed that they overvalued the work done, making it impossible for any other contractor to make an arrangement with Savin's inspectors in bankruptcy and complete the railway. LeFevre applied for an abandonment order in 1869 but the BoT refused to make it.

LeFevre was to give evidence at the select committee hearings into the NWNGR bill in 1872. As the Hafod y Llan quarry's engineer he had, he said, laid out the inclines and gained landowners' consent for a 2ft gauge railway 'past Beddgelert'. Savin had said that he could build the railway before a bill could reach the select committee by using the licences LeFevre had obtained and took it over. Work stopped when the direct railway scheme failed to pass standing orders and the Cambrian, as the AWCR had become in 1865, took nine miles of sleepers certified by LeFevre for the BR. The BR's directors included the chairman, deputy chairman and secretary of the AWCR. The AWCR line to Pwllheli was opened in 1867.

The most significant strand of the Portmadoc–Carnarvon railway route, the North Wales Narrow Gauge Railways

Borth y Gest, proposed terminus of the Croesor & Portmadoc Railway, looking eastwards. The railway would have swung around the promontory and terminated slightly to the right of centre. Cnicht and the Moelwyns are ranged behind.
Salmon/Author's collection

(NWNGR), came from a bill deposited in December 1871. The prime function of the railway then built was to serve the Moel Tryfan quarries. The scheme was masterminded by C. E. Spooner, who became its engineer, although McKie, 'acting engineer' in the 1871 prospectus, signed the Parliamentary estimates. Spooner's motivation was probably two-fold. He owned a slate quarry that came to be served by the Bryngwyn branch and perhaps thought he could recreate the FR's success. His involvement with the CPR has already been noted. In addition to the FR he had other railway interests, having been engineer to the Carnarvonshire and Nantlle railways at different times.

By 1871, the FR was making substantial profits from its monopoly of the Festiniog slate traffic but in the same Parliamentary session the London & North Western Railway sought powers to construct the Bettws & Festiniog Railway, a 2ft gauge line intended to undermine it. In 1870 the LNWR had acquired the Carnarvonshire Railway, giving it access to the Nantlle slate traffic at Penygroes.

The NWNGR bill proposed eight 2ft gauge railways, the objectives being to link Porthdinllleyn with Corwen, via Pwllheli,

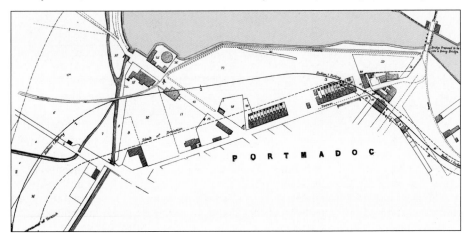

An extract from the plan of the Aberystwyth & Welsh Coast Railway's Portmadoc public wharf branch deposited in 1864. The Croesor Tramway route is highlighted in red. The draftsman appears to have made an error in the 3ft gauge Gorseddau Tramway route near the Britannia bridge. *HLRO*

Portmadoc, the Croesor & Portmadoc Railway (CPR), Beddgelert, Capel Curig and Bettws y coed (Nos 1-3 and 8); a branch to the LNWR station at Bettws y Coed (No 4); a branch to Penmachno from Railway No 2 (No 5); a branch from the LNWR (Carnarvonshire Railway) near Llanwnda to Bryngwyn (No 6) and a branch from Railway No 6 to Rhyd Ddu (No 7).

The link between Pwllheli and Portmadoc would have been achieved by making the Cambrian line between those places mixed gauge. Railway No 8 seemed to have been an afterthought, the bill contained no clauses for junctions and the deposited plans no explanation for dealing with the Carnarvonshire Railway junction at Afon Wen. The Cambrian objected, although it admitted that its service was sparse. The LNWR objected to the link that the NWNGR would have provided between Bettws y Coed and Corwen and its view

prevailed, as did the Cambrian's about railway No 8. In rejecting railways Nos 2, 3, 4 and 5, the select committee expressed a wish that the NWNGR should have access to Bettws y Coed.

Spooner said that Railway No 6 was for quarry purposes although there was a large population. Of No 7 he said it 'runs up the Bettws Garmon Valley and taps another slate district'. He also anticipated carrying slate from Blaenau Festiniog to the GWR at Corwen via Portmadoc and Nant Gwynant, 'a small source' of traffic.

Accordingly, Railways Nos 1, 6 and 7 gained approval on 6 August 1872. Railway No 1 was defined as the general undertaking and Railways Nos 6 and 7 as the Moel Tryfan undertaking. The former was to be capitalised at £150,000, the latter at £66,000. An amount equal to a third of the capital was

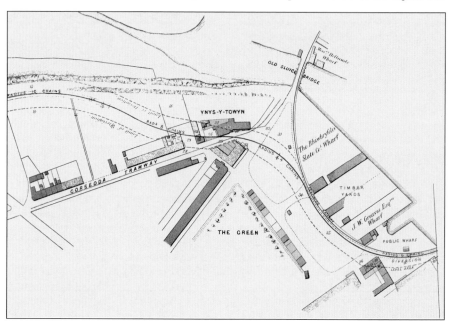

Right: **Contemporary with the AWCR plan is this plan deposited in support of the Croesor & Portmadoc Railway Bill. The Gorseddau route is highlighted.** *HLRO*

Below: **The 1864 terminus of the Croesor Tramway was located on the far bank of the Afon Glaslyn as seen c1950. Ironically, the Croesor formation, which was rejected by the WHR's engineers as impracticable in 1921, is now occupied by the revived WHR. The overgrown Gorseddau wharf was behind the boundary wall.** *Valentine/ Author's collection*

Right: **Beddgelert, the target of so many railway schemes, starting with the Beddgelert Railway in 1865, as seen in an early 19th century engraving from a location near Bryn y Felin. The Goat Hotel is on the left.** *J. Newman/Author's collection*

Below: **Hafod y Llan Quarry, the target of the Beddgelert Railway, was located to the right of this photograph. The incline of the South Snowdon Quarry, the objective of the Portmadoc, Beddgelert & South Snowdon Railway, is prominent in the centre.** *A. W. Hutton/Author's collection*

permitted to be borrowed on mortgage when all the capital had been subscribed and half of it paid up. The undertakings' capital and revenue accounts were to be kept separately. The company incorporated by the act was legally plural, The North Wales Narrow Gauge Railways Company, because there was, then, more than one undertaking but the final 's' was often omitted on the company's own letterheads and even on the company's official seal.

The Act identified the promoters as Livingston Thompson (a director of the FR), Sir Llewelyn Turner (a trustee of the Carnarvon Harbour Trust), James Hewitt Oliver (managing director of the Rhosydd Slate Company Ltd, in the Croesor Valley) and Roberts; the latter had sold the CPR to Spooner, McKie and Thompson in 1871 for £12,500 to facilitate Railway No 1; 'it was the key to it' he said. The sale agreement was dated 2 October 1871 but subsequent events suggest that the sale was not completed. Roberts also said that he had spent £14,000 on developing the tramway.

The prospectus issued in October 1871 must have failed, for on 30 December 1872 the financiers Grant Brothers & Company agreed to make an advance against the Moel Tryfan

undertaking's share and debenture capital of £88,000 on payment of 10%. A 12-month option to place the general undertaking capital was renounced on 31 December 1873. Baron Albert Grant, né Abraham Gottheimer, had been born in Dublin; his title was Italian; his brother Maurice was a partner in the business. In the 1860s, Albert Grant had been accused of fraudulent company promotion. MP for Kidderminster from 1865 to 1868, his re-election in 1874 was declared null and void due to his corrupt practices. He was bankrupted in 1877, when there were 89 actions outstanding against him, and he was on the verge of bankruptcy again when he died in 1899. Despite his reputation he moved amongst the upper echelons of London society and had paid for the development of London's Leicester Square in 1873/4. He also had some involvement with the Wye Valley Railway. Portraits of him are kept in the National Portrait Gallery.

On 23 December 1872, a contract was let to McKie for £56,160. In another prospectus issued on 20 January 1873 it states that McKie had 'given security' to build the 'Moel Tryfan line' within 12 months and the 'Bettws Garmon line' within 18 months. During the 1860s and 1870s McKie had been involved with an attempt to develop the Croesor United slate quarry.

The 1873 share issue was opened on 20 January and closed on 28 January. The prospectus offered £66,000 in ordinary £10 shares on the basis that the railway would serve the same function as the FR and that that railway had demonstrated how successful and profitable a narrow gauge line could be. The NWNGR's dividend was guaranteed, investors were informed, by an arrangement entered into between the company and Roberts, whereby he would lease the railway when completed and guarantee a minimum 6% dividend. If the railway was as successful as the FR then the dividend could be as much as 10%. To encourage investors to pay for their shares in full on application, two of the directors were to invest a sufficient sum in Consols, long-term government stocks, to cover the interest until the line was opened. The 21-year lease agreement with Roberts was made on 23 April 1873, the NWNGR (Lease) Act 1873 confirming the arrangement. Roberts was also expected to cover the company's administrative expenses. Presumably, any money raised would be used to reimburse Grant Brothers.

Roberts was allocated £10,000 by the company for the purchase of locomotives and rolling stock. Following the success of Robert Fairlie's articulated locomotive, *Little Wonder*, introduced on the FR in 1869, all locomotives (except shunting engines) were to be constructed to Fairlie's patents with Roberts paying a royalty of £300 per engine. The stock was to be returned to the company on expiry of the lease or on determination if sooner, to the full £10,000 value, that is, with no recognition being made of depreciation or wear and tear.

Construction of the railway was started in May 1873, with completion of both lines being anticipated within 12 months. Spooner had signed the plan showing the land required from Colonel Hugh Rowlands at Plas Bodaden on 16 April 1873. At the same time Roberts instructed solicitors to draw up the abstract of title. There appeared to have been a lack of communication between railway and contractor, with the contractor losing interest and slowing down work as payments from the company got into arrears, indicative of problems with fundraising. In 1876, it was said that the NWNGR had had difficulty getting the money promised from Grant Brothers and had in fact only received £83,500, of which £8,800 had been retained by the financiers. It was also claimed that McKie had paid a commission to Grant Brothers for the contract; the amount is not clear.

Work ceased in 1874 and McKie started to remove the track materials he had bought. The company went to arbitration, unexpectedly losing and having to pay an additional £8,000 to McKie. In 1886 Russell (p19), then the railway's receiver, was to claim that McKie was owed only £4,000 of the contract price yet a third of the work was incomplete, requiring a further £20,000 to finish. A prospectus for £22,000 mortgage debentures was issued on 9 June 1874; the events may not be unconnected. Paying 6% interest, the debentures were a first charge on the company and given priority over the £66,000 ordinary shares which were fully paid up.

By 30 June 1875 £66,394 had been spent and there was £3,765 in the capital account. In September the company reported that the 'contractor had continued the works, but had made far less progress than expected ... he had recently increased the number of men at work'. Despite this, little more progress was made and McKie succeeded with a further arbitration award against the company. A new contractor was appointed in August 1876.

An 1876 act authorised the abandonment of the general undertaking, the NWNGR being unable to raise any capital for it, and approved further fund raising, an additional £40,000 in ordinary or preferential shares, or both, the company having declared that the Moel Tryfan undertaking's capital and authorised borrowing had all been spent. Crucially, the act specified that any debts due from the general undertaking could not be claimed from the Moel

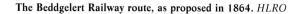

The Beddgelert Railway route, as proposed in 1864. *HLRO*

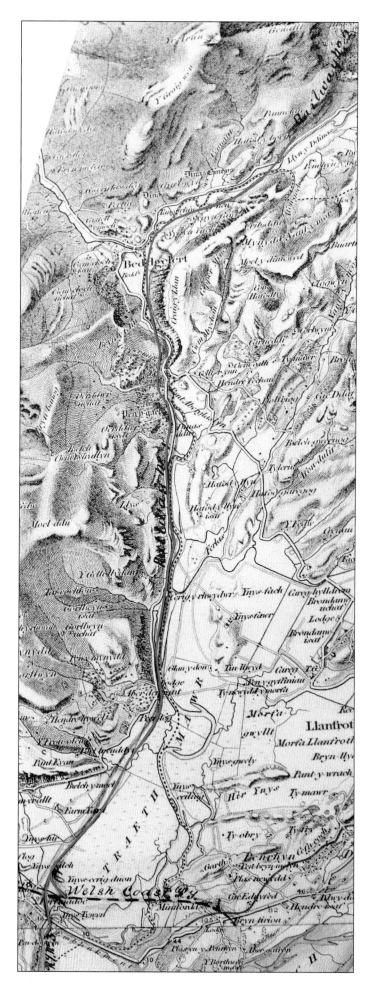

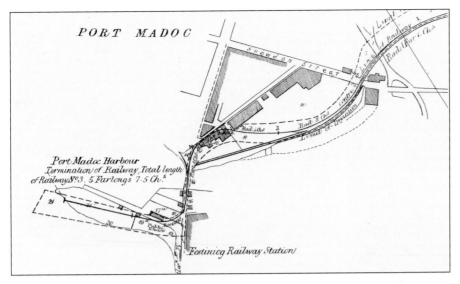

Left: **The Beddgelert Railway's proposed Portmadoc terminus. To reach it would have required crossing the Festiniog Railway station.** *HLRO*

Below: **A plan produced by the North Wales Narrow Gauge Railways to illustrate its proposals. It appears to have been printed before the promoters' ideas were fully formed.** *Author's collection*

Tryfan undertaking. The act also confirmed and protected Roberts's rights under the Lease Act although it was not long before he repudiated the lease. The company did not recognise his right to do so but pragmatically accepted that it was unable to deal with him from a position of strength. A benefit of the formal abandonment would have been the release of the Parliamentary deposit.

As an aside, the general undertaking's promotion had apparently prompted the advancement of the 2ft gauge Ruthin & Cerrig y Druidion Railway to connect with the line between Bettws y Coed and Corwen that had been rejected in the 1872 Act. This scheme gained Parliamentary approval in the 1876 session, just as the NWNGR abandoned the general undertaking. Spooner was engaged as consultant engineer on an occasional basis but took no further part. An extension from Cerrig y Druidion to Bettws y Coed was proposed in 1878, using the NWNGR's proposed route, when there was contact with the Tramways Corporation, then involved with the Croesor Tramway. Some 5½ miles of earthworks, not all within the limits of deviation, were constructed in 1879, but the company was without the skills and resources to complete its undertaking and it was abandoned by an act of 1884.

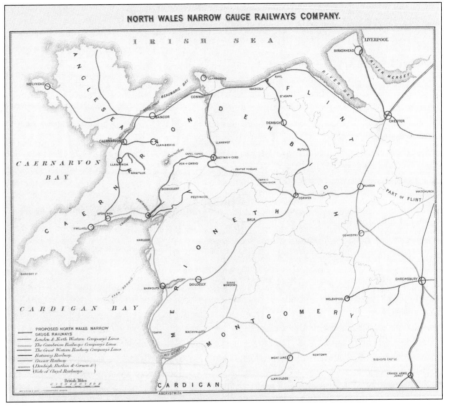

The NWNGR's new contractor made good progress. In February 1876, the FR board approved a request from a Mr Bray to hire one of the FR's small locomotives. The arrangement was subject to a contract made between the companies on 9 May, the NWNGR agreeing to pay £130 for six months' hire, the FR to deliver the locomotive to 'Llanwnda Junction' free of charge. The NWNGR was to be responsible for any damage caused to the locomotive and to use Coed Porth coal; the FR was responsible for maintenance. Having received light repairs at Boston Lodge on 8 May, *Palmerston* was despatched to Llanwnda the next day. It was returned to Boston Lodge by 9 July 1877, taking until 30 July to repair the ravages of its stay on the NWNGR. One of Spooner's sons, Charles Edwin, was the resident engineer during 1876.

The legal relationship with the LNWR was attended to in 1877, an agreement concerning the junction station and exchange of traffic being signed on 16 March. The availability of land was probably the reason for siting a new station less than one mile from that existing at Llanwnda. A plan had been drawn up at the LNWR's Bangor engineer's office and signed by Joseph Oldham, the company secretary, at Caernarfon in March 1877. A shared double-faced platform with the boundary running through it served both railways. On the standard gauge, a single turnout overseen by a signalbox at the Carnarvon end of the site gave access to the exchange yard; there were four slate sidings, two goods sidings, one of which served a platform in the goods shed, and a coal siding that ran the length of the site on its eastern side; a crossover connected one of the slate sidings back to the main line making a short loop. Three NWNGR lines on a raised wharf served the slate sidings; two tracks, one running though the goods shed, were provided for goods traffic.

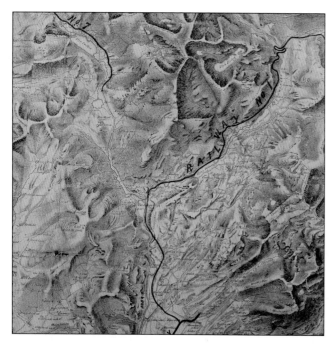

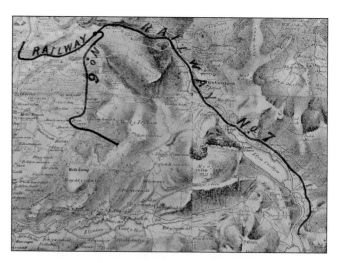

Each company provided its own sidings while the NWNGR provided the 'goods shed, goods platform, loading banks and all other necessary accommodation.' Although the NWNGR was required to provide or pay for the signalling and was responsible for its maintenance the LNWR controlled it; as it turned out, the LNWR provided it and NWNGR failed to meet its financial obligation. Employment costs of working the yard were to be charged to each company in proportion to the amount of traffic exchanged. A copy of an undated printed document that contains calculations of the operating expenses at Dinas, taking into account capital, interest, depreciation and labour costs, is filed at the National Archives with Crown Estates material dealing with a lease of land in Llandwrog parish.

According to the BoT returns, goods traffic was started on 21 May 1877, but it was not until 26 June that Oldham gave notice to the BoT that the line would be ready for inspection 'in about a fortnight.' He signed the bylaws on 6 July and *Palmerston* was returned to the FR by 9 July as noted on page 15.

A few days later, on 23 July 1877, Major Francis A. Marindin, newly recruited to the railway inspectorate, conducted his first inspection. Railway No 6, the Bryngwyn branch, was complete, whilst railway No 7 terminated at Quellyn. There were stations at Llanwnda, to be known as Dinas, Moel Tryfan Junction, Rhostryfan and Bryngwyn on the former and at Waenfawr, Bettws y Garmon [sic] and Quellyn on the latter. The flat-bottom rail, Vignoles section, weighed 35lb per yard in 24ft lengths. The sharpest curves and the steepest gradients were 3¾ chains and 3½ chains and 1 in 40 and 1 in 80 on each line respectively.

There were signalboxes at Llanwnda, Moel Tryfan [Tryfan Junction], Rhos Tryfan, Bryngwyn, Waunfawr, Bettws y Garmon and Quellyn. He noted that there were only two signals and no points at Quellyn, a temporary terminus, which implies that locos could not run round there. He commented that there were no means of implementing the block system of train operation and that the railway would be worked by one engine-in-steam or two engines coupled together, adding that 'slate trains ... run down by their own impetus, being considered in the same light as an engine in steam.'

At Bryngwyn he required the points to the goods siding at the foot of the incline, beyond the end of the passenger line, to be weighted towards the siding, to protect the passenger line from runaways on the incline. The incline here was unusual in being owned and operated by the railway company. It was double track and about 880 yards long; its gradient was 1 in 9.

'Generally speaking,' reported Marindin, 'the works on these lines have been well carried out ...' He found, however, deficiencies under 10 headings, including inadequate clearances under the overbridges, insufficient space allowed for women travelling 3rd class and a lack of public clocks at stations. Until these issues were resolved he could not sanction the use of the NWNGR by passenger trains. Perhaps Marindin did not see the railway's plans, for he failed to comment on the section near Plas y Nant that was built substantially outside the limits of deviation; had he been aware of it he should have required the company to obtain powers to regularise it.

On 6 August 1877 Oldham wrote to the BoT that Marindin's requirements were being dealt with although the bridge modifications would take some time. On behalf of his directors he sought provisional authority to open the line to passengers from 13 August, the company undertaking to make the alterations within two months and to fix bars to the carriage windows and to lock the carriage doors in the meantime. Following consultation with Marindin, who noted that 'bars ... are in themselves objectionable, yet accident is [sic] less likely to result from their adoption', on 9 August approval was given for the early opening. Marindin, being in the area, re-inspected the line on 14 August and found everything satisfactory except the clearances. In the BoT returns the date of opening to passengers was given as 15 August. Turner and Oldham signed the company's sealed undertaking regarding the method of working on 16 August.

During 1877 the railway earned £495 from carrying 18,877 passengers and £1,277 from 5,720 tons of goods, most of which was slate. In 1878, passenger traffic increased to 49,604, earning £1,250, and goods rose to 10,545 tons, earning £2,537. The accounts of the 1877/8 receivership show that Roberts was by far the largest slate-shipping customer, followed by the Alexandra and Moel Tryfan Crown quarries. The busiest day for passenger traffic was Saturday, when the level of business usually surpassed that of the total for the rest of the week. A small operating profit in 1877 was followed by a loss in 1878.

The bridge modifications took longer than anticipated, for it was 3 January 1878 before Oldham reported that the alterations were complete. Marindin reported that the work was satisfactory on 23 January. It is quite possible that the bridges were completely rebuilt. Marindin had described them as having masonry arches and required an additional 12in clearance on their width; he thought this could be achieved by chipping away at the masonry. As existing, the bridges have brick arches founded on masonry abutments that show no sign of having been altered. A civil engineer consulted by the author opined that the increased clearance could only be obtained by taking the bridges down and rebuilding them, which might account for the works having taken four months. It cannot be discounted that Marindin used masonry as a synonym for both stone and brickwork but they still show no sign of having been made 12in wider.

By the end of 1877 the company had been put into receivership by Grant Brothers. Of the money they had advanced, £8,862 had been allocated to the general undertaking's preliminary expenses but had not been repaid so a claim was made against the Moel Tryfan undertaking, contrary to the provisions of the 1876 Act. The company argued that it had no liability for the general undertaking's debts. The money included £7,000 Parliamentary deposit that had been repaid to Roberts and another, unidentified, promoter. Samuel Lowell Price was appointed receiver following a failed appeal on 5 December 1877. The company appealed again and obtained judgement in its favour on 7 May 1878; Price completed the accounts until 7 June. The £7,000 loan from the Grants was shown in the reports until 1913 and £2,647 'spent on the general undertaking now abandoned' remained a balance sheet item until 1922. The reports identified general undertaking expenditure as £4,465 11s 11d on

Parliamentary expenses and £5,146 5s 4d on engineering expenses.

Oldham had notified the BoT that the company was in a position to extend to Snowdon Ranger, the name taken from the adjacent public house, on 11 May 1878; Marindin returned to Wales and submitted his report from Chester on 28 May. The extension was seven furlongs long, the steepest gradient 1 in 79 and the sharpest curve six chains radius. There were no sidings except one beyond the station to permit the loco to run round its train. The only signals were a home and a distant at Snowdon Ranger. The temporary station at Quellyn had been removed and a permanent one provided at the new terminus. Provided that fencing was made good as required, padlocks were fitted to field gates, a name board was erected at the station, an additional waiting room, with conveniences, was provided for ladies and an undertaking was given concerning the method of working, he recommended the use of the extension for passenger traffic be approved. Turner and Oldham sealed the undertaking on 5 June. From this time Dinas–Snowdon Ranger (and later Rhyd Ddu) was considered the main line and Tryfan Junction–Bryngwyn the branch, a reversal of the definitions in the 1872 Act.

The *Manchester Guardian* reported the company's half-yearly meeting held on 15 September 1878 in some detail. Opening the extension to Snowdon Ranger had increased income without increasing the number of staff; weekly income had increased from £4 13s 7d per mile to £6 3s; £5,000 was needed to complete the line to Rhyd Ddu. The company's rolling stock, the shareholders were told, had been obtained on the 'deferred payment system' over periods of three, five and seven years. Because of the company's poor financial position

Below: **The Gorseddau Tramway was regauged and connected to the Croesor & Portmadoc Railway as the Gorseddau Junction & Portmadoc Railway in 1872.** *HLRO*

Below: **With an extension to Beddgelert approved in 1879, the Croesor & Portmadoc Railway became the Portmadoc, Croesor & Beddgelert Tram Railway Company.** *HLRO*

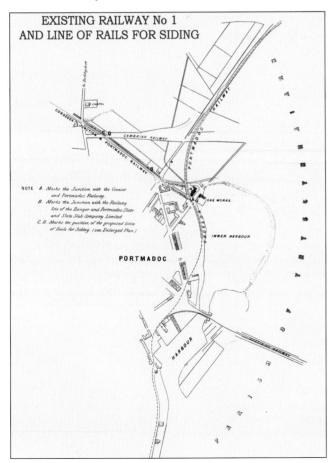

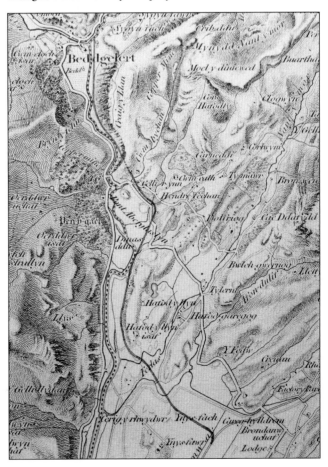

Right: One of several versions of the NWNGR's crest, this one with the singular 'railway'. *Author's collection*

Below: Moel Tryfan and a short train, no doubt typical of many on the NWNGR, at Snowdon Ranger, probably before 1881, when it was the terminus. The two brake/composites are an Ashbury bogie vehicle, next to the locomotive, and a Gloucester Cleminson six-wheeler. *FR Archives*

Bottom: An early view of Dinas, with standard and narrow gauge lines on opposing sides of the shared platform. On the NWNGR, the Hunslet 0-6-4ST *Beddgelert* stands at the starting signal with a train of bogie stock. *Welsh Highland Heritage*

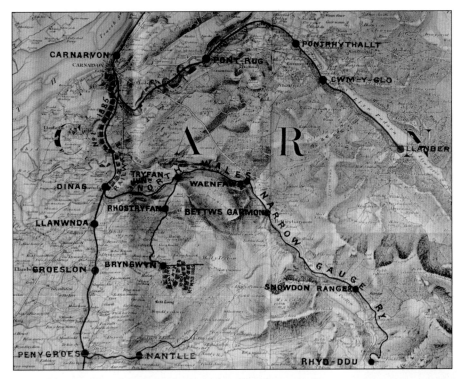

Left: **This plan, deposited in 1884, not only highlights the NWNGR's proposed Carnarvon extension and Bryngwyn deviation but the adjoining railways too. See page 27.** *NA*

Below left: **The NWNGR's proposed Carnarvon extension, authorised in 1885.** *NA*

Below: **The Bryngwyn deviation consisted of a reverse curve and a reversing neck.** *NA*

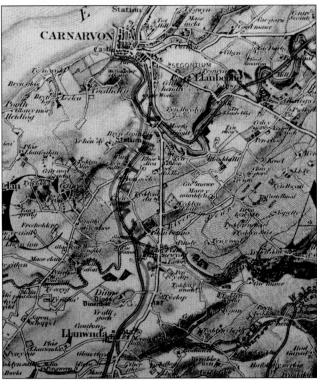

the quarterly rentals had been unpaid on locos since 25 September 1877, on wagons since 1 January 1878, and on carriages since 1 February 1878.

To keep the railway going, James Cholmeley Russell, one of the directors, had bought the three locomotives, three carriages and four coal wagons from their makers and owners. The latter were claiming for the arrears due to them and the company was at risk of losing half of its revenue; what revenue could be earned with no locomotives was not stated. The directors therefore proposed to establish a rolling stock company. Russell seconded the adoption of the chairman's report, saying that raising the money to complete the line would be difficult: the debenture holders had refused to defer the interest due to them. He had advanced 'considerable

sums' to the company and had bought the rolling stock to protect his money. Brown, Marshalls & Company owned the slate wagons and would not wait for ever for their money, he said. Costs had been reduced; some stationmasters were paid only 10s or 12s per week and had no house to live in. The line could perhaps be leased to the LNWR but the terms would be poor. Shareholders could invest in the rolling stock company.

Accordingly, the Moel Tryfan Rolling Stock Company Ltd (MTRS) was established in December 1878; seven partners, including Russell, capitalised it to £10,000. Russell sold 'his' stock to MTRS for £3,630, assigning the £1,000 arrears of interest due to him to MTRS at the same time. MTRS promptly sued for the arrears and succeeded in putting the company into receivership, with Russell appointed receiver.

Russell, a barrister, was to influence the fortunes, or otherwise, of the NWNGR until his death on 29 August 1912 at the age of 71; he became company chairman in 1879. From 1880 until 1904 he was also the receiver of the Manchester & Milford Railway. (The MTRS was to be wound up in 1889 and was dissolved in 1894.)

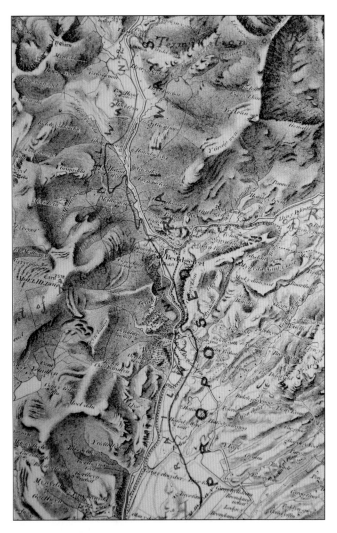

Fund raising remained a problem for the NWNGR. On 17 April 1879 it entered into a scheme of arrangement with its creditors whereby it could raise £5,000 'A' debentures and £40,000 'B' debentures and convert existing debentures into 'B' stock; this move suggests that the debenture holders had been threatening the company over unpaid interest. In 1880 another scheme was arranged, replacing the first, whereby the 'A' debentures were increased to £6,000, the 'B' debentures reduced to £30,000 and £14,000 of 'C' debentures were created. R. S. Guinness was elected to represent the interests of the 'B' debenture holders; he was to resign, to be replaced by Russell, in 1888. The directors' report for the first half of 1881 reveals that £4,564 11s for 'instalments of hire of rolling stock previously charged to revenue' was now covered by the £6,000 'A' debentures. At the expense of £127 interest incurred the railway saved £481 6s 10d on hire charges and £171 1s 4d 'interest on arrears of hire'.

Later in 1879, the company entered into an agreement with the Glanyrafon Quarry, near Rhyd Ddu, whereby the quarry's proprietors would subscribe for 80 £10 preference shares in exchange for certain rights. The money was to be paid in four monthly instalments from September 1879, providing that the last only became payable when the railway was completed and opened for goods and passenger traffic.

Left: **The concept of reverse curves to maintain an even and workable gradient between Beddgelert and Rhyd Ddu was introduced in the Portmadoc, Beddgelert & Rhyd Ddu Railway proposals deposited in 1891.** *HLRO*

Below: **Photographs suggest that NWNGR trains were usually lightly loaded but that was not always the case and on special occasions every item of rolling stock and every locomotive would be put into action, as in this 1892 scene. Steam from the third locomotive is just visible at the rear.**
A. G. Symons/Welsh Highland Heritage

The initial objective of the contract was to complete the railway to a point where a junction could be made with the quarry's internal tramway, the target date being 31 January 1880. When the NWNGR was completed to Rhyd Ddu the quarry company would contribute half the cost, not exceeding £50, of any signalling required at its siding.

In return the NWNGR was to stop one train in each direction at the siding daily, except Sundays, Christmas Day and Good Friday, and to run workmen's trains, or suitable public trains, timed to arrive at the quarry from Dinas between 6.30am and 7am in summer and 7am and 7.30am in winter and to leave between 5.45pm and 6.15pm, provided the quarry guaranteed a minimum of 40 3rd class passengers travelling daily from Waenfawr and beyond. Workmen's tickets were to be made available at a single fare for the return journey. The 21-year agreement was signed by John Owen and Edward Humphrey

Owen for the quarry and Russell and Robert Henry Livesey, secretary and manager, Oldham's successor, for the NWNGR.

Despite this influx of capital it was to be 14 May 1881 before the line to Rhyd Ddu was opened. Livesey notified the BoT that the line was ready for inspection on 29 March that year but the line was still not ready. James Cleminson, the railway's new civil and mechanical engineer, submitted the required technical data and drawings on 25 April; the covering letter survives but none of the enclosures.

Marindin made his inspection on 5 May. There were just the two stations with a siding at Glanyrafon. He noted that 'the line follows the surface of the side of the hills and the cuttings & embankments are few and of little importance'; that is, it followed the contours. The gradient from Snowdon Ranger varied between 1 in 332 and 1 in 74 and the sharpest curve was 3½ chains radius. The only substantial work was a 'viaduct' that

Right: **The signalling diagram submitted to the BoT when the NWNGR wished to make Waenfawr a passing place in 1895 — see page 30.** *NA*

Below: ***Moel Tryfan*** **and a mixed train at Rhyd Ddu. The purpose of the wagon is not known. The passenger stock includes an Ashbury and a Gloucester brake/composite at each end and the 'Gladstone' car, the latter delivered in 1891. A glimpse of the Rhyd Ddu nameboard is visible; the station was renamed 'Snowdon' from 1893. Continuous brakes have been fitted and the driver seemed to think that two buckets of sand would be a wise precaution.** *FR Archives*

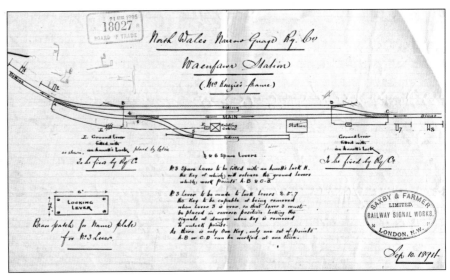

Top left: **A postcard view of Rhyd Ddu with the station in the centre and Snowdon behind. One of the single Fairlies is running round its train.** *Author's collection*

Top right: **The Carnarvon-end of Rhyd Ddu station showing the access to the Rhyd Ddu path to Snowdon. Judging by the sleepers and stone piled on the ground that station was barely complete, if that, when the photograph was taken. The rock behind the fence, by the gate, was engraved by villagers in the 19th century.** *Author's collection*

Above: **Perhaps the imposing headlamp signified that *Moel Tryfan* and its train were expecting to be out after dark when photographed c1900.** *FR Archives*

Left: **Bryngwyn is very likely the location of this photograph, with an incline rope and other components in the foreground.** *FR Archives*

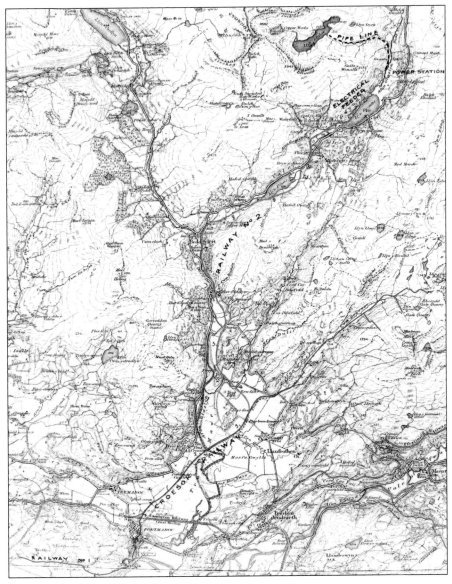

The Portmadoc, Beddgelert & South Snowdon Railway proposals of 1901, with the power station and its associated feeder and pipe line. For the purpose of this book, the non-statutory Croesor Tramway has been highlighted in blue. See page 32. *HLRO*

the same day and approval for passenger operation given.

Livesey reported that Marindin's requirements had been completed and that the line was available for inspection on 11 August. Marindin did not hurry; it was 14 September before he reported that he had re-inspected the line, finding it satisfactory except for the lack of guards on the bridge. Cleminson submitted a drawing showing his proposals on 25 November but had shown inside instead of outside guards as required by Marindin. Livesey reported that the work had been carried out on 3 July 1882; the company's half-year report included capital expenditure of £88 15s for it.

There is as yet no indication of an earlier goods service to Glanyrafon. A handwritten notice of 'rates for goods & mineral traffic between Dinas and under mentioned stations', signed by Livesey, was dated May 1881; added later, minerals could be despatched to 'top of incline' and packages to 'Moeltryfan (for slate quarries)'. The debentures issued under the terms of the agreement were issued on 20 February 1880 (80) and 12 October 1881 (5).

An indenture between the railway company and the West Snowdon Slate Company Ltd made on 1 July 1885 reveals that the formation between the Dinas end of Rhyd Ddu station and the boundary with Assheton-Smith land at Clogwin y Gwin, some three acres, cost £80. Reconstruction of the trackbed here revealed a lack of drainage, a demonstration that funds were still in short supply during its original building.

These works completed the NWNGR's Moel Tryfan undertaking. It was a basic railway, with loops only at the termini, although the stations were fully signalled with appropriate interlocking. It was not until 1882 that train operating became profitable but revenues remained insufficient to pay debenture interest. Slate was and remained the prime source of traffic, followed by passengers. The railway published timetable guidebooks for tourists, making much of Rhyd Ddu's proximity to the summit of Snowdon. Other features promoted were 'elephant mountains', near Plas y Nant, Quellyn Lake, Betws Garmon Valley and Nant Mill waterfall. Connecting coaches for Beddgelert met trains at Rhyd Ddu. Because of the inconvenience and delay caused by transhipment at Dinas, merchandise traffic never developed as it might have done. Despite all its earlier, and later, ambitions nothing more was achieved by the railway. Quite why Beddgelert, with a population of 1,423 in 1871 and only 3½ miles from Rhyd Ddu, an obvious link with the general undertaking, was never targeted at this stage is not known.

carried the railway across a ravine, and had stone abutments and wrought iron girders, a height of 56ft and a 'span of 94ft,' he said; actually it is 100ft. Referred to by the railway's engineer, James Cleminson, as the Dingle bridge, it spans the Afon Treweunydd, close to the site of Glanyrafon Quarry, which name it has taken. Its remote location and the effort required to build it would have contributed to the final delay in completing the railway.

The culverts, Marindin continued, had been in place for several years and although only one had shown evidence of being inadequate he thought that they were too small. Once again he found the works incomplete, fencing, a buffer stop at Snowdon Ranger, nameboard, point lock and incomplete station buildings at Rhyd Ddu, and lack of outside guard rails on the bridge were the main items, and recommended refusing permission for use by passenger trains.

On 13 May 1881, Marindin submitted that Cleminson had informed him that some of the requirements had been met and that others were in progress. Cleminson had also told him that it was 'of great importance to this line to open tomorrow', Whit Saturday, and had undertaken that speed on the bridge would be restricted to 10mph until the guides had been installed. Marindin therefore recommended approval subject to re-inspection and an undertaking concerning the method of working. Signed by Russell and Cleminson, the undertaking was delivered to the BoT

Right: **An extract of the plan showing the PBSSR's proposed Queen's Hotel branch, showing also the location of the Cambrian and Beddgelert exchange sidings.** *HLRO*

Below: **A 19th century photograph of the Aberglaslyn Pass depicting the scree through which the railway was to be built in the centre.** *Author's collection*

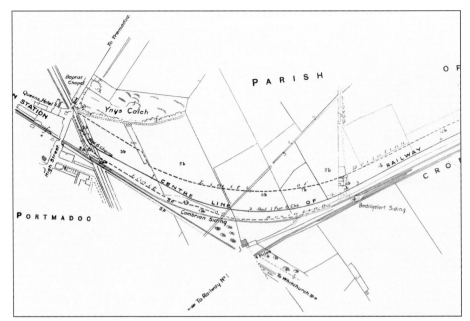

Beddgelert had been the target of a second CPR Act obtained in 1879, authorising a three-mile extension there, with £23,000 capital to pay for it. The company was allowed to enter into agreements with the Cambrian Railways and/or the FR for 'working, use, management and maintenance of their respective railways' and to change its name to the Portmadoc, Croesor, & Beddgelert Tram Railway Company (PCBTR). If the extension was maintained as a separate undertaking it was to be known as the PCBTR's Beddgelert Extension.

The inspiration for this Act had come from the Tramways Corporation Ltd which promoted the CPR and its Beddgelert extension as a railway that could match the FR for traffic and dividends. The identities of the corporation's backers are unknown. Despite possibly having sold his interest in the railway in 1871, Roberts now became its secretary. Perhaps the corporation had greater ambitions than Beddgelert, for it had also been in contact with the Ruthin & Cerrigydruidion Railway's promoters. PCBTR shares were offered to the public shortly after the act was obtained. Neither extension was carried out but the target of Beddgelert and sanction for Festiniog co-operation established a pattern for the future. In 1883, Roberts was to try to encourage the FR to operate the proposed railway, but without success. In 1882, the PCBTR had established a further link to the NWNGR when a second mortgage was obtained, this time from Russell, for £330.

The earliest NWNGR directors' report currently available, for the first half of 1881, has already been mentioned. Severe weather in January closed the line for two days and caused 'considerable loss and damage' whilst increasing expenses. Including only a few weeks of operation to Rhyd Ddu, a profit of £18 9s 5d was made, compared with a loss of £540 2s 11d for the previous half-year. Slate tonnage had increased but receipts from that source had declined because the rate had been reduced by 14%. Efforts had been made to develop tourist and goods traffic with Beddgelert and £345 12s had been set aside for a rolling stock renewal fund. £1,016 18s 4d was allocated for the LNWR signals at Dinas.

It seems to have taken the NWNGR a while to realise the true value of Snowdon as a destination. In July 1881, Snowdon station was renamed Snowdon Ranger and then Quellyn Lake in July 1893, when Rhyd Ddu was renamed Snowdon. Maybe this was responsible for the big increase in the number of passengers carried in 1893. It certainly played a part in the

decision to build the Snowdon Mountain Railway shortly afterwards. The WHR was to rename Rhyd Ddu 'South Snowdon' in 1923.

Traffic was improved by 1882, when Russell reported increasing business in the carriage of slate, coal and lime. On the passenger side a decline in 3rd class passengers was accompanied by an increase in those travelling 1st and 2nd. Extra trains ran on Saturdays, but the railway never ran on Sundays.

An incident that occurred on 24 February 1883 took Marindin back to the railway. The 8.25pm from Rhyd Ddu consisted of a Cleminson brake/composite next to the locomotive and two four-wheeled carriages. Shortly after the train had left Snowdon Ranger one or both of the four-wheelers derailed and then became detached from the train, about half a mile from the station. The guard noticed the carriages were missing as the train reached the overbridge at Quellyn and ordered the driver to return to find them, this occurring at such a speed that a collision took place; it would have been 'very' dark too. The train's sole passenger, riding in the composite, escaped injury, as did the train crew. At Dinas, Livesey found the driver asleep on the loco and sacked him. The fireman, he told Marindin, was sober and the guard was not as drunk as the driver.

Left: **Snowdon, seen from Nant Gwynant. The PBSSR power station site was at the lower left.** *Author's collection*

Below left: **The location plan of the NWNGR's 1903 proposed extension to connect its 1900 extension at Beddgelert with the PBSSR.** *NA*

Below: **Moel Hebog and the Goat Hotel, Beddgelert. The railway eventually tunnelled behind the hotel and the station was located in the field to the right of it.** *C. N. & Co/Author's collection*

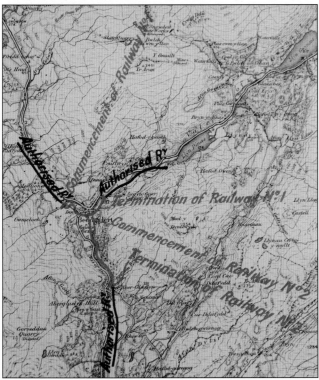

Marindin found that the collision was caused by the carelessness of the driver and the 'stupidity and disregard of rules' of the guard. The guard was 'unfit for any position of trust', he reported. He thought that the problem of train crew drinking at Snowdon Ranger would be avoided if the railway appointed a stationmaster there although he recognised that there was probably insufficient work for one. In their half-year report the directors attributed the increase of expenditure to 'damage to rolling stock, caused by the carelessness of some of the company's servants.' The NWNGR was to maintain its reputation for poor operating. In accidents that occurred in 1878 and 1901, employees were killed.

Despite the agreement that the railways would share the cost of transhipment at Dinas the LNWR refused to make any contribution. Russell had taken up the issue when he became chairman but it was 9 June 1884 before a new agreement was made, being applied retrospectively to 1 July 1882. The NWNGR was to bear the cost of the transhipment of slate with traffic for Caernarfon Quay being charged at 10d per ton from Dinas, the LNWR paying a rebate of 1d per ton to the NWNGR. Slate bound for inland destinations was charged at 4d per ton between Dinas and Carnarvon Junction, a longer distance, to discourage use of the harbour. For goods passing through Dinas the NWNGR could raise a 1s per ton terminal, the fee chargeable in addition to the carriage rate for the use of the infrastructure, except for goods from Carnarvon where it would be paid to the LNWR. The NWNGR could charge 3d per ton for coal and other minerals delivered at Dinas. One third of the agent's wages was to be attributable to the goods traffic. From 1 July 1882 the LNWR was to pay the NWNGR £25 per annum to cover expenses '... including maintenance of station.' The cost of maintaining the telegraph from 1877 to 31 December 1883 had been £54 6s 7d; the NWNGR agreed to pay half of this amount and to pay half of the cost in future, providing the sum due did not exceed £4 10s in any one year; this change was a consequence of the LNWR making Dinas a block post in 1878 and allocating the cost to the NWNGR although that company had no benefit from the alteration.

Regardless of its indebtedness the NWNGR deposited a new bill in Parliament in December 1884. Its objectives were to

Top: **A family scene Rhyd Ddu, c1900. The ladies stand by while father and son pose on the loco.**
Peacock/Author's collection

Right: **Photographed at Rhyd Ddu on 23 June 1909, *Gowrie* was barely a year old and the Pickering brake composite next to it two years old.**
H. L. Hopwood/Author's collection

Below: **Another view of Rhyd Ddu with *Gowrie*, taken from the other side; it shows the train ready to leave although the token, left foreground, is still in the point lock. The stationmaster's house is on the right; it was rented by the WHR for 10s per month.** *FR Archives*

Right: **An LNWR train at Dinas early in the 20th century. The board on the Carnarvon-bound platform reads 'Dinas change here for narrow gauge line'.**
Author's collection

bypass the Bryngwyn incline and to build an independent line to Carnarvon. The Bryngwyn deviation would be formed by sweeping curves up the hillside whilst the Carnarvon extension would have run close to the LNWR line, crossing under it at Bontnewydd, where a station was planned, and using a part of the Nantlle Railway formation before terminating opposite the castle, 'near the boat-house in the occupation of the Carnarvon Rowing Club'. Having the railway on that bank of the Seiont would justify the provision of additional wharfage although public access would require using the existing ferry, for which powers of purchase were sought, or a proposed bridge. The only objection was to the Carnarvon extension, from the LNWR.

The bill was examined by the House of Commons select committee in April 1885 and by the Lords in July. Russell was examined at some length. The railway had eventually cost £106,500 to complete, more than double the contract price. He attributed the 'excessive cost' to commission and litigation; of the original £56,000 contract £16,000 had been paid to Grant as commission. The line had been poorly built, said Russell, and £200 per year had been spent on improving the track. It had also been necessary to replace the original wagons.

He had, he went on, invested £19,000 in the company and had been a director since 1876. The £6,000 'A' debentures, which paid interest at 4% or 4¼%, represented the rolling stock, originally hired from the manufacturers; the total expenditure on rolling stock was £11,230. The £30,000 'B' 4% debentures replaced the same amount of 6% debentures. £15,000 'C' debentures were for allocation to ordinary creditors. The company owed £5,800, including £1,016 18s 4d to the LNWR for the signalling at Dinas and £2,000 to himself. Interest on the 'A' debentures was cumulative, on the 'B' debentures it was cumulative from 1886 and on the 'C' debentures from 1889.

It cost 6d per ton to tranship goods, including slate, at Dinas, Russell explained. For slate, the railway charged an inclusive rate of 2s per ton, including wagons used in the quarries and transhipment. The LNWR had overcharged for goods originating beyond Carnarvon by charging as if they were being delivered at Carnarvon instead of being transhipped at Dinas, he claimed; the terminal was actually chargeable by the NWNGR at the delivery station. Russell had got the LNWR to reduce the rate, but he still thought it was overcharging.

Connections were poor, and as an example, a passenger on the 4.20pm from Bryngwyn changing at Dinas would arrive at Carnarvon at 5.30pm if the trains were on time, 70 minutes for eight miles. The 49,000 passengers carried in 1878 fell to 27,060 in 1879 as a result. There had been some improvement in numbers since, but not to 1878 levels, because the company had advertised the summer service to tourists – in 1884 'people did not go abroad on account of the cholera, and there were more people travelling in North Wales than there had been for some time.' Slate traffic had shown some increase but goods traffic remained static: 760 tons in 1877, 720 tons in 1884, because of the delay caused by transhipment; it took two days for goods to be transported from Carnarvon to Waenfawr, a distance of six miles. Around 2½% of slate was lost to breakages at Dinas.

When the LNWR's barrister claimed that his company could provide transporter wagons, which could carry loaded slate wagons and then being constructed for use on the Conwy Valley line, to reduce breakages, Russell claimed that a design for such a wagon had been submitted to the LNWR c1877 and rejected. Neither party appeared to know of the transporter wagons used by the LNWR to carry Nantlle wagons for five years after the latter's route had been converted to standard gauge in 1867. The barrister demonstrated that on the current level of business, and assuming that the LNWR did not retain any traffic, the new line would only make £207 profit annually against the £720 required to pay 4% interest on the £13,000 capital required to build it. Russell claimed that he had examined the figures closely and was satisfied with them but was unable to produce any evidence to counter the QC's assertion.

The 1877 agreement overlooked the allocation of passenger traffic expenses at Dinas. Russell said that he tried to get the LNWR to agree to pay half of the expenses and half of 5% interest on the capital cost of making the station. This was appropriate, he thought, because the NWNGR was bringing the LNWR traffic from areas that it did not serve. Failing to reach agreement, on 17 April 1883 the LNWR threatened to discontinue stopping its trains at Dinas. In 1884, the station had 8,000 originating passengers bound for Carnarvon, worth, together with some originating parcels traffic, £271 to the LNWR yet the NWNGR only received the £25 payable under the 1884 agreement, the LNWR even refusing to make a contribution towards the cost of consumables and lighting. He estimated that the station's net benefit to the LNWR, even allowing for the initial cost of the sidings and the signalling, was £2,500.

Livesey explained how the delay in transhipment occurred at Dinas. The LNWR's morning train (6am) from Carnarvon left wagons in the loop before proceeding to Afon Wen; when that train returned from Afon Wen (around 1pm) the wagons were shunted into position for the NWNGR to unload; sometimes an earlier train from Afon Wen did the shunting. During the summer most of the LNWR passenger trains ran late, contributing to the decline in passenger numbers between 1878 and 1884. Russell added that the LNWR collected the loaded wagons during the morning but would never take more than five.

Edward Humphrey Owen was a member of the Carnarvon engineering company H. Owen & Sons and involved with Glanyrafon Quarry. He explained that it was cost effective to cart the quarry's coal and other goods from Carnarvon to the NWNGR at Dinas to avoid the delay caused by the LNWR.

William Charles Whiskin of Hughes & Co, supplier of paints, oils and petroleum, estimated that his company delivered some 300 tons of goods a year to places in the vicinity of the railway by road. Under cross-examination he explained that usually if there was a station then people would use it for their goods. In the case of Beddgelert, however, goods from Carnarvon were being sent via the LNWR and Portmadoc, 27 miles from Carnarvon, at customers' request, because it was quicker despite the greater distance, and the eight miles cartage still needed instead of 2½ miles from Rhyd Ddu, 16½ miles from Carnarvon. The LNWR also offered an advantageous rate, 10d per cwt for parcels to Portmadoc compared with 7d per cwt to Dinas; Livesey thought that the existence of sea-going competition between Carnarvon and Portmadoc accounted for it.

William Arthur Darbishire, principal owner of the Pen yr Orsedd Quarry and partner in Pen y Cryn at Nantlle, complained of the lack of space on the wharves at Carnarvon. There was space for just three wagons and only 15 tons of slate on each wharf so that loading a ship with 180 tons could take two to three days. The Nantlle quarries had not been able to compete with Festiniog and Penrhyn for foreign trade since the 'old Nantlle tramway' had ceased to exist. The quarries served by the NWNGR would have an advantage with direct connection to Carnarvon. He also was unaware of any working system involving the use of transporter wagons, but he did not think that the LNWR would invest in the slate traffic because it automatically got all the inland traffic on offer, whereas at Blaenau Ffestiniog it had to compete for the traffic.

The LNWR's general manager, George Findlay, was brought in at the end, admitting that although the NWNGR's Carnarvon extension would have little effect on his railway his company did not want to lose even a small amount of traffic. He could not explain why the company had spent so much objecting to the bill.

The Act was given the royal assent on 31 July 1885. The use of Crown lands at the incline summit was permitted by a 998-year lease, annual rental of £5 being payable – the official receiver was still paying this rent on behalf of the WHR, in receivership, until the FR acquired the assets in 1999. The extensions were to be maintained distinctly from the Moel Tryfan undertaking and known as the Carnarvon and Bryngwyn extensions undertaking. This undertaking was to be capitalised at £28,000, with powers to borrow further sums on mortgage. The extensions were not built despite an extension of time being obtained in 1890. In 1886, Russell was to tell the shareholders that several months of illness had prevented him from concentrating on the company's affairs and progressing the extensions.

Earlier in 1885 the company had resolved an outstanding debt of £340 for legal expenses and costs incurred in the legal action against Grant by issuing 'C' debentures at par, 'an arrangement very favourable to the company.'

By July 1887, it is possible that the directors thought the NWGR was at last heading in the right direction. Traffic and revenue were steadily increasing, making a small profit, with 'A' debenture interest being paid in full, along with some of the 'B' debenture interest. As the Fairlie locomotives had been overhauled, three miles of track relaid with new materials, the Bettws Garmon and Nant Mill river bridges retimbered and the stations and signalboxes repainted, it is possible that Russell, acting as receiver, decided that the maintenance was more important than the interest, especially as he was probably the largest holder of the 'B' class stock. The arrears were accumulating, though, and approval was sought to make a payment on account.

The Regulation of Railways Act 1889 brought with it obligations for all railways, to install block working, interlocking signals and points, fit continuous brakes and print the fares on tickets, but despite the 1886 Act giving the NWNGR borrowing powers to fund some of them, they were obligations that the NWNGR tried to avoid.

Following receipt of a BoT circular, on 24 December 1889 Livesey wrote: 'Without therefore going into detail into the special circumstances of this line I am desired to add that they are such, that if the proposed regulations were put in force, it would be difficult if not impossible to work the traffic, and to ask ... special consideration in the case of this company.'

On 4 March 1890 he submitted a draft order asking that the Bryngwyn branch be worked by train staff only and to be given three years to comply with the other requirements because 'the company does not possess any communication by telegraph or telephone along its railway.' Except for sidings, which were locked by an Annett's key on the train staff, all points and signals were interlocked. It would not be possible to separate the passenger and goods traffic without 'diminishing the number of

passenger trains to such an extent that the accommodation to the public would be greatly reduced and the revenue ... so severely affected that the present small net earnings would disappear', he claimed. He also claimed that although the line's maximum speed was 16mph it was usually 12mph or less, passenger accommodation on the mixed trains was usually a composite carriage with brake compartment and the trains were light and could stop quickly. The considerations, he said, applicable to standard gauge railways did not apply to the NWNGR. He concluded by asking for the railway's case to be specially heard.

On 24 June 1890, Livesey asked for an extension to the time allowed to print the fares on tickets until 31 December. 'The company is very poor,' he explained, and 'there are a considerable number of tickets in hand.' Tanner acknowledged the BoT's approval on 5 September. No doubt Russell was instrumental in Tanner's appointment for the latter had been previously employed by the Manchester & Milford Railway. Livesey had been appointed the secretary and locomotive superintendant of the Finn Valley Railway in Ireland.

A printed version of the draft order was submitted to the company on 10 October 1890. Although 18 months was given to adopt the block system and the interlocking, the main line was excluded because it was worked with train staffs without tickets and the branch because it was worked one-engine-in-steam, or two coupled together, with a train staff. Compliance with interlocking was not required where points were locked with an Annett's key. Two years were allowed for equipping passenger trains with continuous brakes. The exception made for the use for vehicles belonging to other railways was the same as that applied to standard gauge lines and was irrelevant to NWNGR conditions. A limited number of mixed trains were permitted for which the wagons did not require continuous brakes, but the loco and passenger carriages did.

Russell replied on 30 October. He complained that the railway could not afford to comply with the mixed train requirements, the expenditure would be unproductive and unnecessary. The railway had, he said, no separate brake vans and four 'large passenger vehicles' with guards' compartments and brakes. 'Frequently, one passenger vehicle with wagons form a train. The passenger vehicle

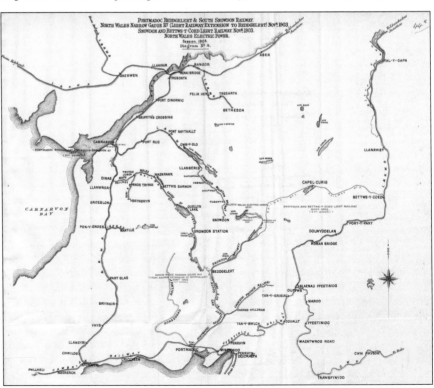

The position regarding the various railway proposals in November 1903. *NA*

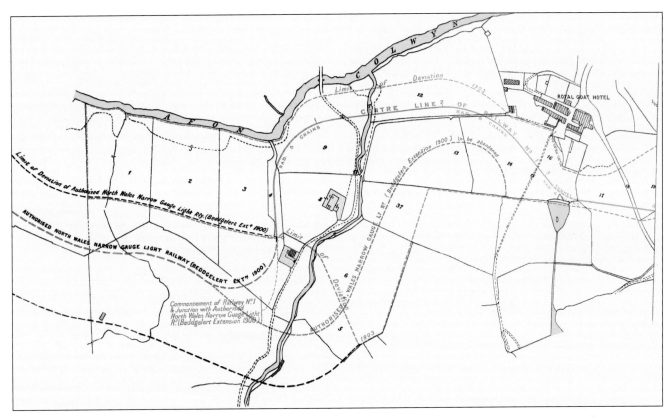

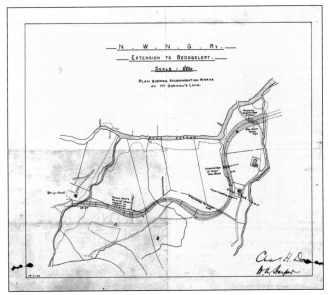

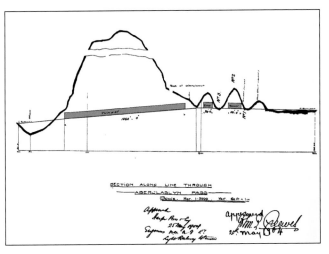

Above: **The NWNGR 1904 detail plan for the area at the rear of the Goat Hotel defined both the proposed route and the 1900 route to be abandoned.** *NA*

Left: **Dated 14 July 1904, this plan shows the accommodation works agreed with the Cwm Cloch owner, Charles H. Dorman and the NWNGR's engineers, and signed by both parties.** *NA*

Below left: **A section showing the tunnels in the Aberglaslyn Pass, as approved by the County Lieutenant in May 1904.** *NA*

is used as a brake van and is placed at the rear of the train behind the wagons. If the passenger vehicle be fitted with a continuous brake it must be placed next to the engine, in which case it cannot be used as a brake van at the rear of the train ...' He asked for an interview before the order was made.

General Charles Scrope Hutchinson was deputed to see Russell and made notes about the meeting on 5 December. He was prepared to allow the NWNGR three years to comply and agreed that the brake carriages could be used in the mixed trains. With the railway's steep gradients there was no guarantee that 12mph would not be exceeded by ascending trains and there was the risk of runaways from descending trains. The order was made on 31 December 1890 and the telegraph was installed during the second half of 1891.

Jumping forward to complete this topic, on 13 June 1892, Russell wrote to the BoT about the railway's six-wheeled Cleminson carriages. They were incapable of being fitted with continuous brakes and had been equipped with through pipes, but were they allowed to be used? The BoT did not see its way to making an exception for them. At the date of Russell's letter the NWNGR had fitted four bogie carriages with Westinghouse air brakes.

In 1890, the NWGR had obtained powers to raise money to fund the 1889 requirements, to convert the 'A' debentures to 'A' debenture stock and to extend the time available to complete the 1885 extensions. £10,000 'A' debenture stock was authorised, £6,000 of which was to redeem the 'A' debentures issued when the rolling stock was bought from the MTRS in 1881. The remainder was to raise funds for continuous brakes, additional rolling stock, a telegraph/telephone system, turntables, additional buildings, sheds, signals and 'other matters and things for the permanent improvement of the Moel Tryfan undertaking.' In March 1891, the shareholders were told that additional carriages and a carriage shed were also required and that the estimated cost was £1,400; approval to spend £2,000 was sought on 8 September. The telegraph had been installed between Dinas and Rhyd Ddu by the end of the year. Installation of Westinghouse brakes was completed by 1894, at which time the last of eight new carriages funded by the 1890 debentures was delivered. There were never any turntables.

Capital expenditure
December 1890 to June 1895

	On line open (*works, sheds and telegraph*)	Working stock (*rolling stock and continuous brakes*)	
December 1890	£440		£440
June 1891	£473 4s 3d	£401 8s 3d	£874 12s 6d
December 1891		£196	£196
June 1892	£12		£12
December 1892	£76 18s	£44 17s 9d	£121 15s 9d
June 1893	£184 1s 9d	£254	£438 1s 9d
December 1893		£140	£140
June 1894		£649	£649
December 1894	£129 3s		£129 3s
June 1895	(£205 4s 3d)		(£205 4s 3d)

In an analysis of a bout of severe weather that had swept the country in January 1892, *The Times* reported that the NWNGR had, again, been blocked by snow.

More attention was paid to the railway on 12 September 1892. The Prime Minister, William Ewart Gladstone, had arranged to visit Sir Edward Watkin at Beddgelert to inaugurate the footpath to the Snowdon summit now known as the Watkin Path. Travelling by train, he was greeted at Carnarvon by the major and corporation, the local MP, Lloyd George, and a large crowd. After speeches, the party rejoined the train for the short journey to Dinas, where it transferred to the NWNGR to travel onwards to Rhyd Ddu, giving rise to the speculation that he travelled in the semi-open carriage that now bears his name.

A passenger timetable for 1893 allowed 50 minutes between Dinas and Rhyd Ddu and 15 minutes from Tryfan Junction to Bryngwyn. Connections between the LNWR and the NWNGR were as short as one minute. At Tryfan Junction most trains had

a connection for Bryngwyn. Fares were quoted from Dinas and Carnarvon. 'Amateur photographers' were solicited with the exhortation that they would 'be delighted with the views obtainable along this popular route to Snowdon and Beddgelert.'

A need for increased operating flexibility was felt in the 1890s, when the railway decided that a loop at Waenfawr would help deal with summer tourist traffic. There was no obvious sense of urgency as it took three years from the time that Russell first approaching Marindin with the proposal in June 1894. His idea was to have the main line used by passenger traffic in each direction and to restrict the loop line to goods trains. No doubt he was aware that the station only had one platform and wished to avoid paying for a second one. Two-lever ground frames, one of them located in a corner of the signalbox, would interlock with the signalling and be released by an Annett's key. Russell thought that there was no need for starting signals. When the BoT asked Tanner on 21 September 1894 for a plan it was 16 August 1895 before Russell supplied one — page 21.

Colonel H. Arthur Yorke was deputed to make the inspection, submitting his report on 28 November 1895. Requiring facing point locks at each end of the loop he also thought the station should be properly signalled as a passing place. On 18 December, Russell was given until 1 April 1896 to complete the alterations. Due to delays in getting tenders, Russell informed the BoT on 12 May, the contract had not been awarded to Saxby & Farmer until 1 April. On 31 July 1896 Tanner reported the installation ready for inspection. Submitting his report on 21 December 1896, Yorke explained that at a meeting he and Marindin had had with Russell it had been agreed that starting signals were unnecessary. The home signals could only be lowered when the points were set for the left-hand road. He required just two minor adjustments to the locking to approve the installation. Operationally, he instructed that when two trains approached the station from opposite directions both home signals were to be kept at danger until the trains had come to a stand, when they could be lowered. Finally, Tanner notified the BoT that the alterations had been made on 11 June 1897.

Tanner was replaced as secretary and manager by Gowrie Colquhoun Aitchison, holder of the same position with the Snowdon Mountain Railway, early in 1898. On 12 March the SMR board approved Aitchison taking the appointment in addition to his SMR position providing the SMR's interests were not affected.

In 1898, the NWNGR's net revenue was £971, an increase of more than 50% on 1897, but the balance sheet revealed a sorry story, chiefly arrears in debenture interest of more than £16,000. On the positive side, a Parliamentary deposit of £845 14s 9d had been returned and the renewals reserve had reached £1,329 0s 7d, but the £2,647 0s 2d due to the Moel Tryfan undertaking from the general undertaking was still shown as an asset. Without comment, the £1,016 18s 4d for the LNWR signalling at Dinas, that had probably been carried since 1877, was reduced to £972 3s 7d.

In contrast to the drawn-out processes that brought the Waenfawr loop into use in 1897, approval of an additional siding in 1901 and the moving of an existing siding in 1902 were quite straightforward. In December 1901 Russell sought approval for a siding connecting to the iron ore mine at Bettws Garmon. Aitchison reported the works completed on 14 April 1902 and Major E. Druitt submitted his report on 7 May. There were two connections worked by separate ground frames locked by an Annett's key. He required the key to be attached to the Waenfawr token and the points to be fitted with facing point locks; they also required a second coupling rod and the stock rails required gauge ties. Aitchison reported the work complete on 25 July.

In October 1902, Aitchison requested approval for moving the Snowdon Slate Company's siding to a location 17 chains from its original position. The old site was on a short straight located between curves of 3½ and 4 chains and on a gradient of 1 in 128; the new site was on a similar short straight between curves of 3½ and 5 chains but on a gradient of 1 in 89. The change was required because the land the quarry used to access the railway had changed hands and its new owner refused a wayleave. The siding was 29yd long in total and Druitt approved it on 28 March 1903.

Apart from its link with the LNWR at Dinas the NWNGR operated in isolation, a situation that had started to change from the 1890s as others saw untapped opportunities to complete the gaps between Rhyd Ddu, Beddgelert and Portmadoc. From this point most of what happened to affect the NWNGR was as a result of the activities of outsiders, but first there was some fruitless legal activity.

The Portmadoc, Beddgelert & Rhyd Ddu Railway was first proposed to link the FR to the NWNGR in 1891, when an intention to promote an act of Parliament was announced. Nothing happened until 1897, however, when a Light Railway Order (LRO) application was lodged by Richard Davies, Robert Isaacs and J. William Jones, Portmadoc businessmen. Their 1ft 11½in gauge 11½ mile-long steam railway was estimated to cost £24,720.

The application was withdrawn due to objections by some county council members to proposals that the council should give financial support to the project, but two sets of plans were produced, the first with a route starting on the Gorseddau Railway formation opposite the Queen's Hotel at Portmadoc and running parallel to the Croesor Tramway before diverting to the abandoned formation of the Beddgelert Railway. Reaching Beddgelert via a 280yd tunnel in the Aberglaslyn Pass and a river crossing lower than that later built at Bryn y Felin, the route climbed to Rhyd Ddu via a series of reverse curves, including five of 2 chains (132ft) radius, on gradients as steep as 1 in 41. This route stayed to the east of Pitt's Head and dog-legged across the road to join the NWNGR at the south end of Rhyd Ddu station.

The second set of plans incorporated the Croesor Tramway in the route, starting at Portmadoc Harbour and with a spur serving the Queen's Hotel terminus, before heading off to Beddgelert from a point in the locality of the later Croesor Junction.

In May 1898 Davies, together with A. Bromurch and D. Morris, submitted an application for the Portmadoc, Beddgelert & Snowdon Light Railway (PBSLR). This railway also used the Croesor route and was estimated to cost £24,720. The promoters intended to use their LRO to gain powers to purchase the Croesor, then allegedly disused, but the application was rejected by the Light Railway Commissioners (LRC). They felt that they had no powers to authorise the sale and transfer of a railway operating under Parliamentary sanction. It must have been this application that caused Canon Hardwicke Rawnsley, secretary and a founder of the National Trust for Places of Historic Interest or Natural Beauties, to inform Trust members, at its AGM in July 1898, that 'opposition had been decided upon in the case of the ... light railway projected to pass through the pass at Aberglaslyn', not the only time the Trust would take an interest in proposals to route a railway through the pass.

The NWNGR then submitted, in November 1898, its own LRO application for an extension to Beddgelert, terminating near the Goat Hotel and with no intention of going further. From Rhyd Ddu the 4½ mile railway was level or rising slightly for nearly a mile but the remainder fell 426ft towards Beddgelert with a succession of tight (up to 4 chains) curves on gradients

Above: **Construction of the PBSSR started in 1904 and this postcard of the Aberglaslyn Pass illustrates the temporary bridge made across the river. The message is dated 6 May 1906 and reads 'We are at present making the railway in this Aberglaslyn Pass ... it is a very beautiful place. ... This last week has been terribly wet and the River Glaslyn is in flood. ... This is the north end of the pass, the huts belong to the railway contractors ...'**
Wrench/Author's collection

Below: **Amongst the PBSSR works completed was this bridge over the Cwm Cloch lane. It was altered when the gradient was reduced by the WHR in 1923 and again when the line was being rebuilt in 2007.** *P. G. Thomas/ Welsh Highland Heritage*

Right: **Another section of work completed for the PBSSR was the stone structures near Bryn y Felin, c1913.**
Valentine/Author's collection

Below: **Abandoned track at what became the Beddgelert station site, 1920.**
Author's collection

varying between 1 in 45 and 1 in 42. The proposed Beddgelert station site was criticised by the ministry, being on less than 200ft of level ground at the foot of the incline and itself on a 4-chain curve. Engineers James W. Szlumper and William W. Szlumper signed the estimate of expense totalling £11,496. As the former had been the Manchester & Milford Railway's engineer since 1864 it is most likely that, as with Tanner in 1890, with Russell being the MMR's receiver, that was the link that brought him to the NWNGR.

Charles Breese and William George, who were both to participate in the WHR story some 20 years later, were somehow involved in the PBSLR scheme. In April 1899, they were party to an agreement reached with the NWNGR, whereby they agreed not to compete with the NWNGR scheme provided the latter raised the site of its proposed Beddgelert station by 5ft to facilitate a junction with any subsequent railway from Portmadoc, and granted running powers to Rhyd Ddu.

The LRC held an inquiry into the NWNGR scheme at Carnarvon on 16 December 1899, a Saturday. The commissioners were told that the extension capital would be kept separate from that of the Moel Tryfan undertaking and that the NWNGR would work the line for 60% of its revenue. As the NWNGR had been generating an income of £7 10s (£7.50) per mile per week the extension ought to produce £1,700 annually on the same basis, 40% of which would pay 5-6% interest on its capital.

At the 1891 census Beddgelert's population had fallen to 672. It was presently rising, it was claimed, due to the existence of quarries and mines although copper mines had closed due to transport difficulties but it was hoped the railway would alleviate this. Glanyrafon, the largest quarry in the locality, employed 500 men, 30 of them living in Beddgelert and who could be expected to use the railway daily.

The North Wales Narrow Gauge Railways (Beddgelert Light Railway Extension) Order was made on 3 August 1900. The order specified that rails should weigh at least 41½lb per yard and that check rails should be used on curves of less the three chains radius. It was extremely detailed on the fixings to be used on flat-bottom rail.

Although a special general meeting was held on 16 April 1901 to pass the special resolutions necessary to bring the extension undertaking into effect, it was 14 April 1903 before Russell was able to tell the shareholders that 'agreements have been made for the purchase of nearly all the land required ...' An extension credit shown in the balance sheet had reached £505 by 1904. As it happened, the impetus for linking Rhyd Ddu and Beddgelert was being taken away from the NWNGR by the Portmadoc, Beddgelert & South Snowdon Railway (PBSSR).

The PBSSR was the creation of an Act of Parliament obtained by the Northern Counties Traction Company Limited (NCT) on 17 August 1901. The Act authorised the following: construction of Railway No 1, 5 furlongs 1 chain long, from Pen y Mount, parallel to the standard gauge Cambrian siding, to a location on the former Gorseddau Railway, opposite the Queen's Hotel at Portmadoc and which would have given the railway a public face; No 2, seven miles long, commencing at a junction with the PCBTR three miles from Portmadoc and terminating near Llyn Gwynant where it would have served a proposed power station and South Snowdon quarry; purchase of the PCBTR for £10,000 within one year and the dissolution of the PCBTR; use of the Parliamentary section of the Croesor Tramway by passengers as well as by goods and mineral traffic; the undertaking of agreements with any or either of the Cambrian, FR, NWNGR and the Snowdon Mountain Railways; the supply of electricity to Portmadoc, Criccieth and Beddgelert and the working of the railway by electricity. The estimates reveal an intention to build a line from Portmadoc to Borth y Gest, an 1865 objective of the CPR. See page 23.

NCT was not the only organisation planning electric railways in the area. In 1900 and 1903 the North Wales & District Light Railway & Electric Power Syndicate made applications for three light railway orders for a standard gauge railway between Pwllheli and Porth Dinlleyn. The May 1900 Pwllheli & Nevin LRO application was withdrawn, to be replaced by a Pwllheli, Nevin and Porth Dinlleyn LRO application in November 1900. After a public inquiry this was withdrawn because the promoters could not get a treasury grant. In May 1903 they returned with a second Pwllheli, Nevin & Porth Dinlleyn application which was provisionally approved but was struck off due to a lack of response by the promoters.

PBSSR Railway No 1 was estimated at £8,004, refurbishing the Croesor Tramway at £39,413 and Railway No 2 at £75,407, these prices including electrification. Capital was set at £270,000 in 54,000 £5 shares, with a further £60,000 borrowing sanctioned, supplemented by an additional £30,000, in share subscriptions or loans, from four local authorities, to be repaid within 40 years.

There would have been exchange facilities with the FR and stations at Portmadoc, Pont Croesor, either end of the Aberglaslyn tunnel, Beddgelert, Llyn Dinas and Llyn Gwynant. The PBSSR was forbidden to tip debris or rubbish on the banks of, or into, the Glaslyn in the Aberglaslyn Pass without the sanction of the Lord Lieutenant – these requirements, with the extended tunnel referred to hereafter, being early examples of enforced environmental protection.

The passage of PBSSR trains over the standard gauge line was to be regulated by the Cambrian so as not to interfere with its own traffic. The hydro-electric power station was to be located at Cwm Dyli, separated from Railway No 2's terminus by an overhead electrical feeder. It was to take water from Llyn Llydaw, a lake of about 100 acres at 1,400ft above sea level.

Portmadoc and Criccieth UDCs asked for concessions on the price for lighting and the Cambrian and the FR asked for protective clauses. Mary Roche, the Tremadoc estate beneficiary, originally made a substantial objection but following negotiations conducted by solicitors concentrated on the route through the Aberglaslyn Pass, as did the National Trust. Mrs Roche withdrew her objection but the trust succeeded in extending the length of the Aberglaslyn tunnel from the 270 yards of the deposited plans to 700 yards, to conceal the railway from observers at Pont Aberglaslyn; the promoters agreed to the change, at an estimated cost of £3,000, without consulting its engineers to secure an unopposed reading in the House of Lords.

The trust, having said that it was satisfied with the bill in committee, then decided, with the support of the Commons Preservation Society, to object again at its third reading in the Commons on 6 August. This was contrary to convention because at that stage there was no opportunity for any objection to be examined properly.

Devoting its energies to the Aberglaslyn Pass, the trust had failed to notice the significance of the power station. Now it claimed that the high-pressure water pipes and culverts would 'destroy two waterfalls in the cwm and disfigure it. The landscape of Llyn Llydaw will be permanently injured.' Others said that the population was too small to justify the scheme and that coal generation of electricity in Portmadoc would be better.

Lloyd George spoke for the railway, saying that local people supported it: 'An electric tramway to Snowdon would be a great convenience not only to tourists but also to the locality. It would certainly be better to have a nice little electric tram up Snowdon than a steam engine.' The next day this was reported in *The Times* as: 'Besides, it would be good for the tourists to be able to ascend Snowdon by a nice electric tram instead of by a shaky charabanc, as at present.' The motion to retain the power to take water from the lake was carried 162 votes to 52. The PBSSR later claimed that it had organised its own Parliamentary whip to ensure the bill's success in the Commons.

The Gorseddau Railway was at this time abandoned. From 1856/7 it had been a non-statutory 3ft gauge horse tramway and, with the benefit of Parliamentary powers obtained in 1872, it was converted to 2ft gauge being connected to the Croesor line at Portmadoc, where, after the main line fell out of use in the 1880s, a small part survived at Portmadoc to give access to the Moel y Gest Quarry and a stonemason's yard.

Electricity could be supplied in bulk to any of the Cambrian, Festiniog, NWNGR and Snowdon Mountain railways or 'any local authority, company or person authorised to supply electrical energy'; the Portmadoc and Criccieth councils could buy the installations after 36 years had elapsed from the passing of the act. The accounts of the electricity undertaking were to be kept separately from those of the railway.

The engineers were Bennett & Ward Thomas of Manchester and Alfred M. Fowler of Westminster. The solicitor was Evan Robert Davies of Pwllheli, a name of some significance later in this story. After the act had been obtained he continued to work for the PBSSR, on 24 February 1902 asking the FR's manager, J. S. Hughes, if the FR would use electricity for 'lighting or any other purpose' in order that the PBSSR could produce estimates of likely revenue – were there no revenue estimates before the act was obtained? The FR board decided that no definitive answer could be given.

The PBSSR became the subject of a takeover in 1903, with representatives of consulting engineers Harper Brothers and electrical engineers Bruce Peebles Ltd driving the company and changing its direction from being a railway company with generating powers to being a power company with a railway. The North Wales Power & Traction Company (NWPTC) was registered on 30 July 1903, capitalised at £1 million, to own the PBSSR and to develop the generating business. A prospectus was

The only success of the PBSSR enterprise, the Cwm Dyli power station.
Author's collection

issued on 4 August 1903. To cater for future expansion the company was to buy 1,300 acres and the water rights around Llyn Eigiau, Dolgarrog, from James Tomkinson MP and Henry Platt, the electrical engineer; they were to be paid £40,000, alleged to be less than they had paid for the property. Both were members of the NWPTC board from its second meeting on 8 August.

Preliminary expenses of £80,000 included £3,000 cash due to Tomkinson and Platt as part of the £40,000: £36,000 payable in cash or shares to NCT, and £25,000 for brokerage and other expenses. On 30 July 1903, NCT had taken an option to subscribe the PBSSR capital and the latter had agreed to reimburse £500 to NCT on account of the interest payable on the Croesor purchase. The £36,000 due to NCT was effectively in respect of the PBSSR, including surveys, reports, plans etc. NCT undertook to pay all expenses payable by the PBSSR, except the Croesor interest and stamp duty, up to 30 June 1903, and £15,000 to the Electric Conversion Syndicate for assistance.

A total of 33,500 £5 shares were underwritten by William Windle Pilkington, the glassmaker, Joseph Beecham, the pill maker, Peebles and others, including the directors. If Peebles was allotted shares they would be allocated in proportion to the value of work undertaken as certified by the engineers. Pilkington and Beecham had advanced the Parliamentary deposit of £10,717 15s 9d. Beecham owned half of the issued capital of the St Helens Cable Company, which was in a position to supply Peebles with electric cable if its price and quality was acceptable.

The NWPTC issued the cheque for £10,000 to purchase the PCBTR on 29 September 1903, somewhat later than the 12 months allowed by the 1901 Act although 5% interest was due as a result; a balance sheet dated 4 August 1904 showed the total expenditure under this heading at £11,518 4s 5d. Roberts had been, again, the tramway's sole proprietor when the sale was completed. Russell's £330 mortgage was settled by NWPTC on 22 October, when the transaction was reported as being complete. On 23 November NWPTC had paid £500 to NCT as a refund on interest paid to the PCBTR.

Aitchison was to report that he took over the PCBTR from 1 January 1904; his appointment as manager of the PBSSR, with a salary of £600, started the same day. Despite the change in ownership the tramway continued as it always had done. The busiest section was between Portmadoc harbour and the Beddgelert siding, including carriage of slate from the FR before the exchange yard was built at Minffordd in 1872, and afterwards when Minffordd was too busy.

To achieve the company's objectives new Parliamentary powers were needed, two bills being deposited in November 1903. The second PBSSR Act gained royal assent on 15 August 1904, at the same time as the North Wales Electric Power Act. The former authorised the construction of further railways, extending the NWNGR to Carnarvon, agreements with the NWNGR, working the lines by electricity, additional time to build the 1901 railway, and the transfer of the generating powers to the NWPTC.

The objection of main line railway companies, the Cambrian and the LNWR, had prevented the PBSSR from applying for an LRO. The LNWR had most to say, claiming that completion of the Portmadoc–Carnarvon narrow gauge route would be in competition with its own route and such competition was 'unnecessary and uncalled for, more especially as it will be established by means of piecemeal legislation', implying that the promoters had been underhand and had previously disguised their intentions.

Cross examination in the Lords on 10 March 1904 identified other PBSSR backers, including its chairman, James Ernest

Rawlins, who had experience in power transmission in America, and another director, Percy Tarbutt, who was a mining engineer with experience in South Africa. According to Rawlins the PBSSR had £170,000 already subscribed, sufficient to complete the 1901 railway, he said. Actually slightly less than £170,000, as this was the value of the underwritten NWPCT shares.

The Power Act increased the area to which power could be supplied and at the company's first annual meeting, held on 9 December 1904, a jubilant Rawlins claimed that it was the first power company to obtain Parliamentary powers, previously the province of local authorities. He told shareholders that the Dinas–Carnarvon railway would be a valuable asset and that the board 'hope to make arrangements shortly to build this extension'. Regarding finances, Rawlins explained that the time was not right to issue debentures and arrangements would 'probably be made for a temporary loan sufficient to complete the works and railways at present contemplated.'

Sir Douglas Fox, the company's consulting engineer, paid tribute to the 'very satisfactory way' in which the contractor, Bruce Peebles & Company, was working in North Wales. The engineer, W. A. Harper, explained that it was important that the railway between Rhyd Ddu and Beddgelert should be completed 'at the earliest possible moment' so that the transmission line to the Nantlle quarries could be routed along the permanent way and not on adjacent land at extra expense.

At the same time that the bills were deposited in 1903, NWPTC had submitted two LRO applications, one for the Snowdon & Bettws Railway under its own name, the other for NWNGR. The latter sought extra time to complete its Beddgelert extension, to link it to the PBSSR, to work the Moel Tryfan undertaking as a light railway and by electricity, to sell any part of the undertaking to the PBSSR, to transfer the Beddgelert extension powers to the PBSSR, and to make various capital adjustments.

One of NWPTC's customers for power was the Marconi radio station at Waenfawr. *Marconi/Author's collection*

The PBSSR link comprised two lines totalling two miles in length, one starting a quarter-mile short of the 1900 line's proposed Beddgelert terminus and passing through a tunnel 100 yards long at the rear of the Goat Hotel before crossing the Portmadoc road by a bridge to reach the Glaslyn meadows, crossed on embankment, then passing around the village and crossing the river before making a connection to the PBSSR in the Nant Gwynant direction. The other line was a realignment of the PBSSR in the Aberglaslyn Pass before crossing the river near Bryn y Felin and making a junction with the first in the Rhyd Ddu direction near the church. Perversely, this layout removed the through route from Portmadoc to Nant Gwynant. See plan on page 25. The river crossings would have been 60ft and 80ft long and gradients as steep as 1 in 20. The second line was to cause problems when the order came to be processed.

By this stage, NWNGR revenue was down to £6 per mile per week with costs of £5 per mile per week, producing a surplus of £600 per annum; it had carried 39,000 passengers and 28,496 tons of slate in 1902. In March the shareholders had been told that the Beddgelert extension's centre line had been set out and that negotiations over the land needed had been started. By September, agreement had been reached for more than half the land concerned and by April 1903 for nearly all of it.

The LRC held an inquiry that lasted two hours in Beddgelert on 2 February 1904. The NWNGR had been unable to progress its 1900 extension due to lack of funds. The Portmadoc-facing spur was intended to supersede the PBSSR's 1901 route through the Aberglaslyn Pass, the engineers saying that the proposed long tunnel was impracticable and dangerous and should be replaced by two shorter bores. Due to the nature of the rock, a tunnel on the original centre line would have brought the railway over the river, with no means of support. Solicitor Randal Casson, appearing for the Tremadoc Estate and the Lord Lieutenant, said that he had drafted the 1901 amendment and agreed that it had been accepted by the PBSSR without due consideration, to get the bill before Parliament on the unopposed list.

Russell gave evidence that electric working would save the NWNGR £1,000 a year, even if there was no increase in business. Richard Davies, one of the 1897/8 promoters and now chairman of the county council, attended the inquiry to support the application on behalf of the surveyor's committee. The secretary of the National Trust, Nigel Bond, said that the pass was too narrow to accommodate the railway, the road and the river and that if it was possible the 1901 route should be adhered to. The NWNGR's solicitor said the NWPTC had already entered into contracts for carrying out the proposed works and the contractors were ready to start work. Engineers Harper Brothers & Co and consulting engineers Douglas Fox & Partners signed the estimate of £10,291.

The modified route started what became a longstanding dispute with the owners of the Goat Hotel estate at Beddgelert. In this instance agreement was reached, whereby the railway sold back some of the land purchased in 1900 whilst it bought additional land for the extension, both transactions taking place at the 1903 rate per acre. Amongst other conditions the railway agreed not to use any of the land as tea gardens or to build any other station within a mile of the hotel, except for a passenger platform on the eastern bank of the Glaslyn. The railway was to be built as far from Gelert's grave as permitted by the limit of deviation and the embankment across the Portmadoc road was to be planted with trees, shrubs or evergreens. The only access to the station was to be through the hotel's yard.

An agreement between the NWNGR, the PBSSR and the NWPTC 'containing the bases of working arrangements between the companies and the construction of railways' was

made on 4 November 1904 and approved by NWNGR shareholders at an extraordinary meeting held on 2 November 1905. Under the terms of the agreement, the NWNGR proprietors were told, their railway would be worked by electricity by the PBSSR in perpetuity. The meeting was the third occasion that the agreement had been put to the NWNGR proprietors; there is no explanation for its deferment but it did require court approval before it could be made.

As the order processing stretched into 1905 without the LRO being made, the NWNGR's solicitors maintained pressure on the BoT, asking when it was going to be confirmed as their clients 'desired to proceed at once with the reconstruction' and were 'anxious to commence electrification.' The draft order turned out to be defective and did not include powers of abandonment for the former Beddgelert station site and the affected section of the PBSSR although a fresh set of plans produced in 1904 did indicate the sections that would be abandoned. However, when the NWNGR (Light Railway) Order was made on 6 June 1905 it had only powers to work the existing lines as light railways, by electricity, to raise £12,000 '1905' debenture stock, of which £2,000 was to be allocated to the appointment of a receiver, and to be leased to the PBSSR. No extra time was given for the 1900 extension, although in August 1903, Aitchison had secured a 12-month extension from the BoT. The LRC reported that the missing components would be the subject of a separate application by the PBSSR.

The NWPTC November 1903 application for the Snowdon & Bettws y Coed Light Railway (SBLR) LRO would have made an 11½-mile extension of the PBSSR with gradients as steep as 1 in 19 and curves down to 6 chains. An inquiry was held at Bettws y Coed on 3 February 1904, the day after the NWNGR inquiry. The application attracted considerable numbers of objections, the National Trust and the Co-Op Holidays Association chief amongst them, and letters published in national newspapers. A petition attracted 2,400 signatures, few of them local.

Amongst the objections were criticisms of the order being awarded to a limited company, leading to an agreement to make the order in favour of the PBSSR, a statutory company. Although the LRC submitted the order to the BoT for confirmation on 18 August 1904 there were concerns that the PBSSR would be governed by two acts and three LROs. A combination order to amalgamate the powers and to give the PBSSR authority to operate the NWNGR was proposed, when the deferred aspects of the NWNGR 1903 application could also be dealt with. The application was therefore held over by the BoT.

The SBLR application seems to have triggered a simultaneous application from the Penmachno, Corwen & Bettws Light Railway Co. This 28-mile 2ft gauge electric railway would, with the PBSSR and the SBLR, have completed the NWNGR's original general undertaking proposal along with its Penmachno branch. Its promoters, A. Carter and J. L. Owen were named in the application, were apparently independent of either the PBSSR or the NWPT. Following an inquiry held at Corwen on 28 July 1904 the LRC approved the order but it was not confirmed by the BoT and the application was struck off in 1910 because of lack of response from the promoters.

The PBSSR returned to the LRC in November 1904 with an application to work its 1901 and 1904 lines as light railways and to modify the 1901 route through the Aberglaslyn Pass. An inquiry was held in Carnarvon on Saturday, 15 April 1905.

There were some misconceptions about the purpose of the order, with Ynyscynhaiarn (Portmadoc) and Deudraeth councils asking that as the public had become accustomed to walking along the Croesor Tramway trackbed for more than 20 years, the commissioners should protect this 'right' in the order. Not unnaturally the commissioners explained that this was beyond their remit.

Again the National Trust objected to the modification of the tunnel, saying that it had been approved by Parliament and could only be changed by Parliament. It was generally felt that a shorter tunnel would bring the railway into view of those admiring the pass from Pont Aberglaslyn and spoil their enjoyment of it. It is difficult to appreciate this now, due to the considerable tree and rhododendron growth over the intervening period that has seriously reduced this perspective. As railway enthusiasts, we would take the view that the appearance of a train would only enhance the scenery!

The trust could not say why its view should prevail over anyone else's and the LRC, in its report, did not think it was well founded, saying that even as modified the railway would still be unseen from Pont Aberglaslyn. Despite the recommendation that the order be made the BoT decided to hear further objections in London on 24 October 1905.

Whilst these applications were still outstanding the PBSSR made two further LRO applications in November 1905. The first was to resolve the outstanding extension at Beddgelert. In addition to transferring the 1900 powers, diverted at Beddgelert to suit a through railway, the application sought approval to connect to the PBSSR and to obtain extra time to build the 1900 extension. The NWNGR proposal to have a Nant Gwynant-facing connection to the PBSSR was abandoned, the connecting line being about three-quarters of a mile long, deviating from the 1900 line at Beddgelert and taking the line behind the Goat Hotel in tunnel and giving rise to the now-famous abandoned road overbridge and abutments standing isolated in the field nearby. The county council was allowed to advance up to £2,000 by share subscription or loan. As the issue had already received a public airing at the 1904 inquiry the order was processed without too much delay, being made on 24 October 1906 when it was signed by the president of the BoT, David Lloyd George.

The second 1905 application was to amend the PBSSR's 1904 route at Carnarvon, abandoning the last quarter-mile on the quayside and substituting a tramway half a mile long along St Helen's Road to the wharves alongside the castle. Harper Brothers estimated that it would cost £3,241; £500 was allowed for a station to be located beneath the castle walls. A public inquiry was held at Carnarvon on 30 January 1906.

The original terminus was to have been on the site of the disused de Winton foundry, de Winton & Company being in liquidation. The extension was needed because the river there was too shallow for sea-going craft to access and therefore to eliminate double handling of slate in transit to the wharves. There was some debate about the rate to be charged for freight carried over the extension, the railway wishing to charge more, on a pro rata basis, to allow for the expense of installing wagon turntables on the wharves. Darbishire, now the mayor of Carnarvon and owner of the Pen yr Orsedd Quarry in the Nantlle, said his quarry was being electrified, using power purchased from NWPTC, and he was considering connecting it to the NWNGR at Bryngwyn. He told the inquiry that the LNWR charged 1s 7d per ton for carrying slate between Nantlle and Carnarvon but if the slate were being exported from Carnarvon by sea the rate was increased by 1s 1d. Aitchison, speaking for the PBSSR, said the rate by narrow gauge would still be less and breakages would be reduced. The LRC passed the order to the BoT for approval on 11 October 1906 but due to a question arising over the interpretation of a clause on the application of capital it was 8 July 1908 before the PBSSR (Light Railway Extension at Carnarvon) Order was made.

Two days after the Beddgelert Extension Order had been made, 26 October 1906, there was further action on the SBLR and PBSSR applications, when the BoT remitted them to the LRC for consolidation and for revision of the capital and borrowing powers of the PBSSR. By this time the PBSSR had raised £50,000 share capital for railway construction under its 1901 powers. It now sought an authorised share capital of £100,000 and borrowing of £100,000 in respect of Portmadoc–Rhyd Ddu, and £90,000 plus £30,000 for the SBLR.

This order was made on 7 July 1908. Its powers included bringing the 1901 and 1904 railways within the ambit of the Light Railways Act, giving until 24 October 1909 for the construction of the 1900 Beddgelert extension, authorising the SBLR and sanctioning the changes to the 1901 Aberglaslyn tunnel. The works in the pass were to be built according to plans countersigned by the county's Lord Lieutenant and the National Trust.

On the financial front the PBSSR's capital was reduced to £190,000 from £270,000, despite the additional expense of building the SBLR, because it no longer needed capital for the power station. The county council was allowed to advance £10,000.

The legal results of eight years' effort to connect Portmadoc with Rhyd Ddu, recognising that that was not always a priority, may be tabulated as shown opposite.

While all this legal activity was in progress construction work had actually started. The PBSSR, in its half-year report to 30 June 1904, stated that works 'in connection with the construction of the PBSSR from Portmadoc to Beddgelert, and the junction railway at Beddgelert and the Beddgelert extension railway ... have been in progress since February 1904' but Douglas Fox & Partners and Harper Bros, in their joint report to NWPTC dated 4 August, declared that 'for all practical purposes, the date for starting the works was really about 1 June, in fact, the contractors only got possession of some of the land ... as recently as ... last month.' Considering that both companies had the same directors, were addressing the same audience and received information from the same source, the difference in approach is intriguing.

NWPTC had accepted Bruce Peebles & Company's £145,000 tender for 'the alteration, extension and electrification of the railway, the construction of dams and hydraulic works and erection and equipment of the power station ...' on 31 July 1903. Peebles had the manufacturing licenses for the railway patents of the Hungarian company, Ganz & Co. The tender included the 'alteration, extension and electrification of the railway, the construction of the dams and hydraulic works and erection and equipping of the power station.' The civil engineering and permanent way was sub-contracted to Strauss & Co, a Bristol-based contractor with tramway-building experience, with Peebles acting as main contractor, erecting at least one board to inform passersby that it was acting for the North Wales Power & Electric Traction Co.

The engineers' report already mentioned reads as though the section between Beddgelert and Rhyd Ddu was an afterthought, with 'the' tunnel in the Aberglaslyn Pass now only 450yd long instead of 700yd; 'this will effect a large saving on this portion ... which will go towards paying for the additional section being constructed ...' Strictly speaking, at this date the PBSSR had no authority to build towards Rhyd Ddu. It was, the engineers reported, very difficult 'on account of broken peat bogs.' The cuttings and embankments 'necessitate a considerable number of culverts and accommodation works, the latter on account of the smallness of the holdings.' There were also problems in recruiting labour; there was no accommodation and the best labour was already employed in the quarries. The contractors forecast that the line would be completed in eight or nine months, at the same

Act or Order	Date	Railway authorised	Share capital	Borrowing	Remarks
NWNGR (Beddgelert Light Railway Extension) Order	1900	From Rhyd Ddu terminus of existing NWNGR to Beddgelert	£13,800	£4,600	Powers transferred to PBSSR, 1906, when capital and borrowing powers repealed.
PBSSR Act	1901	From Portmadoc to Beddgelert	£270,000	£60,000	Capital authorised included capital for power station scheme, reduced by 1908 Order.
PBSSR Act	1904	From Dinas terminus of existing NWNGR to Carnarvon	£24,000	£98,000	Borrowing powers of 1901 Act repealed, powers given to borrow not exceeding one third of capital authorised by 1901 and 1904 Acts repealed by 1908 Order, share capital repealed by 1908 Order.
PBSSR (Beddgelert Railway Light Extension) Order	1906	At Beddgelert, connecting railways authorised by 1900 Order and 1901 Act	£24,000	£8,000	Also transfer of powers of 1900 Order to PBSSR. Share capital and borrowing repealed by 1908 Order.
PBSSR (Light Railway Extension at Carnarvon) Order	1908	Deviation and extension at Carnarvon	None	None	
PBSSR	1908	From Beddgelert connecting with railway authorised by 1901 Act to Bettws y Coed	£190,000	£130,000	More than £100,000 share capital not to be raised until resolution on commencement of SBLR carried.

In railway terms it can be summarised as:

Act or Order	Route	Miles
1901 Act	Portmadoc–Beddgelert, including Croesor Tramway	11
1900 and 1906 Orders	Beddgelert to Rhyd Ddu NWNGR	5
1904 Act and 1908 Carnarvon Order	Dinas–Carnarvon	3

time as the tunnel. In another report, dated 29 November, they merely say, of the railways, that 'the contractors are making satisfactory progress ...' Peebles' first request for payment, of £2,500, was made on 9 February 1904.

Details of the proposed electrical installation were sent to the BoT in 1905. The overhead rail electrification was to be a twin-wire, three-phase, 630 volts, ac system because it would be more cost effective than using dc; the rails would have carried the third phase. Ten 100kVa substations were proposed, located at the Beddgelert Siding, Croesor Junction, Beddgelert, Hafod Ruffydd, Rhyd Ddu, Bettws Garmon, Tryfan Junction, Bryngwyn, Dinas and Caernarvon. Two extra high-tension primary cables, one for the railway and the other supplying lighting power to Portmadoc and Criccieth, would pass through the Aberglaslyn tunnels in a protected trough. One BoT officer commented: 'The scheme has been carefully worked out and all reasonable precautions have been taken ...'

In 1904, the NWPTC had taken over responsibility for the 1901 PBSSR Act's Parliamentary deposit, £10,970, and had paid the £1,118 deposit for the railway's 1904 Act. On 30 December, the PBSSR obtained a loan of £10,810 from the Excess Insurance Company that was paid to the power company, both companies securing the loan with debenture stock, when issued, and guaranteeing the interest. The loan was to be repaid within 18 months or 'upon completion or abandonment of the works authorised.' According to the BoT returns, the PBSSR never issued any debentures.

Throughout 1904 Peebles received payments when due for work carried out on the power station and the railway; the figures were not broken down. By 6 January 1905 £39,506 had been paid. Peebles had to pay 35% of the monies received back to NWPTC to purchase shares.

The first signs of financial problems came on 3 February 1905, when Harper Brothers submitted a certificate valued at £10,000. There was only £6,952 16s 9d in the bank so the board decided to pay Peebles only £5,000. W. A. Harper, present at the meeting, warned his firm would be certifying another £8,000 in a few days and more within a few weeks. The secretary was instructed to authorise Peebles to draw two bills of £7,500 on the company, payable on sight when the certificates had been received. In his report Harper said that works were progressing well 'except for the railway' – this last remark was not explained.

Peebles accepted the revised payment arrangements and informed NWPTC that it had signed a works contract with the PBSSR and requesting a £7,500 bill be issued. Peebles also agreed to sign another contract before the second bill was issued. As Peebles was owed £19,876 2s 6d the board decided that the first bill would be payable on 7 April and the second on 7 May. As the work progressed these bills were cancelled and replaced by new ones for larger amounts.

Despite the shortage of funds, the omens for the power business seemed good. The minutes for 1905 contain regular reports of quarries agreeing to take supplies when available and in November the board was in a position to decide to advertise that it had power for sale. During the summer, Lloyds Bank advanced a total of £38,000 and arrangements were made to borrow £120,000 from the Law Debenture Corporation; six shareholders had to guarantee £30,000 before this advance was made. Peebles' outstanding account of £27,275 19s had been paid in July. The sting in the tail for Peebles – the cheque was accompanied with a request for £12,000 for NWPTC shares. The only progress in Carnarvon had occurred on 15 August, when the board had agreed the purchase of the land required from the harbour trustees for £3,000, a deal negotiated by Aitchison. The price was substantial, nearly that estimated for the diversion of half a mile of railway. The land included the station site located between the castle, the slate quay and the harbour office, a prime position (page 41).

The engineers reported on 29 November 1905 that two-thirds of the railway was completed but the necessity of additional powers and bad weather had delayed progress. The heaviest works were, however, completed and the remainder could be done in five or six months. Tenders had been requested for the Carnarvon extension. In his report to shareholders at the annual meeting on 8 December 1905, Rawlins said that there was a problem with the railway contract, 'a misunderstanding on the question of the quantities' without making any further comment. There was another problem with the railway that had nothing to do with the contract that came to a head later in the month.

Not content with its objections to the LRC and the BoT, the National Trust returned to Wales and succeeded in getting the work stopped before the end of 1905. Lloyd George's involvement, as president of the BoT, was noted on an internal briefing memo dealing with the SBLR application: 'Mr Lloyd George himself visited the place, and saw the objectors' but more details are contained in a report published in local newspapers. Lloyd George 'saw the objectors' at the Goat Hotel, Beddgelert, on 30 December 1905. With Aitchison,

Francis Fox of Douglas Fox & Partners, resident engineer L. D. Taylor, a Mr Wells from Peebles and his newly appointed Parliamentary secretary Hudson Ewbanke Kearley MP, he faced Canon Rawnsley, previously encountered in 1898, and Bond, its secretary.

Fox explained that concern about the stability of the scree, to be seen by the mouth of what became the long tunnel, had prompted the deviation. The revised plans had the Lord Lieutenant's approval, reported Aitchison, adding that proposals made by the company in response to the trust's objections had been rejected by that personage. The trust's representatives had nothing more to add to the objections already made in London, saying that now they had 'been over the points of the line ... [they] could now see a reason for the deviation' – had they not visited the location previously? The meeting ended with consensus on the work proceeding and a site visit.

Work resumed soon afterwards and on 30 March 1906 the NWPTC board was informed that only two bridges were needed to complete the railway between Portmadoc and the 'Glaslyn Pass'. Aitchison was asked to get an estimate of the costs with a view to opening this section of line. As the long tunnel remained unfinished it was probably the intention to have had a temporary terminus at Nantmor or Cwm Bychan. Aitchison was also asked to investigate the cost of completing the 'Rhyd Ddu extension'.

Russell, meanwhile, had apparently become concerned about the lack of progress with the NWNGR electrification for on 29 January 1906 he had told the NWPTC that he wanted to discuss terms for agreeing to its postponement. On 13 February he had written again, saying that pending a meeting with Rawlins, he felt compelled to ask the contractors to stop work on erecting transmission lines where they crossed the NWNGR, near Quellyn, but 'as negotiations were pending ... do not object to the work proceeding but ... reserve ... the right to take [it] all down as ... think fit.' Rawlins had met him and his conditions were put to the NWPTC board on 20 February 1906:

Construction of the railways could be deferred for two years but the PBSSR must undertake to recommence construction on or before 1 March 1908.

The NWPTC to restore the NWNGR for steam working and to provide one steam locomotive at a cost not exceeding in total £2,500.

If the Carnarvon extension was not started by March 1908 all agreements between the companies were to be cancelled, the NWPTC paying the NWNGR £5,000 in cash in liquidated damages in addition to the £2,500.

Salem, near Betws Garmon, seen from above, c1905. The NWNGR route is in front of the house at the lower left of centre. *E. D., Bangor/Author's collection*

Mynydd Mawr (Elephant Mountain), at 2,290ft, dominates this view from Waenfawr as it does the railway. The station house, now the Snowdonia Parc public house, is visible on the right and the back of the station building and goods shed can be seen to its left.
Author's collection

The PBSSR was to pay £250 per year to the NWNGR until the Carnarvon–Portmadoc railway was completed or until the agreements were cancelled.

Aitchison was to be manager of the combined railways for at least 10 years from the date of his appointment as the NWPTC's general manager.

NWPTC was to guarantee the construction of the railways 'if and when construction be recommenced'.

Subject to approval by the Law Debenture Corporation, the NWPTC had accepted the terms without demur on 20 February 1906. Russell had then written to fine-tune his demands on 21 February and 28 February, concluding the second letter, 'it must be clearly understood that no arrangement will be entered into with the Portmadoc company. The power company is the company with which the narrow gauge company deals and to which it looks for carrying out all arrangements &c. The Portmadoc company is mere paper and no contract or undertaking entered into by it would be of the slightest value.' This letter had been taken to the NWPTC board on 2 March when it was 'discussed and finally approved.'

There is something slightly odd about the sequence of events here, for Aitchison had apparently obtained a specification for a locomotive on 31 January and had placed the order, via the PBSSR, on 13 February. NWNGR shareholders were informed of the 'postponement' on 12 March 1906. The Hunslet 2-6-2T named *Russell* was delivered to Dinas in June 1906. On 8 June the NWPTC had hoped the £1,435 due to the Hunslet Engine Co would be financed by the Law Debenture Corporation, but on 3 August it ordered a cheque be drawn against an advance expected from Lloyds Bank. The first instalment of the annual payment to the NWNGR, £125 for six months to 30 June, was paid on 3 August 1906.

With the power station and transmission lines in the throes of commissioning, on 17 June 1906 Rawlins informed Aitchison that the power station had cost more than anticipated and 'that there are not sufficient funds to complete the railway' – all work was stopped. Aitchison was instructed, on 16 July, to investigate the company's affairs, to ascertain its liabilities, to terminate any expenditure that he considered unnecessary and to report to the board in 14 days. Although the report was typed up, at a cost of £2 19s 6d, it was only discussed when incomplete, and the details of its content have not come to light.

On 30 July 1907 Peebles and NWPTC agreed to cancel the works contract, Peebles transferring the assets it had acquired for the railway, including transformers, switchgear and six locomotives, to NWPTC and accepting £60,000 in NWPTC 7% second charge debentures to discharge all liabilities. Power

generation and supply is very profitable but capital intensive in its early days so it is hardly surprising that in this case there was no spare cash to build narrow gauge railways, electric or otherwise. On 16 October 1906, shareholders were told that the company had 'now come to the end of its resources.'

One of the PBSSR locomotives had been exhibited on Peebles' stand at the Third International Electric Tramway & Railway Exhibition held at Crystal Palace in July 1905. It seems that five of them had been built by Ganz in Hungary so possibly the sixth had been built by Peebles under licence; ten had been ordered. On 31 May 1905 the NWPTC board had agreed to pay £15 towards W. A. Harper's expenses incurred in visiting Budapest, no doubt in connection with equipment to be supplied by Ganz. The locomotives were advertised for sale until at least 1910; the contact was a man named Jack, who will be encountered again in 1919.

When Peebles entered voluntary liquidation in March 1908 it held £119,744 NWPTC shares amongst its assets; its difficulties were ascribed to being undercapitalised and the company was reconstructed. Examination of contemporary newspaper reports suggests that the company had been trying to expand too quickly.

To tie up the loose ends over the £2,500 it had agreed to spend on the NWNGR, on 7 September 1906 the NWPTC agreed that the £346 balance could be spent on the NWNGR's permanent way and that after payment of wages it should be taken in materials to clear the account. To account fully for the £2,500 there must have been other items not recorded in the NWPTC minutes and in addition to the £46 that had been spent on NWNGR ballast in July. This was not the first time that the NWPTC had assisted the NWNGR financially, for on 8 July 1904 it had paid £300 to the LNWR in settlement of a NWNGR debt of £972 although the full debt remained as a separate item in the NWNGR's balance sheet until 1912.

The NWPTC board tried to terminate the contract with the NWNGR when it met on 12 February 1908. Russell had submitted draft contracts to bring about the completion of the railways and to settle other claims and wayleaves, 'the gist of which was that the power company should enter into a binding obligation to his satisfaction for the completion of all railways within a period of two years.' By this time the NWPCT was generating and selling power, costs had been reduced and its debt had been rescheduled. The directors were in no mood to bow to pressure from Russell.

They countered by deciding to offer to complete and hand over for the NWNGR to work until the railway to Beddgelert was completed, the one-mile section of railway beyond Rhyd Ddu, to Cae'r Gors, and to cancel the NWNGR's LNWR debt.

The option of offering £500 in cash for a perpetual wayleave for the Nantlle transmission line was also considered. 'Failing an amicable settlement with Mr Russell, it was decided that the company's position be legally defended against any interference with their transmission line.' At the same meeting it was agreed to ask if the Aluminium Corporation was interested in buying any of the electric locomotives.

Russell did not take the bait and issued a notice requiring the transmission line to be removed by 31 March 1908. The company's solicitor suggested that as the transmission line was constructed with the NWNGR's approval the NWPTC should apply for an injunction to deal with any threat to it. The directors decided to continue negotiations whilst seeking counsel's opinion on its legal position. It took until 23 October 1908 before agreement was reached. Unfortunately, the full details were not recorded but in November the payment of £25 for 'half year's wayleave on new terms' was reported. When the agreement expired in 1913 NWPTC failed to reduce the amount paid and accepted renewal for another year at £50.

Despite this posturing by Russell, the NWNGR shareholders had already, on 12 March 1908, been informed that the NWPTC and PBSSR 'have been unable to carry out the proposed agreements ... and that consequently the matters contemplated thereby are at an end.' Perhaps Russell could see no benefit in taking on the incomplete formation south of Rhyd Ddu but patience might have rewarded him. On 12 November 1912 the PBSSR made a three-year agreement with Thomas Parry & Co, timber merchants of Mold, permitting its use to carry timber from Coed Mawr to Rhyd Ddu for £30 per annum. The company was required to make any repairs necessary to make the railway suitable for its purpose and was allowed to use any rails on the site. Haulage was to be by horse; bolster wagons were obtained from the FR. The PBSSR retained the right to resume construction at any time, avoiding any interference with the timber traffic.

On 26 November 1912 the PBSSR gave Parry permission to use a 'light engine'. Haulage of 1,273 tons of timber generated £161 15s 5d revenue for the NWNGR in 1913. On 21 October 1915 the agreement was renewed for another year with provision made for further extension on an annual basis. NWNGR reports distinguish no more revenue from timber although the traffic was 'quite satisfactory' in 1915 and acknowledged as the reason for traffic increasing in 1918.

As the NWPTC's connection with the NWNGR came to an end, the last of the LROs had been made and it was finally time call a halt to the PBSSR. On 16 December 1908, having considered a letter from Aitchison concerning the local authorities and the borrowing powers they had been given for railways, the directors decided they could do no more. It is best to use their words: 'Full authority was given to inform anyone finding cash to complete [the] railways, that the power company and the Portmadoc company would take a deferred position in respect of land, materials and partly constructed work. Unused materials would be handed over for new construction.' It was no doubt hearing this information that prompted the local authorities to form a joint investigative committee in 1909, the consequences of which are described in the next chapter. The other constant in this story, Aitchison, was given six months notice by NWPTC in April 1909.

It is ironic that, as the railway was being abandoned, the Carnarvon land purchase was completed. The prolonged transaction had been dependent on the 1908 'extension at Carnarvon' LRO being made, two legal agreements with the harbour trust and payments of two deposits. The first agreement had been made on 1 May 1906 and made the £300 deposit forfeit if the sale was not completed by 1 January 1907.

It identified two plots that would together be sold for £3,000 and stated that the station site, no more than 38 x 140ft, would be sold at 15s per square yard, just under £500. When the deadline was missed NWPTC increased the deposit to £500 to maintain goodwill with the trust. The second agreement, made on 20 May 1907, required payment of £1,500 by 24 June 1907 and the remaining £1,000 to be placed in a joint account set up in the names of one of the trustees and NWPTC; subsequently £2,500 was placed in the joint account. Completion of the station site was deferred until 31 July 1908. If the LRO had not been made by 31 December 1907 then £2,500 would be refunded to NWPTC. The LRO was made on 8 July 1908 and sale completed by 11 November that year. It is not clear from the records seen whether the extra money due for the station site was ever paid.

In June 1910, NWPTC hoped to raise between £1,200 and £1,500 from the sale of surplus PBSSR materials and determined that the money should be set against interest, credit being given to the PBSSR in the intra-company accounts.

Meanwhile, the existing railways had continued in operation. Despite the exchanges following the 1889 Regulation of Railway Act in the 1890s, the NWNGR's relaxed attitude towards officialdom and regulation had continued. On 12 August 1902 Aitchison informed the BoT of two derailments that had occurred. On 9 August a privately owned iron ore tip wagon derailed and overturned, derailing two other wagons also, between Waenfawr and Tryfan Junction, and on 11 August the loco of the 7.50am departure from Waenfawr 'fouled the points' and derailed. Asked about the first incident, Aitchison informed the BoT that the wagons formed part of a mixed train 'of several wagons next the engine and composite carriage with brake compartment in the rear.'

When the BoT asked why the train had not been worked in accordance with the order made under the 1889 Regulation of Railways Act, Aitchison had responded, on 11 September: 'The writer only came onto the railway in 1898 and found matters in a very mixed condition with no records to assist him. He is unable to trace the order you refer to and would be greatly obliged if you would cause copies ... to be supplied. The working of the line since my management commenced has been based on the lines I found in vogue on my appointment and I am pleased to state singularly few mishaps have occurred. If you will kindly favour me with copies ... The official receiver ... gave me many particulars both verbally and in writing of regulations affecting this line ...' Copies of the orders were sent to him.

There was a more serious accident on 31 July 1906, when the coal wagon attached to a mixed train approaching Rhyd Ddu ran away and collided with the locomotive of the following excursion train near Plas y Nant, both trains being improperly in the same section. Seven passengers and the train crew reported injuries and the locomotive's trailing bogie derailed. Investigation revealed that it was not practice for the stationmaster at Rhyd Ddu to send 'train arrived' to Waenfawr, the NWNGR's rules only requiring it 'when there are "special reasons" for so doing'.

Notwithstanding any deficiencies in the rules, it may be surmised that, with Aitchison based at his Snowdon Mountain Railway office in Llanberis, the number and type of incidents indicate a lack of direct management supervision on the railway. It is equally possible that Aitchison had rather a laissez-faire attitude towards safety. When the Regulation of Railways bill, with its proposal that rolling stock should be fitted with automatic couplings, to avoid the risk of staff being crushed when coupling up, was going through Parliament in 1899 he wrote to John Sylvester Hughes, the FR's manager, suggesting that they get together with other narrow gauge railways to gain an exemption.

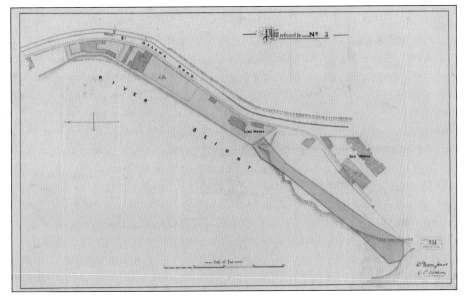

Left: **This plan, showing the strip of land acquired from the Carnarvon Harbour Trust by the NWPTC for the PBSSR in 1908, was countersigned by Aitchison.** *NA*

Below: **Also countersigned by Aitchison was this plan of the wharf at Carnarvon and the proposed PBSSR terminus.** *NA*

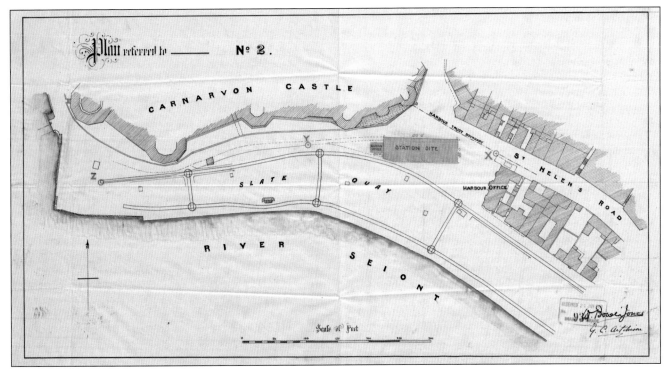

The requirement to adopt byelaws to cover the handling of explosives developed into an ongoing correspondence with the BoT, starting in 1904. Aitchison explained, on 8 December, that all the railway's trains were mixed so he would propose carrying gunpowder in metallic cases placed in slate wagons attached to such trains. Further he could not meet the requirement for a special vehicle because such a vehicle would not go up the (Bryngwyn) incline nor would it reach the 'places where the quarry companies require the powder delivered.' At the BoT this generated a flurry of remarks, including: 'This company is not authorised to run all its trains as mixed trains' and 'Can you trace any papers … for the Festiniog Railway, probably in 1867?' The Home Office was consulted and, on 26 December, refused to allow any modification.

Aitchison responded by asking, on 10 January 1905, if a wooden van or wagon that had its iron work protected were designed, which could get into the quarries, would it be acceptable? By return he was told that the byelaws in question applied only to explosives packed in metallic cases or cylinders so he let the matter rest.

A year later the BoT pursued the matter again. On 17 January 1906 Aitchison replied: 'As the railway is about to be reconstructed and run in conjunction with another company which is being built, the company has decided to refuse to carry explosives until they had obtained suitable vans for the carrying of explosives. Under these circumstances I issued an order to that effect, and at present the only explosives which we will deal with are those contained in such kinds of cylinders as will enable us to deal with it in the ordinary traffic'!

The frustrated BoT returned to the Home Office for advice, to be told on 22 February 1906: 'In the circumstances there is no need to press the company to make byelaws at present, but as soon as reconstruction is completed the new company should be called upon to make byelaws.' Nothing more was heard on the subject.

Simultaneously the railway had been asked to adopt new model byelaws for ordinary traffic, some of the earlier byelaws having been superseded by the 1889 Regulation of Railways Act. This resulted in an exchange between Aitchison and the BoT on the reason for the Moel Tryfan undertaking appellation

The PBSSR station building would have been located somewhere in the centre of this view of Carnarvon Castle. The train on the right is headed for Llanberis; the Afon Wen line is to its left.
Photochrom/Author's collection

22573 Carnarvon. Castle and Slate Quay.

added to the railway's name. The board had unilaterally removed it and then sought an explanation. These byelaws were signed and sealed on 3 April 1906.

In 1899 the NWNGR had been able to deposit £1,000 with 'the paymaster general, for investment', further deposits creating a fund of £3,200 by 1905. The money was probably operating surpluses that were insufficient to settle debt or debenture interest and would have been protected by court order. In 1907, £780 of it was applied to the company's renewals reserve account and used to purchase two 'composite and brake van bogie carriages' from R. & Y. Pickering, replacing two similar vehicles that had been in use since 1877. The fund also provided £1,300 to purchase the Hunslet Fairlie *Gowrie* in 1908. No further additions were made to the fund which, reduced to £500 by 1912, was eliminated during 1914.

Not all incidents that occurred on the NWNGR were attributable to slapdash operating. On 20 March 1909 an attempt to derail a train by putting stones between the rail and check-rail in a crossing near Dinas was reported in *The Times*. The last carriage of the train was derailed but none of the 40 passengers was injured.

Aitchison resigned as manager in 1910 and accepted a seat on the board. He continued as secretary and became the receiver after Russell's death in 1912.

In spite of appearances operating costs were covered most years; indeed, the railway would not have gone on for so long in receivership had this not been the case. The first operating loss since 1881, of £10, was incurred in 1910. The best year for in cash terms was 1898, with an operating surplus of £971.

In 1913, when there was a loss of £205, shareholders were informed that whilst excursion traffic had been satisfactory, local traffic had been affected by competition from motor charabancs. The 1912 passenger figures, despite that statement, had actually been almost the same. A six-week national strike by coalminers in 1912 had caused problems when the LNWR gave notice that it would not accept any slate traffic. Initially the service had been reduced but after a while it was withdrawn and most employees laid off for an unspecified period.

There had been, however, a big turndown over earlier years. Until 1892 the railway consistently carried between 30,000 and 40,000 passengers annually. From 1893 until 1899 it experienced a boom, probably because Rhyd Ddu station had been renamed Snowdon, carrying less than 50,000 passengers only in 1898 and over 55,000 in 1893 and 1895. From 1900 to 1911, the first year was the worst with 36,450 passengers carried. Traffic peaked in 1905, with 52,256 passengers, before declining

to 40,636 in 1911. In 1912 and 1913 10,000 of the 23,000 passengers carried did not originate on the railway. The 10,000 passengers lost in 1914 were evenly divided between tourist and local traffic and even in 1915 and 1916, when 5,000 passengers were lost each year there was still a good proportion of incoming traffic. However, in 1917 traffic fell away completely, with only 211 passengers carried, earning £11.

Slate traffic revenue fluctuated at around £2,000, 20,000 tons or so, until 1903, when it started a gradual decline. At 7,017 tons in 1913 it was half what it had been the year before, attributed to the largest quarry that sent traffic being closed down for much of the year.

In 1914, a deficit of £387 was attributed to various causes. Owing to the outbreak of war all excursion bookings from other companies had been cancelled during August, 'thus the most profitable part of the passenger traffic for the year was lost.' Local traffic was further decreased, with slate traffic 'very much diminished', reduced by 20% on 1913, which itself had shrunk by 22% on 1912. The Bryngwyn branch passenger service had not been operated since 1 January.

The 1915 deficit was £283, with all excursion traffic lost and local traffic further decreased. Slate was 60% down but iron ore, from Bettws Garmon, and timber, from Beddgelert, were satisfactory. In 1916 the results were judged to have been slightly better than in 1915, with a loss of £2 3s 8d. Traffic in iron ore and timber was greatly increased. A report published in *Railway & Travel Monthly* in 1917 described the railway at this time, everything was run down and holes seen in the panelling of carriages. The writer commented: 'A motor bus service along a road which follows the line bids fair to prove the proverbial "last straw".'

'Practically no passenger bookings' contributed to a loss of £166 in 1917. The slate trade was still further decreased owing to the 'stoppage of building.' The termination of loading facilities, the location is not known, had affected the iron ore traffic.

In 1918, the last year for which returns have been found, the deficit was £177. Aitchison reported that the traffic had been larger than for some years, mainly owing to the timber traffic. Expenses had increased due to higher wages being paid and 'repairs necessitated by the nature of the traffic.' No repairs to either locomotives or rolling stock had been recorded since 1915.

A shortage of visitors to the Snowdon summit from Rhyd Ddu was attributed to the NWNGR's 'stoppage' in a *Times* report on 25 July 1921, its writer apparently unaware that no passenger trains had run since 1916.

As a part of its planning for what became the 1921 Railways Act the Ministry of Transport established a Light Railways Investigation Committee, asking light railways to complete a 27-page questionnaire. The NWNGR's was completed by the company's assistant secretary and accountant, based in Liverpool, who said of the NWNGR's history: 'From its inception difficulties appear to have occurred with regard to finance and for many years the undertaking has been in the hands of a receiver.' Of train formations he said that passenger trains had run with a maximum of 10 vehicles and an average of three; freight trains contained a maximum of 40 wagons but averaged 20. Regarding wages, he said that they were 'very far below' standard, main line, rates and were governed by the amount of money available.

The situation of the PBSSR, in the guise of the Croesor Tramway, was no better than that of the NWNGR. In 1904 it had carried 9,035 tons of slate and 698 tons of merchandise, back traffic to Croesor and the quarries. Thereafter, the slate traffic was consistently around 7,000 tons until 1914 when it started to decline to around 1,000 tons although in 1918 and 1919 it carried less than 400 tons. The best operating profit was £204 in 1911; most years it made a loss of less than £100. Annual mileage was constantly 2,772, equating to 308 journeys, six per week. An intriguing entry: 'Wayleave rent for the use of railway, £80', appears in the 1918 returns under the heading of merchandise receipts. During that year the railway had carried no merchandise or coal and only 346 tons of slate. Whether the £80 is Parry's payments for use of the unfinished railway at Beddgelert is not clear. He was to have paid £30 annually from 1912 but was recorded as a year-end debtor to the extent of £15 10s for each of the three years from 1919. This might have been a half-year payment for it cannot be discounted that his rental was increased after 1916.

Two new sources of traffic came to the PBSSR right at the end of its independent existence. In 1920 and 1921 road stone was carried, 191 tons in 1920 and 11 tons in the second year. Also in 1921, five pigs were carried, earning 10s 6d.

Until 1921 the PBSSR's returns showed a sum rising to £1,981 as being due to NWPTC whilst the auditors' report also noted an unknown sum owed to the NWPTC 'for construction'; the identified money probably included rental, shown at £50 annually. Over the same period £767 17s 10d due to Aitchison in settlement of the action that he brought over unpaid fees remained in the balance sheet. He had started the action in 1908/9 when he had been dismissed; in 1910 the PBSSR had been advised to settle

by paying him £150 per year until 1913; most likely he went unpaid.

Expenditure on 'lines not open' had reached £37,674 by 1916. NWPTC had agreed to the sale of surplus materials, steel rails, bridge components and sleepers, all deteriorating, to Marple & Gillott and R. White & Sons in June 1910. Listed as items sold 'in connection with line under construction' in the PBSSR's returns, £310 was raised in 1918 and £374 in 1919. The FR had bought 2,000 sleepers for £90 in 1911.

A shed located on the Beddgelert Siding and used by the Portmadoc Flour Mills Company to tranship flour came under the Cambrian Railways' scrutiny in 1919. The Cambrian's engineer complained that the shed was 'practically falling to pieces and dangerous' to which the mill replied that until it had been damaged by 'your men' during shunting operations it had been perfectly safe. No one knew who owned the shed but the flour company thought that the Cambrian had supplied the materials used for its construction. It was suggested that the shed should be replaced by a canopy but the matter was left unresolved. Of note is a comment made by the Portmadoc agent on 19 July: 'It is rumoured that the Croesor Railway is to be electrified and if that is carried out the mill people will be prohibited to make use of the tramway with their horses as at present ...' It may not be that the flour mill used its own horses, for the railway was to carry 79 tons of flour in 1921 and 89 tons in 1922.

Looking back a little, in November 1918 the Dolgarrog-based Aluminium Corporation had acquired a controlling interest in NWPTC, still struggling financially, and thereby acquired the PBSSR and its tramway. The consequence of this change in control showed in the returns in two forms. The cost of management services, which had declined from £100 in 1914 to £15 in 1919, was increased to £60 in 1920 and the corporation owed the railway £310 2s 11d in 1919 and 1920, the debt reducing to £84 3s 9d in 1921. The 1921 return shows that the NWNGR, 'per Sir John Stewart', was a debtor to the extent of £230 6s 2d.

The corporation extended its interest in railways in April 1920, when it paid bought £36,100 of NWNGR debentures, thus acquiring control of that railway, too. For although the NWNGR and the Croesor Tramway were all but derelict and carried very little traffic, behind the scenes a great deal of effort was being made to bring them together to complete the long-held dream of completing the railway link between Portmadoc and Carnarvon.

The Hunslet single Fairlie 0-6-4T *Gowrie* with the Bryngwyn goods at Dinas, c1911. *G. M. Perkins/ FR Archives*

2

The Creation of the Welsh Highland Railway 1914-22

Whilst the origins of the WHR as we understand it today date back to 1830 the final pieces of the jigsaw started to come together on 27 November 1914. That was when Evan Robert Davies, town clerk of Pwllheli and alderman and secretary of education of Carnarvonshire County Council, a solicitor and friend of David Lloyd George, and who was to work in George's private office during the forthcoming war, published a notice of intention to submit an application for an LRO to unite the NWNGR with the PBSSR. This was the verbosely named Portmadoc, Beddgelert & South Snowdon Railway (Light Railway) and North Wales Narrow Gauge Railways (Light Railways) Revival and Transfer of Powers Order.

Submitted on 19 December, the order was to revive existing powers and to transfer them to a new, unnamed, company. In submitting the application Davies was acting on behalf of the Portmadoc, Beddgelert & Carnarvon Light Railway Committee. Established in 1909, the committee represented Carnarvon County Council, Carnarvon Town Council, Carnarvon Harbour Trust, the Urban District Council of Ynyscynhaiarn (later renamed Portmadoc) and the Rural District Councils of Gwyrfai and Glaslyn.

The local authorities had charged the committee with investigating the scope for developing the areas through which the railways ran, or would run, to the benefit of the community.

Snowdon Ranger **arrives at Rhyd Ddu with a large sandbox on its running board, c1914. The Snowdon Ranger–Rhyd Ddu token is locked into the point mechanism.** *Welsh Highland Heritage*

The representative for Ynyscynhaiarn was the solicitor William George, who has already been encountered.

By June 1910 the committee had established that the government might be the source of a grant that could be used to complete the railways. To qualify, a mainline railway company was required to construct, finish and work them. If *The Times* of 20 April 1910 is to be believed this had already been resolved, for the newspaper announced that the LNWR was to acquire the NWNGR. How seriously the LNWR took this idea is not known, but by 2 June the NWPTC had received a formal notification of the LNWR's interest. In 1911 the committee learned that NWPTC was prepared to sell, for cash, the PBSSR, including railways finished and unfinished and all powers, a variance of NWPTC's position in 1908 (page 40). The NWNGR needed to agree to the LNWR involvement but Russell would not give his consent.

The committee then proposed that the authorities should take appropriate action to complete the rail link between Carnarvon and Portmadoc, bringing it under a single ownership/management, supporting the scheme by means of loans, hence the 1914 application. To meet the LRC's bi-annual deadline for submission of applications, actually 'by November' and 'by May' so the application was late anyway, it was found necessary to submit it before the joint committee members could obtain approval from their respective councils. The committee members therefore obtained a loan from the LCM Bank and personally guaranteed the £50 fee payable for the LRO application.

In comparison with other orders applicable to the route, or part of it, and the order eventually made, the draft order was relatively straight forward. Unusually, the name of the company to be granted the powers was not specified. The new company was to be granted permission to enter into agreements with either the LNWR or the Cambrian Railways regarding the construction, maintenance and management of the railway or the working and conveyance of traffic thereon as well as the usual commercial agreements. A leasing clause would have permitted leasing the railway to any other railway with which the company was authorised to enter into a working agreement.

A justification for the application which accompanied it described the background and objectives of the order, pointing out that capital expenditure on the NWNGR had totalled £108,291, while that for the PBSSR was £102,668. The latter sum was broken down as follows: purchase of Croesor Tramway – £11,518; purchase of land – £6,150; construction of railway – £73,000, and legal and engineering expenses – £12,000.

The parishes through which the completed railway was to pass were listed with acreages and population; the largest by acreage being Beddgelert at 26,060 and by population, Ynyscynhaiarn with 4,445. The smallest on both counts was Bettws Garmon – 2,723 acres with a population of 440.

A total of 52 slate quarries and lead, copper, ochre and iron mines which had been active during the previous 50 years were listed by parish and name, along with the approximate number employed, totalling 3,500, but not simultaneously. It was estimated that transport costs ranging from 3s 2d to 15s per ton could be reduced by three-quarters if a railway serving either Portmadoc or Carnarvon were available. Transport costs were said to contribute to the failure of several undertakings and handicapped others. It was anticipated that several properties could be developed given adequate transport facilities. The document commented that with the coming of mains electricity to the district, from the NWPTC's Cwm Dyli power station four miles from Beddgelert, the facility to establish manufacturing industries would be further advanced if transportation was improved.

Agriculture was also a significant activity in the district, with some 1,500 tenant farmers or smallholders active. Some land had gone over to pasture because transport costs were cheaper, presumably because the animals were herded to and from market.

The interests of tourism were not overlooked, attention being drawn to the attractiveness of the Rhyd Ddu path to the summit of Snowdon, the Aberglaslyn Pass and Beddgelert as well as claiming that Rhyd Ddu 'is also regarded as one of the healthiest holiday resorts in Wales.' The tourist catchment area was forecast to include the North Wales coast as far as Rhyl or Prestatyn and the Cambrian coast as far as Aberystwyth, a pool of some half a million tourists annually. The development of rail-based circular tours from the North Wales coast was proposed, using the proposed railway in conjunction with either the Festiniog Railway or the standard gauge Afon Wen line.

The owners of the NWNGR and the PBSSR had agreed to sell their undertakings for either £30,000 in cash or £10,000 in cash and £30,000 in shares in the new company, two-thirds for the NWNGR and one third for the PBSSR, the committee reported. The cost of completing the PBSSR was estimated to be £50,000, with a further £1,500 required for additional land. Additionally, £5,000 was needed to refurbish the NWNGR and £3,500 for legal, engineering and contingent expenses, producing a conveniently rounded £100,000 total. Observe that there is no suggestion that the new railway should invest in any rolling stock; an estimate of expenses dated 28 November 1914 had £5,000 for rolling stock but nothing for additional land or

The first page of the 1914 draft LRO, with a blank space for the name of the proposed operating company. *Author's collection*

the legal, engineering and contingent expenses, so still producing a total of £100,000.

To finance the scheme the promoters anticipated obtaining funds from three public sources. Section 5(1) of the Light Railway Act of 1896 made funds available for the construction of light railways provided, inter alia, that the Board of Agriculture certified the proposal would benefit agriculture or that the BoT certified that it would improve communications. A budget of £1 million was available for this purpose, specified in the Act, which could be advanced as a free grant or by loan. The committee sought a £30,000 interest-free loan and a £25,000 loan at 3½% interest.

As the Light Railways Act funds could only be applied to new construction Davies also made application to the Development Commission for a loan of £9,500 to be used to acquire the undertakings. Unspecified local authorities were expected to lend £15,500. The shortfall would be met by selling £30,000 in ordinary shares.

Government rules for proportionate funding, that any advance should not exceed 50% of construction costs, led to the promoters seeking to have the £6,150 PBSSR land purchase and the £73,000 spent on PBSSR construction taken into consideration, claiming therefore a total expenditure of £130,650 on land and works. With a net cost of £100,000 for 25 miles of railway it was implied that the new undertaking was a bargain. The document concluded with the statement that the LNWR was prepared to work the railway on terms to be arranged and to provide such facilities that would 'minimise the inconvenience, delay and loss now experienced at Dinas Junction.'

The joint committee appeared to have gone into limbo, for on 21 May 1914 the county council re-appointed its existing members and added three more. On 14 October 1914 the council learned 'with satisfaction' of the efforts being made 'to revive the scheme for the completion ...' and offered its support.

The war brought an end to the application's progress and there was no further action on it until 1919. It is not clear why the committee, having been considering the railways' position since 1909, was in such a hurry to submit an LRO application in 1914, just after the outbreak of war. Perhaps it is unfortunate that it had not taken action 12 months earlier, for then there would have been a good chance of obtaining the grant and loans with lower interest rates so that raising £30,000 by selling shares might have worked and the railway could have been completed during 1915, in time to provide a useful transport function during the war.

The LRO application was reactivated after the Aluminium Corporation acquired control of the NWPTC, and therefore the PBSSR, in November 1918. Before following the application's progress it is necessary to look at how the PBSSR and the NWNGR became the Welsh Highland Railway.

The corporation obtained control of the NWNGR in April 1920 by buying £36,100 of debentures for £6,219. On 19 January 1921 NWPTC agreed to accept 338 preference shares and £1,094 ordinary shares in the NWNGR from Sir John Henderson Stewart Bt in exchange for 285 ordinary PBSSR shares. It also agreed to give Stewart an option to purchase the PBSSR and the NWNGR in exchange for £50,000 ordinary shares in a new company to be formed to acquire them. Stewart was also to indemnify NWPTC against any claims made regarding the PBSSR's 1904 Parliamentary deposit.

How Stewart came to be involved in this saga is not known. He was not, as previously suspected, a director of the corporation. His baronetcy had been awarded in 1920 'for public services' and might have been connected with a £50,000 donation to an unidentified political party. The owner of a Dundee distillery, it seems likely that he was brought into the WHR in the belief, mistaken as it turned out, that he was a man of substance. The complications of his personal business activities (he was to be described as a conman after his death in 1924), undoubtedly account for some of the share transfers.

Along with Davies and Stewart, the third player in the WHR story was the corporation's managing director, Henry Joseph Jack, who held the same position with the NWPTC. He had become an elected member of Carnarvonshire County Council in 1920.

Jack was appointed the NWNGR's receiver on 8 April 1921. By this time the WHR proposals were well in hand and perhaps it was felt that the viability of the scheme required the NWNGR to continue operating, even if only with occasional goods trains. The NWNGR had not paid any interest on the 'A' debentures since 31 December 1913 and on the remainder since 1878. Neither had the company repaid £1,749 to holders of Lloyds' bonds and £3,487 in respect of unsecured debts, both sums due since 1888. On 1 January 1921 Stewart had paid £1,500 to Aitchison to keep it going.

Sometime in 1920 the promoters had decided that taking control of the FR would be beneficial, perhaps because it would lend credibility, perhaps because it could lend locomotives and rolling stock. By the time a report from the Power, Transport & Economic Department had been compiled on 23 August 1920 Jack had said that 'he' had made an offer for a controlling interest in the FR for the 'success of his project depended very largely upon close working with that line.' On 29 March 1921, Davies and Jack acquired £500 of FR ordinary stock each and Stewart had £13,843 of three classes of FR stock.

According to an affidavit to be made by the assistant general manager of the National Provincial Bank in 1933, during April 1921 the PBSSR used £10,000 borrowed from the bank, guaranteed by Stewart, to purchase £34,243 NWNGR debentures.

After Jack had given the NWPTC board a report on the acquisition of the FR on 31 May 1921 he was authorised to obtain a loan of £15,000 against the security of 40,000 ordinary

A Dick, Kerr petrol-electric locomotive on test at Dinas in February 1917. Two women are posing alongside the wagons.
Brian Webb Collection/Industrial Railway Society

stock and 25,000 preference shares in the FR. The loan was to be guaranteed by Stewart and when it had been repaid the shares were to be transferred to him.

Stewart, Davies and Jack took control of the FR on 16 July 1921 and on 30 July Jack was elected chairman. By 14 July Stewart's shareholding had increased to £42,999 ordinary stock, £3,660 4½% preference shares and £23,340 5% preference shares. On 15 July it was transferred to Davies and Jack on a one-third/two-thirds basis, leaving Stewart with just £999 ordinary stock.

Acting for Stewart, on 10 October 1921 Jack offered to take over the PBSSR shares from the NWPTC in exchange for £25,000 in FR shares instead of £50,000 in the new, WHR, company. 'The matter was considered at length ...' and accepted. On 22 December, the NWPTC agreed the terms of the agreement that would transfer the NWNGR and the PBSSR to the WHR that was to be incorporated into the LRO.

The corporation's interest in the PBSSR was assigned to Stewart on 25 January 1922. In February doubt was cast on the legal ability of the PBSSR to hold the NWNGR debentures so the £10,000 loan was transferred to Stewart with the bank accepting £38,255 in NWNGR debentures as security. The bank expected the loan to be settled in June 1922 but on 1 December it accepted £9,950 in WHR debentures from Stewart in substitution for the NWNGR debentures.

A significant reallocation of shareholdings took place on 16 May 1922. Davies and Jack transferred their FR ordinary stock to NWPTC, which transferred £9,723 PBSSR shares (nominal value £48,615), to Stewart and he had them shared between himself, Davies and Jack. As Davies and Jack only accounted for £24,875 of FR stock, transfers for £25 holdings from five other shareholders were also lodged with NWPTC. The NWPTC board exercised its control over the FR stock by approving a proxy in favour of Davies, Jack and Stewart in respect of an FR Company general meeting to be held on 29 May.

These transactions and transfers were just one of the components required for the WHR scheme to be completed.

Russell at Waenfawr with a goods train in 1920, when the NWNGR's independent existence was almost expired. *Author's collection*

Now it was necessary to secure the finance, the LRO and to employ a contractor. Returning to March 1919, the news that the Aluminium Corporation had acquired control of the PBSSR had resulted in two very different responses from local authorities in letters to government departments.

The first, from the Glaslyn RDC, urged that the BoT should use its influence to bring about completion of what it called the Portmadoc & Beddgelert Light Railway. The second, from Carnarvonshire County Council, asked the Treasury to reimburse the £50 1914 LRO application fee. The bank had pressed for payment, with interest, and the council had paid it but was concerned that the arrangement might not meet with the district auditor's approval and that the committee members might have their guarantees invoked. On 6 May 1919 the request for reimbursement was refused because the LRO application had not been withdrawn; this story might have been very different if it had been.

Jack appears to have been the instigator of the LRO application's reactivation. On 9 July 1919 Sir Robert McAlpine & Sons, a partnership then undertaking work for the corporation at Dolgarrog, had given him an estimate of £68,559 to complete the railway between what became known as Croesor Junction and Rhyd Ddu. Jack wrote, as the corporation's managing director, to Davies, at Downing Street, instructing him to take the necessary action on 18 October 1919. Carnarvonshire politics must have brought Davies and Jack together. Jack's rationale for the railway scheme and an anticipated £75,000 of public funding was enclosed with his letter.

Agreement had been reached, he explained, to sell the NWNGR to the PBSSR for £26,000, payable £20,000 in PBSSR shares and £6,000 in cash, but the solicitors had been unable to find any existing legal means whereby its receiver could transfer the NWNGR as a going concern. The PBSSR was anxious to award the contract to McAlpine but 'difficulty has been experienced in the present conditions of the money market in obtaining the necessary finance.' Therefore, an advance of £75,000 was sought from the government 'at a reasonable rate of interest.' Annual revenue of £10,000 and 60% working expenses was conservative he thought and sufficient to produce £3,750 interest.

After extolling the virtues of the railway for serving both agriculture and various quarries and mines Jack went on to say how advantageous it would be for developing tourism in the locality. The NWNGR had lost out, he said, because it did not serve 'a place of sufficient importance', Rhyd Ddu being 3½ miles from Beddgelert, but the completed PBSSR would not only link Carnarvon with Portmadoc through 'one of the most picturesque districts' but at Portmadoc it 'connects physically with the narrow gauge railway running ... through the Vale of Ffestiniog to Blaenau Ffestiniog while it also connects ... with the Cambrian Railway', giving opportunities to attract passengers not only directly from Barmouth, Pwllheli and Bala but also as far as Rhyl using various combinations of circular tours. He claimed that North Wales attracted one million visitors each year; if it were established how many made excursions within the area an idea of the likely market might be calculated for 'it is confidently anticipated that a very large percentage of the visitors would make the journey at least once during their stay.'

He went on to assert, briefly, that the scheme would provide employment 'where work is badly needed' and add 12¼ miles of railway to the nation's infrastructure at a cost of £6,100 per mile, or 26 miles at £3,000 per mile if the NWNGR was brought into the equation. Jack concluded that the final benefit lay in the extension of the NWPTC's transmission lines along the railway route and therefore there was 'every prospect' of attracting new industries to the locality as a result.

The county council had other ideas for the improvement of railway facilities in the county, proposing several new lines, including the conversion of the NWNGR to standard gauge and its extension to Portmadoc. Its deputation to London on 2 December 1921 was treated courteously but perhaps it should come as no surprise that a report on the meeting noted 'all departments of government concerned declined to entertain this proposal'.

The rough-and-ready reckoning that the railway could be completed for £75,000 was to be a great problem for the promoters. Neither Jack's calculations nor McAlpine's estimate made any provision for fettling the NWNGR, making the Croesor Tramway fit for locomotives, for a station at Portmadoc nor providing any additional rolling stock. Yet once they had floated the idea of £75,000 there was no way that it could be exceeded.

The Ministry of Agriculture examined the case for the railway and concluded, on 28 May 1920, that 'in spite of the local support ... and of the advantages which it would undoubtedly provide ... the ministry does not feel justified, in view of the very low figure for agricultural produce available for transport in classifying it higher than ... desirable at a future date.'

The report from the Power, Transport & Economic Department dated 23 August 1920 has already been mentioned. It also included or commented on several claims made by Jack that were not included in his rationale. It would be necessary to extend the NWNGR to Carnarvon in order that all the slate quarries, including those at Blaenau Festiniog, would have access to the harbour because Portmadoc harbour was silting up, a claim denied by the experts consulted; the channel had moved and could be improved but any decline in use was more likely caused by the fall in slate production during the war than by any difficulty in using the harbour. At Carnarvon, a quayside transhipment site had been purchased for £3,500; this was probably land purchased by the PBSSR for there is no evidence of any land purchase in 1920.

The report's writer concluded that there was no point in the railway relying on any mineral traffic, as most of the mines and quarries were derelict, but as the NWNGR had carried 24,000 passengers 'in spite of the fact that it went nowhere in particular' Jack's 'suggestion that 150,000 passengers might be carried ... does not seem over optimistic.' The purpose of development schemes, the writer went on, was to open up industry and mineral resources, not the provision of improved holiday resources but 'in this particular case the prospects of heavy tourist traffic are relevant ... they would justify the construction of the line which, if based on the expectation of mineral traffic alone, would be highly speculative ...'

On behalf of the Ministry of Transport, the GWR undertook a traffic analysis, with a report submitted on 28 January 1921 taking a more cold-blooded approach. 'The success of Jack's scheme depends on these schemes [building the Carnarvon extension, taking over the NWNGR and the FR and finishing the PBSSR] being carried through and without them the prospect of earning £10,000 per annum on [the NWNGR and the PBSSR] to pay interest at 5% on the government loan desired ... is doubtful.' Analysing the available rolling stock,

Moel Tryfan **at Rhyd Ddu in WHR auspices in 1922.** *Author's collection*

including the FR's quarrymen's carriages, the report's writer considered that it would be inadequate if traffic were maintained at 1913 levels. He also suggested that the NWPTC should be asked why its 'cheap and abundant supply of electric power' was not on offer to the railway and thought that the government should not be the only source of funding; 'Should not county funds be also available to help this county scheme?'

The county council, meanwhile, was concerned about the state of the roads on the overbridges at Waenfawr, Bettws Garmon, and Cwellyn, which was the responsibility of the railway. In June 1921 it wrote to the NWNGR's registered office in Liverpool. Getting no reply it did the work for £31. On 15 June 1924 the NWNGR replied: 'This company is not in a position to find either the men or the materials for the repair of these roads and moreover being in chancery the master of the court refuses to allow any expenses except on the maintenance of the railway only. I would suggest that the county council repair these roads themselves.' The county council had been pursuing the NWNGR to repair these roads since at least 1913.

With the promoters controlling the FR, the NWNGR and the PBSSR, they were in a position to declare that they should be handled as a unit and have the FR excluded from the railway grouping in the last hours of the enabling bill's progress through Parliament. Apart from that, the enactment of the Railways Act on 19 August 1921 removed one of the components of Jack's scheme, the authority to make special advances to light railways. The Development Commission was also, it turned out, unable to make the grant anticipated. The promoters would have to look to other sources for funding.

A report commissioned from a consultant, Major G. C. Spring, submitted in the autumn of 1921 on the three operational railways, was clearly intended to inform someone on their condition and future prospects. It is not known who commissioned it, but the Aluminium Corporation or NWPTC are the most likely candidates. Spring noted, inter alia, that passenger traffic on the NWNGR section would be improved if that originating from Carnarvon did not have to change trains at Dinas. He concluded by saying 'The completion of the system, i.e. the connection of the three

systems, Festiniog, Croesor branch, and North Wales Narrow Gauge, would doubtless open up a wonderful tourist route by rail through the heart of Snowdonia and would enable the proportionate cost of rolling stock maintenance to be lowered owing to the larger utilisation of the workshop facilities at Boston Lodge, but since the traffic over the uncompleted portion would be seasonal passenger traffic only, it is unlikely that this traffic alone could provide a reasonable return on the cost of completion of the railway.' Perhaps he was not saying what his client wanted to hear, but his words proved to be prophetic.

The Ministry of Transport reviewed the LRO application on 8 October 1921 and a public inquiry was set for Carnarvon on 18 October. At the inquiry it was revealed that the completed railway was to be called the Welsh Highland Railway (WHR); the origins of the name are not known. By this time the cost of acquiring the PBSSR and the NWNGR had risen from £40,000 to £100,000, to be funded by issuing £10,000 in debentures and £90,000 in ordinary shares to the vendors. The cost of completing the railway was given as £120,000, including £45,000 for constructing the Dinas–Carnarvon line.

The only objector, once again, was the LNWR. The larger company was seeking to guarantee that it would retain any traffic 'arising at or destined to stations on the NWNGR and any other line connected thereto.' The WHR objected to the LNWR's proposed clause as in neither its nor the public's interest, pointing out that the LNWR had argued its case in both 1885 and 1904 but

Above: **Still at Rhyd Ddu, *Moel Tryfan* features with a mixed train in another 1922 view.** *Author's collection*

Left: **Parry's timber bolster wagons, at the Waenfawr end of Rhyd Ddu, c1920. They had been used to extract timber from Beddgelert forest using the partially constructed PBSSR — page 40.** *Author's collection*

had not been able to secure such a clause. The greater debate, however, was regarding the usefulness, or otherwise, of the proposed Carnarvon extension, with both sides admitting that it was unlikely to pay its way. In 1913, a record year the LNWR claimed, passenger revenue between the two stations had amounted to £323, while goods traffic, an average year, in both directions totalled 14,000 tons, including 5,000 tons of slate. Only 250 tons of slate ex-Dinas were destined for the quay at Carnarvon. If slate and other goods were no longer to be transhipped at Dinas the LNWR claimed it would be sacrificing the 'considerable expense' of developing the facilities there, some 40 years earlier.

In presenting the case for the WHR, Jack was identified as managing director of NWPTC, chairman of the FR as well as having a controlling interest in it, receiver of the NWNGR, and a director of the PBSSR. He told the commissioners that the chief advantage of bringing the railways together would be one of unified control and rolling stock, reducing expenses. He did not foresee any difficulty in entering into a working agreement with the FR; given his credentials, it was rather odd that he should have been asked the question.

Whilst Jack was on the stand there was some confusion about the sum required to complete construction, between the £120,000 already quoted or the £132,000 Jack claimed. Jack said it would be financed as follows: £32,000 from government grant; £23,000 loaned from three local authorities; £10,000 from the promoters and the remaining £64,000 from the public, which actually totals £129,000. He forecast that the WHR would be a good security for investment and that the railway would make a profit, adding that the FR had just carried more passengers than ever before, an increase of 92% and therefore demonstrating the demand for railways in scenic areas from tourism.

Earlier, when the inquiry chairman had asked how the development of road transport would affect the railway he was told that with the 'enormous expenditure attached to road maintenance' the railway was the better alternative. Major Charles Breese, MP for Carnarvonshire and member of the county council, explained that before the war traffic was very heavy, it had increased after the war and further increased considerably during the previous two years, saying 'The traffic is too heavy for the roads and it is a danger to horse traffic.' He thought the position would be relieved by completion of the railway, summarising: 'I cannot conceive how it will be possible to widen and strengthen the roads to bear the additional traffic to anything corresponding to the cost of constructing the railway.' (Breese, with William George, also present, had been involved in promoting the Portmadoc, Beddgelert & Rhyd Ddu Light Railway of the 1890s; see Chapter 1.)

Supporting the railway scheme, the clerk of Gwyrfai RDC told how the rateable value of the district had declined by £20,000 to £18,642 since 1907 whilst the population had reduced from 29,000 in 1911 to 24,030.

Other witnesses gave evidence on how they thought the railway could improve mineral-extraction businesses and tourism. At the close of the hearing the chairman declared that the commissioners had found in favour of the scheme except for Dinas–Carnarvon. This was, he said, because the application did not include powers for compulsory purchase for this section.

Notwithstanding its earlier support for a standard gauge railway, the county council had met on 20 October 1921 and voted to support the narrow gauge line and, with government approval, make a loan of £15,000 to the railway company. On 29 October the council sent the Treasury a certified copy of the resolution with a background note and a declaration that the railway was essential to provide work for the 1,000 unemployed men in the county.

The months following the LRO inquiry were a period of great intensity for the promoters, with several meetings taking place in London and a great deal of correspondence generated. Despite noting a number of inconsistencies in the promoters' submissions and having a certain scepticism about the capital and revenue estimates, there was a willingness to support the scheme by the senior civil servants although it is not possible to say how much this is attributable to the influence and pressure brought to bear by Davies and Jack. On 8 November 1921 a high-powered delegation met the Minister of Transport, Arthur Neal MP, at the House of Commons. It included the MPs for Carnarvonshire, Cardiganshire, Carmarthen, Neath and Pontypridd, the clerks to Deudraeth, Glaslyn, Gwyrfai and Beddgelert councils, three of them named David Jones, as well as Davies and Jack.

A briefing note produced by Sir Charles M. de Bartolomé for the minister in advance of the meeting outlined the history of the scheme, commenting 'the matter was dropped when it was decided that no money would be available for development but is now revived on the grounds of providing work for the unemployed.' The surviving records give no indication of when the scheme was suspended – it could relate to the £1,000,000 voted for expenditure on light railways in 1920 but returned to the Treasury before it could be spent because of a depression that started in May 1920. de Bartolomé noted that the promoters thought the railway would attract a substantial tourist traffic estimated at 150,000 passengers annually, a view shared by the GWR and considered excessive by the LNWR. The promoters also estimated that the revenue for goods and passenger traffic would be £34 per mile per week. de Bartolomé commented that this seemed excessive when compared with the FR's £24 per mile per week earned in 1920 adding 'the Festiniog line is fully developed, and ... similar receipts could not be expected from the proposed railway ... for some time after completion.' Under the heading 'cost of working' the compiler concluded: '... it is very doubtful that there would be any net receipts.' Despite that de Bartolomé concluded 'I consider that the scheme is a good one.'

During the course of the meeting Jack provided an insight into the involvement of the FR, saying 'I would like to claim that this is an unusual application for an unusual district, and I would like to set before you ... that we have unfortunately been rather too innocent in our way of bringing the scheme forward. In the first place, there is no railway in existence worth speaking of, that is to say, there is no traffic, and the idea is to establish a railway, and when we first approached this scheme we saw that no railway could be a success unless it included the Festiniog Railway, so as to run from Festiniog to Carnarvon. Emphasis has been put on the fact today that we are asking for this money in connection with this small part of the railway, and it has been ignored completely that we have already found £40,000 in hard cash within the last few months to enable us to get the controlling interest in the Festiniog Railway. (Who?) The promoters of this scheme. It could not be brought forward as a complete and unified scheme until the control in the Festiniog Railway could be acquired. That difficulty has stood in the way for the last 10 years.'

Davies made great play on the capital value, £270,000, of the PBSSR and NWNGR, saying that it should be added to the £23,000 to be advanced by the county council (£15,000), Portmadoc Town Council (£5,000) and Gwyrfai RDC (£3,000) and treated as locally-sourced finance, making the £120,000 being sought from the government look like a minority contribution. Neal responded that he had no money for light railways, only a small amount for the relief of unemployment but the Ministry of Labour would only certify that Carnarvon met the criteria, its position being confirmed by letter on 11 November. He also made it clear that he could take no account of the money that had already been spent and could only consider schemes where there was a good level of local investment, suggesting that he could perhaps get treasury support to advance 50% of the sum found locally.

The meeting ended with Neal advising the delegation to 'go and see how much money you have got in your money boxes and let us hear a little bit more about it.' In thanking Neal for the meeting, Breese said that if the railway was not built it would fall upon the local authorities to spend much more money to repair the damage done to the roads by 'increasingly heavy traffic, from charabancs in particular'. The £40,000 spent to acquire control of the FR was undoubtedly provided by Stewart.

The block caused by the Ministry of Labour's unemployment status certification was removed on 16 November 1921, the ministry writing that 'as a result of further investigation the minister is now prepared to certify that serious unemployment ... also exists in the areas of Portmadoc, Talysarn and Pwllheli.'

On 17 November 1921, when Davies wrote to the ministry to make a formal application for funds, he proposed dividing the scheme into two parts: Portmadoc–Dinas at £75,000, and the Carnarvon extension at £45,000. He proposed deferring the extension, despite local authority support for it, providing the government would find £42,500 for Portmadoc–Dinas; in his calculations he made allowance for an additional £10,000 spent by the promoters 'for the purposes of this scheme.' If the ministry would support the scheme in this way, the promoters would find the balance.

The ministry responded by sending Davies a detailed questionnaire focusing on the impact of the withdrawal of the Carnarvon extension and trying to get some sharper data. After Davies replied, raising the passenger estimate to 250,000, he and Jack attended a meeting at the ministry on 9 December 1921. The increased passenger estimate, Jack explained, was because the area was getting busier, with the LNWR taking 250,000 passengers to North Wales resorts each fortnight during the summer of 1921 'notwithstanding bad trade and high prices.' When questioned about working expenses, which seemed too low, he said that it was intended to work the line 'more as a tramway', with a small permanent staff and additional staff to deal with holiday traffic; 'he finally admitted that if they carried the traffic which they anticipated the figure was too low' the note-taker commented in the meeting's minutes.

Davies and Breese continued to press for a response, turning up unannounced at the Treasury on 19 December 1921. Breese urged that the matter be dealt with quickly in order that he could take good news back to his constituents. Davies outlined the history of the scheme and the current financial status: the NWNGR and PBSSR had cost £270,000 and were to be purchased for £10,000 in debentures and £90,000 in ordinary shares. Completion would cost £75,000 and £10,000 had been spent already; 50% of £85,000 therefore was being sought from government sources.

They were told that whilst the Treasury had not received details of the scheme from the Ministry of Transport, the government was only interested in the scheme from the standpoint of unemployment relief. For that reason the £10,000 already spent could not be supported, as doing so would not relieve unemployment. Davies said that 65%–70% of the expenditure would go on employment. The meeting ended with Breese and Davies being told that the scheme was one that the Treasury might approve, on the recommendation of the Ministry of Transport, and subject to conditions.

Actually, they had already got the result they wanted, for on the same day Cyril Hurcomb, acting on Neal's instructions, submitted the ministry's request for financial support to the Treasury. In his acknowledgement to Neal, Hurcomb pointed out that the case was weak but none of the earlier scepticism made its way into the Treasury submission. It appears that Breese had seen Neal on 19 December, whether before or after the Treasury meeting is not known. Hurcomb went on to become chairman of the British Transport Commission when the railways were nationalised.

Whilst Davies and Breese were badgering the Treasury, Hurcomb produced an analysis of the scheme, dated 20 December 1921. He noted that although the BoT thought mineral traffic would increase he was of the opinion that success would depend on summer passenger traffic which, he said, would be considerable now that the 'scheme is to be intimately linked with the Festiniog Railway' and offering scope for circular tours. Although the promoters estimated annual freight traffic at 21,000 tons, the ministry thought that 31,000 tons was more realistic. The 250,000 passenger figure was finally accepted without question although it was reduced to 200,000 in revenue calculations. It is worth bearing in mind that even when the FR, then at less than half the length of the WHR, was carrying over 200,000 passengers annually in the 1970s it needed more than 20 bogie carriages and a much longer season to do so. Gross receipts of £25,200 were expected to produce net receipts of £5,850, a 3.7% return on capital of £185,000.

Hurcomb recommended the scheme as being suitable for assistance from unemployment relief funds. There were, he noted, 1,429 unemployed men in the district and the railway could give employment to 520 for six months; the fact that the unemployed were not navvies was conveniently overlooked. He didn't comment, but the Treasury did later, on the promoters' claim to be providing three months' work for 310 men on 'manufactured materials' which turned out to be for the building and track materials to be used during construction and therefore not qualifying for support.

Davies returned alone to the Treasury on 21 December 1921, when an official agreed to see him reluctantly, but in order to clarify items arising from Hurcomb's report; protocol should have prevented Davies from dealing directly with the Treasury, at least without Breese, the MP, present. The first item raised was the Carnarvon extension, which had previously been a vital part of the scheme – 'Davies entered into a long harangue, in the course of which he argued with equal conviction of them, that the extension was essential and that it was not'!

The £10,000 already spent was the subject of some discussion, with Davies prevaricating about its purpose, 'acquiring certain interests', a response that was interpreted as being 'made up of sums required to buy out debenture holders in the old undertakings, and Mr Davies's fees for promotional expenses.' He finally accepted that the most the government would contribute was £37,500. With £23,000 committed from three local authorities, the scheme was still short of £14,500 funding, or £24,500 if the £10,000 was to be reimbursed. Davies asserted that the shortfall would be obtained from 'other local sources.'

On leaving, Davies asked for the money to be made available as soon as possible in order that the work could be progressed. On being told that it would be a condition of grant that local funds should be spent before calling on the government, Davies replied that it was not reasonable to expect the local subscribers to take the risk, generating the telling response that if there were risks local subscribers were unwilling to take then the scheme was one to which the government ought not to be expected to contribute.

On 28 December 1921, Hurcomb informed Davies that

The first page of the 1922 LRO as submitted by the Light Railway Commissioners to the BoT for approval. *Author's collection*

there were two outstanding issues to be dealt with before a decision could be made. The ministry required confirmation of the railway's proposed capital structure and wished to know, in detail, the purpose of the £10,000. Davies replied on 31 December 1921. Concerning the £10,000, he said that it represented £6,759 to acquire control of the NWNGR, £1,470 to keep it open for goods traffic 'in anticipation of completion of the larger scheme now under discussion' and the remainder to 'purchase certain interests' in the PBSSR. Costs to complete the scheme were: completing the railway from Portmadoc to Rhyd Ddu – £65,000; refurbishing the NWNGR – £3,000; land purchase – £1,500; engineers' fees – £3,000; legal and other expenses – £2,500. The capital would consist of £85,000 debenture stock and £90,000 ordinary shares. The latter and £10,000 of the debenture stock would be used to acquire the assets of the NWNGR and the PBSSR. Davies closed by soliciting a reply by first post 'next Thursday', 5 January 1922, because the subject was to be discussed at a special meeting of the county council that day. Keeping up the pressure, the mayor of Carnarvon sent a telegram to Neal on 2 January 1922.

Davies's persistence nearly paid off – the offer letter was drafted on 4 January 1922 and sent the next day; Davies had sent a telegram chasing it up at 9.57am on 5 January. The offer, signed by Hurcomb, was subject to 11 conditions: the government's contribution to be secured on debentures; any land required to be conveyed free or paid for in ordinary shares; guarantees to be given that expenditure over £75,000 to be funded locally; government funding to become available when expenditure of £20,000 from other sources was certified; unskilled construction labour to be obtained locally; support conditional on the LRO being made; debentures issued not to exceed 50% of total capital; Carnarvon extension not to be undertaken without prior approval of the Minister of Transport; and no contribution from public funds to be claimed for it.

At the county council's meeting on 5 January, Walter Cradoc Davies, Davies's brother, read a statement describing the scheme. Jack was present as a council member. R. M. Greaves, a disaffected former FR Company director, said that the scheme would have been better 10 or 12 years earlier, 'before the development of road transport.' Narrow gauge railways, he said, were not better than road transport and quarries were reducing their costs by adopting it. He received no answer when he asked why Merionethshire County Council had not been asked to contribute, about a mile of the line being in that county. The proposal to make the loan was approved with three votes against.

Davies and Jack were then faced with the need to complete the funding shortfall. On 9 January 1922 Davies informed the ministry that not only had the county, Gwyrfai and Portmadoc councils confirmed their support, they had been joined by Glaslyn RDC with another £3,000; Deudraeth RDC was to vote £3,000 a few days later. Davies also apologised for 'appearing to press unduly' for the decision but he had wished to give information on progress to the local authorities and counter criticism that had appeared in the local press. One interpretation of the late participation of Glaslyn and Deudraeth would be that Jack, who had the reputation of being a bully, pressured them to join in. The search for funds was not over, however, for the authorities' contribution came to £29,000 and the government would only contribute half of £75,000, a total of £66,500. The promoters had agreed to find it themselves but events were to show that they had not given up on the idea of getting someone else to pay.

When the LRC compiled their undated report shortly afterwards they revealed that the promoters had applied to revive the Carnarvon extension compulsory purchase powers, previously authorised by the 1904 Act; the affected landowners had been informed on 22 November and the notice had been published on 1 December 1921. The commissioners had made a site visit on February 7, meeting landowners and occupiers, the result of which was a decision in favour of the extension although they had been notified that the promoters did not intend to proceed with the extension for the time being. When the LNWR heard that the order had been transferred from the LRC to the ministry for confirmation it asked to be informed of any application for consent because it would wish to make representations on the matter.

The loan offer had been formally accepted on 26 January 1922, the day after the PBSSR assets had been transferred from NWPTC to Stewart. The agreement to transfer the NWNGR and the PBSSR to the WHR had been made on 1 February and a heads of agreement was made between the promoters and the government on 24 March 1922; these agreements were incorporated into the LRO as schedules. Some of the PBSSR's assets were not as secure as they should have been, for on 10 February 1922 a notice was published in the *North Wales Chronicle* complaining that 'rails, sleepers and other materials' had been taken and seeking their return. Anyone with information was solicited to contact the FR.

The Welsh Highland Railway (Light Railway) Order was made on 30 March 1922.

3

Completing the Portmadoc–Dinas Railway 1922-23

Considerably more complex than the 1914 draft order, the 1922 order defined the railway as: 'the railways respectively authorised to be acquired reconstructed or constructed as the case may be by the Act of 1901 and by the Act of 1904 as amended by the Carnarvon order of 1908 and authorised by the order of 1908 to be reconstructed or constructed as light railways ... and the light railway authorised by the Carnarvon order 1908 and the Moel Tryfan undertaking and the light railway authorised by the order of 1906 ...'

Hence, a railway from Portmadoc harbour to Caernarvon, except that there were no funds for the last three miles and no provision for a station in Portmadoc or a link to the FR. The stub end of the PBSSR's 1901 line between Beddgelert and Llyn Gwynant and the 1908 line thence to Bettws y Coed were excluded.

The order incorporated a company to own and operate the railway, the Welsh Highland Railway (Light Railway) Company, with Davies, Jack and Stewart as its first directors; the investing authorities were also permitted to appoint a director to represent their interests. The investing authorities were authorised to borrow money in order to make their advances providing it was repaid over no more than 50 years. The Carnarvon Harbour Trust, although a party in the draft order and a supporter of the railway, was actually excluded from the order because it was not a public authority as defined by the Light Railways Act and did not require the authority of an LRO to invest in the railway.

Three years were allowed to complete any compulsory land purchases and five years, unless extended by application to the Minister of Transport, for construction, except that government funding would be withheld from any work not completed before 1 April 1923.

The company was empowered to enter into working agreements with the LNWR and the GWR and to lease the railway, or part of it, to any railway company with which it was permitted to enter into agreements. Interestingly, in the light of events, a clause in this section declared that 'any such lease shall imply a condition of re-entry if the lessees discontinue the working of the railway leased ... for a space of three months ...'

When the WHR was incorporated, Stewart received £8,500 debentures and £34,540 ordinary shares for the NWNGR debentures and £1,500 debentures for the 1921 advance to Aitchison. Just to clear things up, a further £5,460 in ordinary shares was allocated to the Lloyds' bond holders, the 1888 creditors and Stewart, in respect of interest due.

The WHR's engineering consultant was Douglas Fox & Partners. On 1 April 1922 the firm sent Davies the details of bids submitted by five contractors: Sir Robert McAlpine & Sons, Laing & Son, Alban Richards & Co, Macdonald Gibbs & Co and Muirhead Macdonald. Each contractor had submitted two bids, one

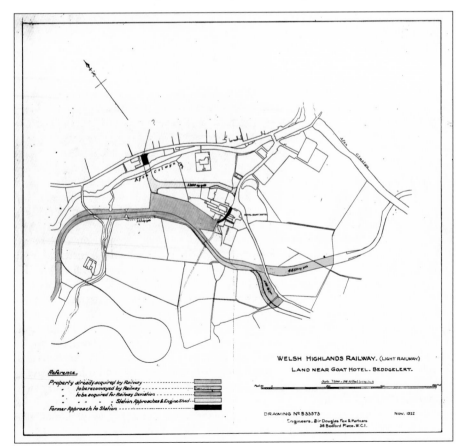

Above: **The Welsh Highland Railway (Light Railway) Company seal.** *NA*

Left: **A plan dated November 1922 showing land required in the vicinity of Beddgelert station as a consequence of the amended route. The PBSSR access via the Goat Hotel is coloured black.** *NA*

Left: **Probably the closest it is possible to get to a photograph of the 1922/3 works in progress is this view of *Moel Tryfan* at Beddgelert in 1923. The station bookstall has not been erected, there are two sedan toolboxes and a skip body to be seen, and the site is unfenced. The building's open door and windows suggest that perhaps the decorator might be in action within. The telephone insulators have been mounted on the roof, but there are no signs of the wires.** *Valentine/ Author's collection*

Right: **Another view of the same train shows loose rock and a spare rail in the foreground and the loco crew peering into *Moel Tryfan's* smokebox. In 1922, the locomotive was reported as suffering from leaking tubes and as the train has just come up from Portmadoc, including some two miles of 1-in-40 gradients, the two might be connected. The locomotive now faces Carnarvon instead of Portmadoc. Although there are at least two passengers in the Pickering brake/composite, the scene has the air of being a trial run for both the loco and the completed railway.** *Valentine/Author's collection*

that included the authorised 1-in-28 PBSSR route at Beddgelert and one that included the unauthorised 1-in-40 route required if the railway was to be worked by steam locomotives. McAlpine was the lowest at £54,171 for the 1-in-28 route and the runner-up, £60,819, for the 1-in-40 route. The positions were reversed: £54,743 and £57,637 for Laing's bids. Muirhead Macdonald's bids were the highest: £85,729 and £93,648 respectively.

Fox recommended accepting the McAlpine quote, even though it was more expensive for the 1-in-40 route, because the partnership's schedule rates were cheaper on items like rock cuttings which could not be estimated accurately. Fox went on to say that McAlpine would undertake to complete the contract within 12 months for a fixed price of £66,500, to include £1,000 for additional land, £750 for station telephones, £500 for additional work at stations and £3,500 for fencing. McAlpine was also prepared to absorb contingencies if it could make Fox-approved changes to make savings.

The ministry was at first inclined to accept the recommendation that McAlpine should have the contract despite being slightly more expensive than Laing. When Davies was asked why Laing had not been asked for a fixed-price quote he replied that Fox was confident in McAlpine's ability to complete the line for £66,500, but that they did not have the same confidence in Laing. Neal, however, insisted that Laing be given an opportunity to quote on the same basis.

By 24 April, Laing had offered to do the work for £60,060. In passing this on to the ministry Fox explained that as there had been changes in the labour rates they had invited McAlpine to requote. Not surprisingly perhaps, the new price was £59,985, £75 less. Fox explained that they would prefer the work to be carried out by a contractor experienced with both railway work and the North Wales terrain, claiming that Laing had no experience in either. Neal gave his approval on 25 April and the contract was made on 30 April 1922. Stewart and Jack signed for the railway, and five members of the McAlpine family for the contractors; the original, impressed with the WHR's seal, is in the archives at Caernarfon.

Under the contract the partnership was required to obtain any land required (clause 13) at its own expense, and to convey it to the railway, for which purpose £1,000 was allowed. Some extra land was required around Beddgelert, where the deviations to accommodate the 1-in-40 route were to be made; despite being included in the contract the railway did not, at this stage, have any authority for these deviations. The railway also obtained ministerial approval to pay £750 (£450 plus interest) for land taken from a Major E. Bowen Jones by the PBSSR in February 1905; Davies claimed they had tried to get Jones to donate the land or to take shares but he had refused, saying that he had been inconvenienced and should be paid in cash.

The minimum radius on curves (clause 34) was to be 198ft and the maximum gradient 1 in 40. Rail in 33ft lengths of 40lb/yd was specified although 'second-hand or reject imperfect material will be accepted provided the engineers are satisfied with the quality of the rails proposed.' All points were to have 1-in-12 turnouts.

The long tunnel in the Aberglaslyn Pass (clause 43) required completion, working from both ends was required providing water did not require pumping, and the others needed opening out to the correct cross-section where necessary.

Clause 56 required exposed steelwork to be given three coats of 'first-class' paint, one before and two after completion; history shows that the contractors defaulted on this item.

Halts, passing places and stations (clause 59) were required at: 'about 3 miles' (from Rhyd Ddu) – halt with 40ft siding, shelter; Beddgelert – 300ft passing loop, 180ft siding, sidings to loco and goods sheds, waiting room/office, goods shed, loco shed, water tank; Nantmor – halt with 40ft siding, shelter; Croesor Junction – 300ft passing loop, 40ft siding; Pont Croesor – 40ft siding, waiting room; Portmadoc – 300ft passing loop, waiting room/office, water tank. Second-hand army huts or similar were permissible. All stations and halts were to have platforms of 6in of rolled stone ballast or gravel 150ft x 10ft, except at Beddgelert where 300ft x 15ft was specified.

Any transport required over the NWNGR section was chargeable at three-quarters of the usual rate. Use could be made of the Croesor section in connection with the execution of the works providing any traffic offering was carried at the normal rate; when the traffic was for WHR use three-quarters of the usual rate became chargeable.

The schedule of prices and quantities divided the contract into three sections: refurbishing the NWNGR, including the Bryngwyn branch; construction between Rhyd Ddu and Croesor Junction, and repairs to the Croesor Tramway from the junction and Portmadoc. The latter was further divided into two parts: from the junction to the Beddgelert siding and thence to Portmadoc.

NWNGR section works were to cost £9,278. They included installing 5,000 new sleepers at £1,666, loosening existing ballast and laying 3in of top ballast at £3,510, replacing one turnout at Dinas and five at Bryngwyn at £20 each and renewing a diamond crossing at Dinas for £50. £1,000 was allowed for repair of rolling stock and £1,000 for fencing.

The new works were costed at £52,492. Trimming the Goat tunnel and the short Aberglaslyn tunnels was priced at 40s per cubic yard for an estimated 190 cubic yards. Excavating and trimming the long tunnel was only 30s per cubic yard for an estimated 2,100 cubic yards – quantity discount?

Diverting the road near Nantmor to pass under the railway, for which there was no approval at the time of the contract, was quoted at £500; a further £100 was the price for remetalling and steamrolling the road. The three lattice girder bridges, crossing the Glaslyn at Bryn y Felin and the Nany y Mor (sic) and Dylif river crossings, were quoted at £30 per ton erected complete, total £1,800.

Ballast was to be laid 10in deep, including no more than 4in of bottom ballast, nine miles at £300 per mile, while 17,000 sleepers were priced at £4,037 with 600 tons of rail and fittings priced at £5,100. The line required 12 sets of points and six catch points costing £288, and £1,000 was allowed for the telephone system. Station buildings, water tanks and gates were to be to be supplied and installed at 'nett invoiced cash price plus 10 per cent', £1,500, and £2,500 was allowed for fencing.

The work to refurbish the Croesor Tramway to Portmadoc was estimated at £4,745. Of this the three miles from Croesor Junction to the Beddgelert siding was to be cleaned and weeded for £40 per mile and existing ballast was to be loosened and improved by the addition of 2in of top ballast for £638. At Croesor Junction 500 new sleepers were required, together with three sets of points and one at Pont Croesor where £1,000 was allowed for reconstruction of eight 24ft spans and £60 for the adjacent level crossing.

From the Beddgelert siding new rail was specified but half the sleepers and half the ballast was expected to be reusable; the inclusive cost, including the loop, was estimated at £1,311 and 400yd of slate sidings were to be relaid with 'light section rails' with ballasting and sleepers as required for £300. Four turnouts were required at the Beddgelert siding and a further six turnouts and passing loops between there and Portmadoc.

The deadlines set for completion were 22 July 1922 for Dinas–Beddgelert and Portmadoc–Nantmor and 31 March 1923 for the remainder. This included a requirement to work at nights and on Sundays if necessary.

The work started on 8 May 1922, and initially, 117 men were employed. McAlpine established an office in a rented house next to the Prince Llewelyn Hotel in Beddgelert. The McAlpine archive records that a local man, Jack Jones, was employed as chainman and interpreter, a reminder that local people had little contact with monoglot English speakers. Bob Paton was the manager and cashier and Frank Harper the timekeeper. Outside staff included Jock Struthers, works manager; Alec Glennie, traveller; Terry Hussey, tunnel foreman; Sam Crosbie, steam boss; and Mrs Crosbie, hut mistress.

Beddgelert station later in 1923, seen from the Goat Hotel cutting. The station building and bookstall are in place with the coal merchant's lorry parked between them. In 1933 W. S. Jones, the coal merchant, was paying 10s per month rent for the 'coal wharf'. Two telephone poles and a bench have been erected since the Valentine photographs were taken.
Frith/Author's collection

Letters dealing with the employment issues in 1923 were signed by J. M. Neilson.

A loan account with the National Provincial Bank was set up to finance construction until the advances were made. The local authorities had to arrange to borrow their contributions as the government money would not be made available until £20,000 had been spent.

On 27 June 1922, members of Deudraeth RDC attempted to rescind its decision to contribute, apparently because they had only just realised that the government contribution was a loan and not a free grant. Councillor R. R. Jones proposed the resolution, saying that he was convinced the railway was doomed to failure and that the council had no power to advance the money as the ratepayers were 'almost unanimously' against it. Reverend J. T. Lewis of Trawsfynydd declared that the council would get no benefit from the railway. The chairman used his casting vote to adjourn the resolution when a vote was taken. Glaslyn RDC members were also concerned about the loan and its impact on the rates they levied. When the council had written to Breese, the MP, about the increasing cost of road maintenance because of escalating heavy traffic he replied that the 'light railway' would be cheaper than what it paid for road repairs. In 1934 Glaslyn was to become bankrupt, being divided between Gwyrfai and Lleyn, the former acquiring the WHR debentures; whether the bankruptcy was due to the burden of its WHR loan is unclear.

To deal with the diversions and some other matters an amendment LRO was applied for in July 1922, while preparations for reopening the NWNGR section were in hand. Colonel J. W. Pringle inspected the line on 22 July and submitted his report three days later. He noted that the permanent way was generally in adequate condition for the class of traffic and speed (15mph) proposed.

He reported that this part of the WHR would be operated in two sections: Dinas to Tryfan Junction and thence to Rhyd Ddu. Control would be by Wise's patent staff-and-ticket for the former and one engine-in-steam (with staff) for the latter. At Tryfan Junction a key on the Dinas–Tryfan Junction staff would lock the Bryngwyn branch points; passenger trains there would use the same track in each direction.

Pringle observed that some of the old sleepers were in a decayed condition and would require changing before too long. He noted that remnants of NWNGR signalling were still in situ and asked for them to be removed. The outlet of a new water tank at Cwellyn Lake halt fouled an open carriage door and had to be moved. Subject to these and other minor works and clarification of some operating rules he recommended that approval be given for passenger trains.

With services starting on 31 July 1922, the reopened railway was promoted as providing '10 miles of beautiful scenery' with streams, waterfalls, lakes and mountains to see, and with observation cars provided. Four passenger trains daily were operated, with goods trains running as required.

Gaumont News filmed the railway for showing in over 500 cinemas, Davies reported, during the first week of operation; regrettably the film has not survived.

Revenue for the week ending 5 August was £94; wages for 22 men amounted to £69 and a pro rata proportion of overheads to £22, leaving a small operating surplus of £3, considered a satisfactory result by Councillor Nee (page 60), although by the end of the year a loss of £571 had been incurred.

The annual return showed that at the end of the year, £24,762 14s 1d had been spent on construction and £23,300 debentures issued. Locomotive-running expenses of £973 included £188 for horse haulage, an item that had cost the PBSSR £154 in 1921. £403 spent on maintaining the permanent way seems high for a line that had just been refurbished, especially as it can only have been incurred since 31 July; £1,018 was to be spent under this heading in 1923.

Glaslyn and Deudraeth councils had still not, in mid-1922, made arrangements to raise the finance required for their loans to the railway; Davies persuaded them to take action by allowing them to consult with the contractors on the use of local labour on outstanding work.

The second LRO application attracted much more attention than that for the first order and, following a site visit the previous day, a public inquiry was held in Portmadoc on 8 September 1922.

In addition to powers of deviation, and abandonment, around Beddgelert the order sought to limit the assessment of the railway to local rates for five years, requiring that the land occupied by the new railway, Rhyd Ddu to Croesor Junction, be assessed on the same basis as it had been before it had been acquired for the railway, as agricultural land. This had been a standard requirement in LROs, intended to stop local authorities benefiting from a government free grant where they had not supported a development. In the case of the 1922 order it had not been included because of the authorities' contribution. However, the Treasury Solicitor required its inclusion in the amendment order. The 1921 Railways Act had extended the provision to allow such relief where a light railway had been constructed with a government loan.

Naturally, it was this clause that excited the investing authorities and all were represented at the inquiry. William George was in attendance again, this time representing the Glaslyn Foundry, R. Newell, owner of the slaughterhouse likely to be affected by the proposed FR station, and the Cwm Cloch owners, affected by a deviation near Beddgelert, as well as Portmadoc UDC.

Trains operated on the NWNGR section before the WHR was opened throughout on 1 June 1923, as represented by this photograph of *Moel Tryfan* hauling a Pickering brake composite and a wagon taken at Waenfawr on 15 May.
FR Archives

Double Fairlie *James Spooner* at Beddgelert. The FR's double Fairlies were used on the WHR in 1923 although they were soon confined to their own line.
Author's Collection

Others represented included the LNWR, Tourist Hotels Ltd, owners of the Goat Hotel, Beddgelert, Carnarvon Harbour Trust, the Tremadoc Estate, the National Union of Railwaymen, the Railway Clerks Association, and the North Wales Quarrymen's Association. Evan R. Davies, Cradoc Davies and Jack represented the promoters.

In its objection the county council sought primarily to rank the debentures authorised by the 1922 order above any others that might be issued by the railway, except in respect of any issued to the authorities supporting the Dinas–Caernarvon extension that should rank equally with the first £85,000, and to reduce the period of rates relief from five years to two without any option for extension.

Davies opened the inquiry by commenting on the 'formidable array … of legal talent' now present but not at the previous inquiry. He said that he thought this indicated support for the scheme on its merits but with objections on detail. He then said that a good deal of progress had been made between Rhyd Ddu and Portmadoc and explained that when the engineers reviewed the engineering details in March 1922 'they found it might be possible to effect considerable improvement in the line of route below Beddgelert'. He justified the proposed route changes, saying that the PBSSR route, an embankment from the road bridge near the Goat Hotel to the Glaslyn, would be 'an interference with its natural beauty' that could be avoided by the route proposed.

Davies went on to say that the deviations below Rhyd Ddu were substantial but gave no explanation for them, commenting only that the landowners had no objections. The road diversion at Nantmor would, he said, replace a level crossing on a busy road with a bridge. The railway's engineers amplified the reasons for the diversions later.

On the matter of rates relief Davies said the promoters had offered to meet the objection by having the relief withdrawn as soon as the railway was in a position to pay both the debenture interest and instalments on the investing authorities' advances. He said that in its early years the railway would have to pay interest on the debentures as well as one fifth of the local authorities' advance of £29,000. He thought rates payable could be in the order of £1,500 but no one really knew. In 1921 the FR had paid £1,630 in rates for a line half as long as the WHR was going to be – he thought WHR traffic would equal that on the FR. He observed that at present the authorities were getting virtually nothing from the railway as it was, implying that they would be no worse off with the clause.

The objection of Tourist Hotels Ltd had some complexity, being based on a covenant entered into when Goat Hotel land was sold to the PBSSR in 1905. Then the station access was to have been through the hotel yard, the hotel presumably hoping to attract additional business thereby. The promoters, noting the unsuitability of the hotel yard as a route for charabancs, wished to build a new access from the Carnarvon side of the village, alongside the village school, as well as providing a better access from the Portmadoc side, on the village side of the hotel, making it possible for charabancs to leave the station without having to turn. Davies said that the promoters would settle for a footpath from the Carnarvon side if they could not have a road. In the event the parties agreed to negotiate further but the improved access was never made.

Davies examined Ralph Freeman, for Douglas Fox & Co, to bring out more information of the need for the diversions. Freeman explained that the PBSSR's route between the Goat Hotel and the Glaslyn would have required some difficult work, with much of the land boggy, whilst the proposed route was shorter, required less earth work and had easier gradients. Fox's plans reveal that two other routes using the PBSSR road bridge and other river crossings had also been considered.

Regarding the route between Rhyd Ddu and Beddgelert, Freeman said, the 1-in-28 gradients would require double heading or split trains to deal with heavy loads; the proposed route would have 1-in-40 maximum gradients – here Freeman rather overstated his case, for only the short section, 2 chains long, connecting the station with the 1900 route at Tyn y Coed was at 1 in 28; other changes to the route were made to reduce the scale of earthworks needed. The modification near Nantmor avoided a level crossing on a sharp bend with limited visibility at the expense of providing a bridge.

Counsel for Gwyrfai RDC cross-examined Jack about the debentures. Essentially he said that as the authorities had to agree to the issue of further debentures he could not see what the problem was – the difficulty for the councils was the proviso 'which consent cannot be unreasonably withheld', which they saw as meaning they would have no say in the matter.

There were questions about the rates assessment, the councils saying that they had been told the railway would be responsible for increased rateable values in the area, and they would prefer the certainty of rates to the uncertainty of

debenture interest. The councils were also concerned that their nominee on the WHR company board could not take his place until they had advanced £15,000, as specified in the 1922 Order; the company agreed to the nominee taking up his post without the financial condition being met, and this modification was incorporated into the new order. The rating clause was withdrawn, too. Notwithstanding their objections it was made clear that the authorities remained in support of the WHR.

The maintenance of and the height of the proposed Nantmor road bridge came in for some comment also. The WHR wanted 14ft whilst the highway authority wanted the 16ft specified by the Railway Clauses Act of 1845 – there was some debate about whether a 'two-deck' charabanc would pass through a 14ft bridge without putting its top deck passengers at risk of decapitation. The county also wanted, for unspecified reasons, a span of 35ft instead of 25ft.

In their report of 16 September 1922 the commissioners approved the deviations without change, noting that McAlpine was already at work on that between Rhyd Ddu and Beddgelert. The WHR lost on the question of the height of the Nantmor road bridge but won on the matter of its span. On the issue of rateable assessment the railway got the clause but it was restricted to two years and with no option to extend it.

Whilst the order was being processed news of the WHR reached *The Times* in London, with the railway forming the centrepiece of a trade supplement published on 11 November 1922. Citing the railway as an imaginative enterprise it called upon the newly formed LMSR and enlarged GWR to follow its example in improving access to Snowdonia.

The condition of the NWNGR buildings was considered on 24 November 1922, when Davies advised the ministry that Fox recommended the expenditure of £990 to repair them and to install toilets at Dinas and Rhyd Ddu, requesting ministerial approval for the expenditure. Briefly, all of the buildings were in a poor state and required repair and decorating. The LNWR had also complained about water draining onto its track from the platform at Dinas. The sidings there also required attention.

Davies made the first application for the release of government funds on 15 December 1922. He submitted an affidavit made by William Richard Huson, the company secretary, on the same date. This reveals that between 19 October and 11 December the local authorities had contributed £20,000 to the WHR and that Fox had submitted certificates totalling £20,316 for work carried out by McAlpine since 23 October; other capital expenses had been incurred in setting up the company. The amount due to McAlpine was subject to 10%

retention; Fox received 4% of the amount paid to the contractor. Hurcomb therefore sent Davies an order for £3,300 on 20 December 1922 and Davies sent a debenture certificate for the same amount on 27 December.

On several occasions from December 1922 into 1923, attempts were made by the mayor of Carnarvon and Davies to secure a government contribution of £18,000 towards the construction of the Carnarvon extension, now estimated to cost £25,000. The ministry was concerned about the consequences of funding the extension if it took traffic away from the LNWR. Following a meeting and some consideration it was decided to inform the mayor that there were no funds available at the present time.

The first interest payment on the loans was due on 31 December 1922. Making the payment from capital, Jack despatched the cheques on 23 January 1923, deducting 25% income tax. The ministry received £3 7s 10d in respect of its £3,300, the interest covering the period from 22 December, the date the debenture certificate was issued, not the date the money was advanced, the difference being noted on the ministry's copy of Jack's covering letter.

The amendment order was made on 7 February 1923, having cost £219 in legal fees to obtain. Deviation Railway No 1 started south of Hafod Ruffydd, 2 miles 2 furlongs from Rhyd Ddu, proceeding in a south-easterly direction and terminating north easterly of Cwm Cloch Isaf, 4 miles 1 furlong from Rhyd Ddu. Deviation Railway No 2 was 4 furlongs 7 chains long, starting by the Goat Hotel tunnel, 4 miles 7 furlongs from Rhyd Ddu, and ending on the east bank of the Glaslyn east of Bryn y Felin, crossing the river by a 75ft bridge. It required relocating some 300ft of the existing road, raising it over the railway on a new bridge. As a consequence of these deviations the railway became 570yd longer.

The FR had also made an LRO application in July 1922, primarily for powers to operate as a light railway but also for new works that were essential to the WHR, a connection between the two lines and a new station. The latter would replace the existing station and enough land would be taken to accommodate a replacement for Boston Lodge Works and an interchange with the Cambrian. The route proposed was split into two for legal reasons, the first replacing part of the original line to the harbour by a new line over a widened Britannia bridge, the second providing the actual link.

Douglas Fox & Partners estimated £13,500 for 10 chains (222yd) of railway: legal and engineering expenses – £1,500, buildings – £3,000; alterations to bridge – £1,500; permanent way and resurfacing roads – £500; land/buildings acquisition – £1,000 and contingencies of £1,000. The FR sought approval to borrow a further £20,000 in consequence, the difference being for working capital and current losses.

The estimate also included £5,000 for rolling stock. Davies was to say, at the inquiry, that the FR's rolling stock was 'pretty old' and the directors thought 'it may be necessary to improve it.'

On 4 September, Davies, Tyrwhitt, from the FR (page 63), and F. W. H. Stileman, from Fox, had met Portmadoc UDC to answer the council's concerns about the proposed orders. In addition to the rating issue already mentioned, the council was concerned about the route through the town and the proposed new station.

The inquiry followed the WHR's amendment order inquiry. Davies explained that the main purpose of the application was to make it possible for there to be a physical union between the two railways under joint direction.

Portmadoc UDC, represented by William George, had objected to the proposal, apparently failing to understand or remember, Davies reminded the inquiry, that the FR already had powers, of which it made regular use, to cross the Britannia bridge and that the Croesor Tramway had statutory authority for its line to the harbour which had been upgraded for passenger use by the PBSSR Act of 1901. The status of the road also caused some confusion as it still belonged to the Tremadoc Estate, owners of the embankment and successors to William Madocks, its builder.

The council proposed an alternative route through the 'Gorseddau yard', the site of the present petrol station, and garden of Ynys Tywyn House, much as the route taken by the restored railway. Ralph Freeman objected to it because it would be more expensive and necessary to start the curve on the bridge. The council said that it would accept the railway's scheme provided there were safeguards for public safety: a flagman leading trains and a bell on the locomotives. The council also hoped that the Croesor crossing would be done away with. When it was pointed out that such a move would require any goods traffic originating from the WHR and bound for the harbour to be double shunted across the Britannia bridge, increasing the use of the road crossings, George responded that the goods could be taken to the FR for shunting.

On the matter of the station, Davies explained that it would be absurd to have two stations for 'these small undertakings' and as they were largely dependent on the GWR for passengers it would not be in the public interest to have the station a mile away from the GWR station – actually the distance is less than three-quarters of a mile. He expressed a wish for the GWR to stop some of its trains close to the proposed narrow gauge station to reduce the walking distance between the railways. The new station would be part of the FR undertaking and replace the existing station at the harbour. The FR would have had running powers over the WHR as far as the GWR crossing.

When asked to speak 'generally' on the linking of the railways, Jack replied: 'The original conception of the WHR was to enable the FR to be of greater service to the district, but it appeared to me when I first went into the figures that there were difficulties facing the railway that might have resulted in defeating the object altogether. A railway of 12¾ miles could not possibly hope to prosper, but if 25 miles of railway were added to it, it would give such an average per passenger as to cover the expenditure, and one might therefore hope to make it a success.' A somewhat different, and almost contradictory, response to the explanation he had previously given to the Treasury.

Top: **All of the FR's surviving England locomotives were used on the WHR and, indeed, the first trains were hauled by** *Princess* **and** *Prince.* *Little Giant* **was photographed with a train of FR stock at the Beddgelert water tower in 1923.** *Author's collection*

Left: **The ex-War Department Baldwin 4-6-0T No 590 was acquired in 1923.** *Little Giant's* **crew has been persuaded to pull it from the shed at Dinas to be photographed.** *Author's collection*

The commissioners' report on the inquiry is undated; they generally approved the FR's application except for a general power of sale to any railway company or the WHR. They said that if there were a proposal for such a sale they could deal with it. They further said that it would be useless to give the FR power to be sold to the WHR as the WHR was not authorised to enter into such a purchase and had no powers to raise the capital required. As the government had invested in the WHR its approval would be needed in any event. The order was made on 30 January 1923.

The FR's ordinary shareholders, incidentally, were only informed of these activities on 17 February 1923, when Jack circulated his annual report and told them about the LRO, working arrangements, through trains, the junction railways and the new station. He said the works were estimated to cost £6,000 and the company expected to issue not more that £10,000 of the £20,000 debenture stock authorised by the LRO. In the meantime, the company expected to borrow on overdraft from the National Provincial Bank. McAlpine widened the Britannia bridge and built the junction railways for a tendered price of £3,640, but in 1924 was paid only £3,000 in cash, the outstanding £966 12s being secured by a debenture.

Before leaving the topic of the FR Company, the NWPTC, renamed the North Wales Power Company since 8 June 1922, had transferred its FR shares to the Aluminium Corporation for £500 on 14 March 1923. In doing so, it was acting on the advice of the electricity commissioners that it should confine its operations to that of a public utility service.

Staying in 1923, Davies reported that WHR work was 'now fast approaching completion' when submitting Fox's fourth certificate on 13 March. The fifth certificate was submitted on 30 April, bringing the value of the work carried out to date to £51,507.

Following the WHR's agreement with the investing authorities, M. E. Nee, a Carnarvon solicitor and county councillor, had been appointed a company director, provisionally, from 15 July 1922. He submitted another report to the authorities on 25 April 1923.

In addition to commenting on the financial results of operating the NWNGR section, page 56, Nee explained that each week he received reports detailing the number of men employed by the company, company progress, construction progress and the number of men employed on the contract. The latter ranged from 250 in July 1922 to 429 at the time of the report.

He closed his report by adding that the WHR and the Snowdon Mountain Railway were producing a guidebook 'showing the beauty spots through which the line runs' and that it would be distributed in 'America and the Colonies'. He concluded, with misplaced confidence: 'It is anticipated that in a few years time the railway will be as popular as any mountain railway in Europe'. The guidebook, the *Snowdon and Welsh Highland Holiday Book*, was reviewed in the *North Wales Chronicle* on 25 May. Accepting Nee's report, the investing authorities resolved that representations be made regarding 'the old bridge embankment near the Goat Hotel, Beddgelert, the removal of which would immensely improve the beauty of the valley.' If only they knew that nearly 100 years later the bridge would remain in situ and regarded as an essential part of the landscape.

Fox had notified the ministry on 11 April 1923 that the railway was expected to be ready for inspection during May, nearly two months after McAlpine's 31 March deadline. On 14 May, however, Fox had to cancel the inspection when it was found that track near the GWR crossing at Portmadoc needed repair. Davies had been concerned when he wrote to the ministry on 10 May because the government loan was limited to expenditure made before 31 March.

Delays had been caused by the need to obtain the LRO amendment order, Davies explained, saying that this delayed gaining access to the extra land required and 'the section of railway above Beddgelert involved a heavy cutting which proved to be ... rock ...' Apart from this, he said, the contract had been almost completed by the due date and would be finished by the end of May. The NWNGR station repair works would also be finished by the end of the month. He closed by saying that the company had no resources other than those originally available and without the ministry's complete contribution 'the company will be unable to discharge its obligations.' The ministry obtained the Treasury's approval to extend the period for qualifying works until 31 May.

Nee had made no reference to the limited amount of local labour used on the contract but on 19 April 1923 the Ministry of Labour wrote to the Ministry of Transport expressing concern on the issue. A survey had shown that of 632 men employed on the contract in March only 361 had been routed to it via the local labour exchange. Most of the remainder were navvies who had moved into the district for the work and some were Irishmen who had previously worked for McAlpine. By April, 415 men were at work, 393 of them unskilled and only 250 local. McAlpine informed Davies that many of those sent by the labour exchange were unsuitable and that some of them left voluntarily when they realised that they were unsuited to the work. Using 'practical' navvies was more efficient. Asked by Davies for more information, McAlpine replied that at one time 807 men were employed, 545 were Welsh, 227 were tramps and 35 were foremen transferred from other contracts. On 8 May 1923 the workforce comprised 205 Welshmen and 95 'outsiders', the latter including the 35 foremen. McAlpine's responses were passed on to the Ministry of Labour and nothing more was said.

The *Cambrian News* of 18 May 1923 reported that the railway was 'practically completed' and that 'an engine travelled over the line from Portmadoc to Nantmor last week.' The FR Company minutes report a trial run over the junction railways at Portmadoc on 12 May – the events could be the same. The newspaper explained that the railway would not be opened by 21 May, Whit Monday, as anticipated.

Following a trial trip with a 'Fairlie and three coaches' on 19 May 1923 Fox gave notice that the railway was ready for inspection on 22 May, Davies having supplied copies of the working instructions for the WHR in general and the junction railways in particular, and a draft timetable on 10 May. The trip, which was reported in the *Carnarvon & Denbigh Herald* on 25 May, was accompanied by Jack, Davies, Tyrwhitt, the general manager, Alfred McAlpine and 'Mr Prendergast' of Sir Douglas Fox & Partners.

Despite the ministry having informed Fox that 10 days' notice was required for an inspection to take place, Lieutenant-Colonel Alan H. L. Mount was en route from Bettws y Coed by car on 24 May. He travelled first to Waenfawr to inspect the loop there. Afterwards he joined a special train, consisting of FR Fairlies *Merddin Emrys* and *Livingston Thompson* and three bogie carriages, one of them possibly substituted by a trolley, at Beddgelert, with departure scheduled for 10am. The purpose of the second locomotive was to test the bridges. Getting Jack's party to Portmadoc required two chauffeurs whose expenses were 7s. *Merddin Emrys*, only, hauled the train returning Mount to Beddgelert. These details are contained in a special train notice issued on 22 May. The speed with which the arrangements were made suggests that perhaps a degree of pressure was applied.

After Mount had returned to London, Tyrwhitt sent him a list of intended stopping places, several more than specified in the contract, and their facilities, and significant locations on the route:

Rhyd Ddu station:
> loop 300ft, three sidings, 100ft, 140ft and 160ft long, brick station building

Pitt's Head halt:
> 1m, no work done, no sidings proposed

Hafod Ruffydd halt:
> 1m 76ch, siding 40ft, corrugated iron shelter

Beddgelert station:
> 4m 52ch, loop 320ft, two sidings, corrugated iron building

Aberglaslyn halt:
> 6m 10ch, no work done, no sidings proposed

Nantmor halt:
> 6m 22ch, siding 40ft

Hafod y Llyn halt:
> 7m 10ch, siding 40ft

Ynys Ferlas halt:
> 8m 7ch, siding 40ft

Croesor Junction:
> 8m 58ch, no halt or station

Ynysfor halt:
> 9m 7ch, siding 40ft, corrugated iron shelter

Pont Croesor halt:
> 10m 13ch, siding 300ft, corrugated iron shelter

Portreuddyn loop:
> 10m 13ch, loop 180ft, old work reconditioned, no halt or station

Gelert Siding:
> 11m 60ch, goods loop 250ft

GWR level crossing:
> 11m 79ch

Portmadoc new station:
> 12m 1ch, loop 150ft, corrugated iron station building

[Corn Mill:
> 12m 10ch, loop on east side, sidings on west, platform for use by goods traffic only]

Commencement of Railway No 2:
> 12m 30ch

Junction with Railway No 1:
> 12m 34.5ch

Portmadoc old station:
> 12m 38ch

The Corn Mill entry is extracted from Mount's report. Seven pages closely typed, it was submitted on 29 May.

He noted that with the exception of 1,000yd south of Rhyd Ddu, where existing track had been reconditioned and ballasted, the section to Croesor Junction had been laid with flat-bottom 40lb British Standard rail in 33ft lengths. The Croesor Tramway section to the GWR crossing was 'old' 41lb flat-bottom material and beyond, to the FR, new rail was used. Ballasting was incomplete on the new line, he observed, and forecast that some sleepers on the Croesor section, damaged by horses, would soon require replacement. Fencing was also incomplete, and causing problems with animals straying on to the track near the GWR crossing.

Working was to be by staff-and-ticket in two sections, dividing at Beddgelert. He had been told that there was no intention to work passenger trains between the two Portmadoc stations but instructed that a staff or a ticket must control any trains over that section. In the vicinity of the High Street the main line had to be protected from

the harbour lines by locked stop blocks. Up was towards Portmadoc.

The highest embankment was near Nantmor (30ft), Mount reported, and the deepest cutting was on the Rhyd Ddu side of Beddgelert (42ft). The Goat Hotel tunnel and the long tunnel in the Aberglaslyn Pass were noted as being on 1-in-40 gradients. Some rock trimming was required and the long tunnel needed two further refuges, making nine in all.

The deflection of the Bryn y Felin bridge was measured under the load of the two Fairlies and found to be 0.35in static, increasing to 0.42in at 15mph. Mount saw that this and the other similar bridges had not been painted and required an application of two coats; despite McAlpine's advertisement for a contractor to paint 25 bridges and culverts, approximately 103 tons of steel, between Rhyd Ddu and Portmadoc being placed in the *Carnarvon & Denbigh Herald* on 8 June, no painting was carried out. Pont Croesor, of a different construction, was similarly tested and gave the result of 0.35in static and 0.47in at 15mph.

The GWR crossing was, he reported, cast solid, he thought of manganese steel. He had met GWR officials during the inspections and had discussed operating procedures with them. During construction there had been 20 horse-drawn movements a day on the WHR, including Croesor slate traffic. The GWR had 40 train movements over it per day, 12 of which were shunting moves. A woman who had worked the crossing satisfactorily previously had been replaced by a porter signalman who had been provided with a telephone. Mount placed the crossing under the control of the GWR and instructed that all WHR trains must come to a stand and wait for a hand signal from the GWR before crossing. He did not make any additional requirements of the GWR.

On the stations front, the loop at Beddgelert required the distance between the lines to be increased from 8ft 6in centres to 13ft to improve sighting for passengers on down trains arriving there. Buildings had not been erected at Hafod Ruffydd, Ynysfor and Pont Croesor.

The maximum speed was to be generally 15mph. Exceptions were 10mph for trains descending the gradients on the 'S' bends between Rhyd Ddu and Beddgelert, up trains traversing the Aberglaslyn tunnels and between Portmadoc New station and Madoc Street and 5mph through facing points, over public road crossings, in Madoc Street and on the Britannia bridge. Mandatory stops were required before the trap points on either side of the GWR crossing, the level crossing over Portmadoc High Street in both directions and the fouling point of the connection at the FR station for up trains.

Mount concluded that despite there being a considerable amount of work to be done before the line was complete he was 'not of the opinion that it would necessarily be unsafe ... to permit operation of passenger trains.' Subject to receipt of undertakings by the company on several outstanding matters he recommended approval be given for the operation of passenger traffic for a temporary period of six months. He proposed that the WHR then be re-inspected to establish what, if any, additional requirements might be necessary.

Mount also inspected the works authorised by the FR's LRO on 24 May, submitting his report on 1 June. For the junction railways he and the WHR party were joined by representatives of Portmadoc UDC, including the town surveyor.

At the station, passenger facilities, waiting room, parcels and ticket offices and conveniences were contained within a 40ft x 12ft corrugated iron building located below the embankment near the GWR crossing. A footpath connection to the GWR station had been made.

Inspecting the junction railways, Mount was unhappy with the timber surface provided between the rails, saying it was unsuitable and would not stand heavy road traffic; tarmacadam should be

Another ex-War Department locomotive obtained in 1923 was this 40hp petrol-engined 'Simplex', photographed when it was about to depart from the FR's old Portmadoc station with a demonstration run on the WHR that was reported in the *Railway Gazette. Author's collection*

used. He agreed with the council's concern over drainage on the Britannia bridge and recommended a kerb with gulleys be installed, having the effect of separating the railway from the road, although he was to change his mind on this point.

Mount approved the station and the junction railways for use by passenger traffic but would not recommend final approval for the junction railways until he had been notified that a settlement had been reached with the council. His report on the loop at Waenfawr, referred to on page 60, was submitted on 4 June. To break up the long section between Tryfan Junction and Rhyd Ddu the existing NWNGR loop had been fettled by replacing some of the worst sleepers; more would need replacing shortly, he forecast. With the station being permanently unmanned, guards would carry a key to gain access to the token instruments. He noted that the station building was in a poor state of repair. Use of the loop by passenger traffic was approved.

The ministry was initially uncertain about the legality of giving approval for opening on a temporary basis but then decided to inform the company, via Fox, writing on 31 May that 'we are unable to sanction opening, but if the company on their own responsibility wish to initiate a service we will, subject to the terms of the report ... take no steps to prevent them doing so ...'

Hauled by the FR's *Princess* and comprising two carriages and a brake van, the first train left Portmadoc for Dinas at 8.10am on 1 June 1923. Cheering crowds watched it go and locomotive whistles were sounded on both the FR and the GWR. The first passenger to book was George Brown, a local man going fishing at, or near, Pont Croesor. After passing another cheering crowd at Beddgelert the first train from Dinas, the 9.50am departure hauled by *Prince*, was passed at Waenfawr.

From Portmadoc, the train crew comprised H. T. Jones (driver), R. Evans (stoker) and Ellis Lewis (guard). The latter was apparently chosen to be the first guard on the WHR in recognition of 32 years' service on the FR. The FR's Portmadoc stationmaster, Henry Jones, was transferred to the new station and the Tan y Bwlch stationmaster, Hugh Jones, transferred to Beddgelert. At Rhyd Ddu, a local woman, Miss Myfanwy Williams had been appointed stationmaster. Representing the company on the first train were Tyrwhitt, Robert Williams, the locomotive superintendant, and A. G. Crick, 'the outside representative'.

Given that this first day was a Friday and that the first train left Portmadoc at 8.10am it may not be too surprising that the trains

were not full. The *Cambrian News* report itemised 10 fare-paying passengers from Portmadoc, some of whom were joined by four more at Beddgelert. At 12.15pm, two minutes later than advertised, some 30 passengers disembarked from the first train from Dinas at Portmadoc, the baskets carried by some of them indicating that their destination was the market. We will never know how satisfied, or not, the promoters were with the day's results.

Fox was not sent a copy of Mount's report on the junction railways until 5 June; as, according to the *Cambrian News* of 8 June, the joint station had been used by FR trains from 1 June, the approval had been overtaken by actuality. The scheduling of the first train to leave when the ministry's letter was still in transit suggests that perhaps use had been made of that new-fangled communications device, the telephone. The opening date had, in any event, been decided sufficiently far in advance for it to be published in at least two local newspapers published on 1 June. At the next FR Company board meeting, held on 27 August 1923, it was reported that the junction railway (sic) had been 'officially' opened on 2 June and that a train had been run through from Blaenau Festiniog to Dinas. This suggests either that the minute taker, writing nearly three months after the event, got the date wrong or that some function took place that was otherwise unreported.

Portmadoc UDC held a special meeting on 1 June, to discuss the issue of the Britannia bridge crossing. The surveyor had agreed that the drainage curb should be located 2ft 3in from the outer rail but Mount had subsequently asked for the distance to be increased to 3ft. Acting on the surveyor's advice, the councillors decided to opt for the original location. The council also dealt with a letter from the WHR's solicitors concerning its requirement for a 40ft roadway to be built along 'allotment field No 7' within six months; presumably this was the access between the WHR and the GWR stations. The existing roadway met present requirements, claimed Davies, asking for a three-year extension. The council determined that it would give 12 months. The road was not built.

On 7 June 1923, Fox gave the required undertakings on the company's behalf. This situation was quite remarkable, for the openings of many railways had been deferred for the want of much less work than the WHR required. The ministry was also uncertain about how much of Mount's report the GWR was entitled to see, but on 9 June sent a copy of the section dealing with the crossing.

4

The Welsh Highland Railway
1923-37

Opened in a glow of optimism, the WHR was always going to struggle. Financed as it was from the public purse, costs had been pared to the bone. The £5,000 contained in the original estimates for rolling stock had gone. The newest locomotive available, *Russell,* had been built in 1906; the newest carriages, two, in 1907. The only shares issued were those used to acquire control of the NWNGR and the PBSSR so there was no working capital. In addition to covering its operating costs the railway had to produce profits of nearly £5,000 annually to cover the debenture interest, £4,238 14s, and capital repayment, £580, to the investing authorities.

Although the construction finances were not finalised until March 1924 it is appropriate to review the capital position here.

Welsh Highland Railway – capital expenditure 1922-24

	£	£
Sir Robert McAlpine & Sons	59,985	59,985
Sir Douglas Fox & Partners	4% on 59,985	2,399
Interest		
1 January 1923	270	
1 July 1923	1,234	
1 January 1924	1,645	
Bank interest to 31 December 1922	68	
Bank interest to 31 December 1923	125	3,342
Land purchases		
Major Bowen Jones	750	
Tourist Hotels	427	
W. Morris Jones	70	1,247
Stamp duty and fees		2,307
Legal costs		
Breese, Jones & Co	45	
(local authorities' loan)		
Stanley & Co (Tourist Hotels)	81	
Jones & Jones (Bowen Jones)	22	
Costs and expenses of order	1,419	1,567
Station improvements		434
Locomotive		267
Total capital expenditure		**71,548**

The matter of the funding shortfall was resolved by, presumably, 'persuading' McAlpine to invest £10,000; W. H. McAlpine was issued with a debenture certificate on 18 April 1923. Jack's involvement is detected in this transaction; W. H. McAlpine was to tell his nephew, Sir William McAlpine Bt, that Jack was not to be trusted. McAlpine lost money on the FR contract, too.

It will be seen that the repairs to the NWNGR buildings had cost less than half the estimate; some of the work was obviously not done. Mount noted that at Rhyd Ddu the station buildings were in poor condition and thought that the floor was about to collapse. £1,267 of the LRO's costs had been paid to Evan Davies & Company. The inclusion of a locomotive (the ex-War Department Baldwin 4-6-0T No 590) in the capital account attracted comment at the Ministry with the observation that the loan was for 'completing' the railway with no mention of rolling

stock; approval was given for the expenditure because the scheme was within budget and it would have been authorised if requested.

The other debentures were issued as follows: Caernarvonshire CC – £15,000; Portmadoc UDC – £5,000; Gwrfai RDC – £3,000; Glaslyn RDC – £3,000; Deudraeth RDC – £3,000; Ministry of Transport – £35,774; Branch Nominees (Stewart) – £10,000; total – £84,774. The interest payable on the debentures, 5%, was intended to match that on the money borrowed by the authorities to make the advances.

No provision had been made for the repayment of the loans by the WHR, terms being subject to agreement when the advances were made. During 1923 the local authorities tried to get the company to execute a mortgage deed, which the company refused as being beyond its powers. With the authorities' QC at odds with the Treasury Solicitor over the terms of repayment, or even if the debentures could be redeemed at all, it was 1 March 1924 before a deed of covenant was made. The ministry's view was that the debentures were irredeemable but that they could be sold 'in favourable circumstances'.

The WHR was managed by the FR, contributing £60 a year to S. E. Tyrwhitt's salary as general manager. A GWR employee on loan to the FR as general manager since March 1921, Tyrwhitt had also been manager of the NWNGR for a short time. He left on 30 September 1923 and was replaced by John May, previously the FR's traffic officer, who was given the title of superintendent. May only lasted until 1 September 1924 and was replaced by Eric H. R. Nicholls, also from the GWR, who had been appointed FR Company managing director and WHR general manager on 17 May 1924; he stayed until 22 May 1925. Initially, the WHR's administration was based at the Aluminium Corporation's Dolgarrog offices.

Lt Colonel Holman Fred Stephens, well known for his links with light, and invariably impecunious, railways, was appointed engineer and locomotive superintendent from 1 April 1923; his salary was £100 per annum plus expenses; he held the same positions on the FR.

In 1923, Moses Kellow, the Croesor Quarry's engineer and manager, was on salary of £60 per annum to provide haulage for the remaining section of the Croesor Tramway, although he also invoiced £37, covering four months, for the same service. The following year he was only paid against invoice for this service, carrying 1,750 tons at 8d per ton during the first six months, earning a total of £117 8s 9d during the year. G. Griffith, or Griffiths, was also paid for haulage in 1923, receiving seven payments that totalled £90 15s.

To work the line the railway employed two three-man train crews, three two-man track gangs, a station master and clerk at Dinas, a carpenter and a loader, the latter paid on tonnage. These were full-time positions; of the three station master positions, that at Rhyd Ddu was most likely seasonal.

From the FR the WHR also received proportional services of the managing director, Nicholls, and his assistant, Robert Evans, shorthand typist Miss E. Davies, storekeeper J. P. Roberts, clerk T. Davies, locomotive superintendent R. Williams, permanent way inspector G. L. Griffiths and Portmadoc stationmaster E. E. Jones.

Above: **The Baldwin about to leave the original FR station at Portmadoc.**
Author's collection

Right: **A Baldwin-hauled train turns into Maddock Street from the Britannia bridge in the 1930s. The direct, ex Croesor Tramway, connection from the harbour was removed by Portmadoc UDC, by agreement, in 1925. This line crossed the road from the lower left and joined the main line where the centre of the train is seen – plan on page 142.**
H. W. Comber/FR Archives

The GWR had issued special instructions for working what it called the 'Croesor Railway level crossing' on 12 May; they were replaced on 13 June. WHR trains wishing to use the crossing had to use a special whistle code: up trains – one long, two short; down trains – two long, one short. Tyrwhitt issued WHR instructions on 28 May, stating that a driver failing to comply would be liable to dismissal.

The first sign of problems with the GWR over the use of the crossing came on 26 July 1923, when the WHR was informed that 'to properly safeguard the working of the traffic over this crossing it is necessary to carry out certain alterations to the signalling at an estimated cost of £150.' It seems that Tyrwhitt, writing on 30 May 1923, had requested the GWR to carry out the protective works at the WHR's expense. In 1928, Stephens was to say that he (Tyrwhitt) had exceeded his authority. In addition to charging for the alterations, the GWR wanted to make a legal agreement covering the use of the crossing and to make charges for its use. It was to install a telephone between the box and Portmadoc signalbox and then said that a link to Penrhyndeudraeth was also required. Other expenses were added, too. One cannot help wondering if the GWR saw the

crossing as an excuse to improve its own infrastructure at the WHR's expense. The affair was drawn out, largely because the WHR would usually ignore the GWR's letters. In 1927, the GWR was to say that its charges, whilst unpaid, were not disputed until Stephens was appointed managing director.

During a period of intense activity Nicholls protested on 13 August 1924, saying that not only had the Croesor been on the site before the AWCR/Cambrian but that there had never been any charge made for using the crossing; further, that the GWR made more use of the crossing, 38 trips per day, than the WHR, 18 trips. He also complained that the crossing box was manned from 8am until 10pm, whereas the WHR's first movement was not until 9.38am and its last 'about' 8pm. He suggested that if there was to be a charge it should be proportionate to the use made by each railway.

James Milne, the GWR's assistant general manager, replied that the institution of the WHR passenger service was entirely responsible for the employment of the two signalmen and therefore the WHR should pay the extra costs. Nicholls responded that as the GWR's, and the Cambrian's, passenger trains had been using the crossing since 1867, and were adequately protected from the mineral trains, the introduction of the WHR passenger service should not have necessitated any alterations. There is no evidence that Mount was unhappy with the arrangements and he made no comment on them when he reinspected the WHR in 1926.

Returning to railway operation in 1923, this turned out to be the WHR's best year, possibly because money was spent on a publicity campaign in the *Carnarvon Herald* and other print media along the North Wales coast. The railway tried to put on a good show for the public, for in 1923 the Snowdon Mountain Railway laid out gardens, perhaps at Dinas and Beddgelert and maybe also at Portmadoc, charging £6 13s 4d for the work. Responding to passenger demand the halt at Ynys Ferlas, near the entrance to Hafod y Llyn farm, had been relocated to Hafod Garregog, where the nameboard posts still survive, in June. Train services were continued through the winter.

To aid inter-working between the FR and the WHR the former NWNGR rolling stock was modified to suit the FR's loading gauge, but in the case of *Russell* this was a wasted effort – the FR guards' logs show that *Moel Tryfan* did reach Blaenau Ffestiniog quite often and it is quite likely that the carriages did too. A compensation claim recorded on 30 September 1923 suggests that some passenger stock was returned to traffic sooner than desirable, with £3 16s being payable for 'damaged coats by paint in carriages.' The FR had charged £6 for the materials required.

Initially there were four return passenger workings throughout, with short workings to/from Beddgelert. Single journey times varied between 140 minutes and 185 minutes between Dinas and Portmadoc and 145 minutes and 205 minutes in the reverse direction. With the first arrival at Dinas at 11.42am and at Portmadoc at 10.18am there was obviously no expectation that anyone should want to use the train to get to work but a service was continued, at a reduced level, after the tourists went home in September.

Tickets were examined and nipped at Portmadoc, Beddgelert and Dinas and collected at all stations and halts. This was important, not least because the GWR had been issuing free passes for the WHR (and the FR). On 27 August 1923 instructions were issued that if any were found their holders were to pay the appropriate fare.

The Bryngwyn goods service ran as required. It was scheduled to leave Dinas at 12.15pm, arriving back at 2.40pm, with an

hour allowed for shunting at Bryngwyn. There was sufficient traffic to justify at least a daily service in the early years. A Croesor goods left Portmadoc at 7.50am, returning thence at 9.10am. In 1924, Porter Roberts was responsible for working this traffic, with the injunction that he 'work sharp to the time shown.'

The acquisition of the Baldwin, No 590, in July 1923 has already been mentioned. Its size restricted it to WHR operations. An armoured 'Simplex' four-wheeled petrol tractor, obtained from the same source by the FR at the same time was used on the WHR for the Croesor slate traffic. It has been said that some of the six Hudson toastrack coaches acquired by the FR in 1923 were intended to be sold on to the WHR, but there is no indication in FR records that this was the case and no transfer was made; this did not inhibit their being used on the WHR, of course.

Beddgelert seems, on the evidence of the goods received book preserved at the NA, to have been established as a handling centre for parcels traffic incoming to the WHR. The first entry, made on 12 June 1923, records a box shipped from Menai Bridge to the Royal Goat Hotel. The hotel received regular shipments of wet fish from Liverpool, too. A picture from Euston for 'Brown' at Beddgelert arrived on 16 June with the glass broken. Mr Till at Beddgelert received a box of live birds from Liverpool on 25 June. Beddgelert's bicycle dealer, Fred Clare, received regular shipments of cycle components and, on 29 June, a Raleigh cycle sign from Nottingham. Perhaps, to 21st century eyes, the most unusual item was a regular delivery of dry ice (carbon dioxide) from Llandudno to 'Griffiths' of Beddgelert.

Above: **The Glaslyn Foundry in Portmadoc's Maddock Street is the backdrop to this photograph of *Princess*.** *Author's collection*

Left: **The Portmadoc flour mill siding, between Snowdon Street and the FR's 1923 station. The FR transported flour from the mill to the bakery next to its station at Penrhyn that survived until 2008. The three vehicles visible belonged to the FR; the one in the centre is the Cleminson iron wagon, the one on the right is lettered 'mill stone traffic'. July 1930.** *K. E. Hartley/FR Archives*

Top: **FR trains at the FR station on the WHR in 1923. The white structure on the left is the station building, with the refreshment room standing behind it.** *Author's collection*

Above: **Moel Tryfan's driver oils round at the 1923 station under the supervision of a small boy in August 1928.** *E. A. Gurney-Smith/Author's collection*

Right: **The GWR crossing, looking towards Beddgelert with the gate closed to the WHR. Two rakes of Pwllheli Granite Co wagons are stabled in the Cambrian siding.** *Author's collection*

Other stations receiving parcels via Beddgelert in the first few weeks were: Waenfawr (H. H. Roberts, parcel of wallpaper from Borough High Street, London, on 13 June); Rhostryfan ('Hughes', boots from Tottenham, on 15 June); South Snowdon (Miss Dyer, one bag, passengers' luggage in advance, from New Barnet, on 22 June); Bettws Garmon (Victoria Quarries, parcel from Camborne on 28 June); Bryngwyn (Amalgamated Slate Association, box from Sheffield on 4 July); Salem Halt (J. Roberts, parcel from Liverpool on 19 July); Tryfan Junction (William Owen (Plas) Bodaden, small box from Birmingham on 31 July), and Nantmor ('Hughes', a bag and a leather trunk from Holyhead on 20 July).

In addition to its 'ordinary' passenger traffic the WHR managed to generate some business from party bookings and special workings. Events included a band contest at Minffordd, a Congregational festival in Carnarvon and Sunday school outings from Rhyd Ddu and Nantmor.

Initially, through trains to and from the FR bypassed the FR's Portmadoc station, the new station was intended to replace it after all. To facilitate engine working a coaling stage, using an FR coal wagon, and a water tank were established outside the FR's goods shed. This failed to meet with everyone's approval and in August 1925 a complaint was received from the residents of Britannia Terrace concerning the nuisance of smoke from locomotives. Instructions were issued for engines to be coaled on the quay.

When, in September 1923, the ministry enquired if Mount's requirements had been met it took three attempts and until 14 December before it got an answer from Fox. The latter 'believed' that the contract works were complete but did not know the status of works that were to have been dealt with by the railway company. A further reminder generated a response from Stephens on 11 April 1924. He said that the FR works had been completed for some time and passed responsibility for the WHR works back to Fox. On 15 May, Fox said that all works had been completed except for the tramway points ordered from Edgar Allan for installation near the Britannia bridge. By 30 October, only some point rodding remained outstanding. On 5 June, more than a year after the line had been opened, the ministry had received the sealed undertaking, signed by Stephens and Huson, regarding the method of working.

The company's own financial records are either lost or as yet undiscovered. However, in response to a request from the investing authorities for information, Nicholls produced an itemised list of expenditure covering 1923 and the first nine months of 1924. The following items have been extracted, giving an insight into operations.

Under the heading of 'rolling stock maintenance' in 1923, the FR retubed *Moel Tryfan*, the brass tubes costing £66 and asbestos 1s 11d. Unspecified work on the loco was undertaken by J. L. Gordon for £47; perhaps for the alterations to enable it to fit the FR loading gauge and/or for painting the loco. The FR also carried out repairs on *Russell*, with unspecified work costing £21, springs from Hunslet £6 and brass tubes £18, these charges being allocated to locomotive running expenses.

In 1924 *Moel Tryfan* received a new injector costing £24 and eight spiral springs costing £3 6s 8d. Electric arc welding repairs to the locomotive's side frames cost £27. In the same year *Russell* was retyred at a cost of £47 and required three more springs, cost £1 10s. Eight cast iron wheels were obtained for carriage bogies (£21) and a further eight for a brake van (£21); four carriage axleboxes cost £4 and four sets of cast iron letters for carriage sides £2 16s. These sums were also charged to maintenance.

A sheep killed in April 1923 cost the railway £1 10s but R. Williams's sheep and lamb killed in August cost £3 5s. Four sheep killed in 1924 cost £9 9s. Damaged slates cost £27 8s 5d in 1923, but £39 0s 11d the following year. Portmadoc Flour Mills received 10s 6d for damaged flour in 1924.

Even at this early date, services did not always run as expected. On 18 September 1923 two carriages of the 10.53am from Portmadoc were derailed on the Bryn y Felin bridge; the guilty vehicle was one of the Hudson toastracks then recently obtained by the FR; adjacent saloon No 8 appeared to have derailed by one pair of wheels when the train stopped, for there were no signs of dragging by them. Perhaps it was another derailment that was responsible for Portmadoc paying 16s 8d out of petty cash for 'hire of cars to carry passengers owing to accident' on 31 January 1924. The incidents naturally resulted in delays to the train service.

Other delays cost the railway money: the WHR paid the Saracen's Head Hotel at Beddgelert £2 16s 8d in 1923 for 'hire of car – lost connection' and in August 1924 the Sportsman in Portmadoc was paid £1 0s 3d for expenses incurred for the same reason. As time passed the railway's reputation for poor timekeeping was to become widespread.

In 1923, passenger revenue totalled £1,914, of which £23 was first class; in 1924 the figures were £1,698 and £20. Revenue from parcels was £99 and £77. Goods traffic earned £3,422, of which £2,074 was from slate and £962 from coal.

Particularly revealing, in the light of the railway's ultimate failure, are the entries under the 'travelling expenses account' heading. On 11 occasions in 1923 cars were hired, usually by the Aluminium Corporation, the cost being totally or partly borne by the WHR. On four occasions chauffeurs received

The Baldwin and its train on the GWR crossing. *FR Archives*

Top left: **Only the meanest of facilities were provided when the WHR decamped to the Beddgelert side of the crossing in 1930. The weighbridge was housed in the stone building on the right.** *Author's collection*

Top right: **Slate stacks on the Beddgelert siding. The white sign on the right indicates the location of the Rhosydd Quarry wharf.** *Adrian Gray collection*

Middle: **Another view of No 590, passing the Beddgelert siding in July 1936.** *H. B. Tours/FR Archives*

Right: **With Cnicht dominating the background,** *Welsh Pony* **and train cross Pont Croesor in 1934. On the left of the bridge is a water tank that could be used to replenish thirsty locomotives.** *R.W. Kidner/Author's collection*

expenses, also. Crossley Colley, the Aluminium Corporation's construction manager and later a WHR director, claimed 're-testing of Fordson tractor' on 27 April 1924 – this machine belonged to the Aluminium Corporation and was tried out on the FR, where it proved too light for the work. Some of these entries are intriguing; on two occasions in 1923 H. Thomas or W. J. West received 'Foden driver's expenses at Dinas' and on 6 June 1923, M. H. Williams had his rail fare paid to Portmadoc 're purchase of sand at Nantmor.'

Councillor Nee spent some time looking after the investing authorities' interests, for he received £11 travelling expenses, not itemised, in 1923, which seems rather high considering that he lived in Carnarvon. His only claim the following year was for less than £5, settled on 21 March.

Nicholls' report concluded with a comment on the request for information on the company's financial position: 'success ... depends upon the development of mineral traffic. A new granite quarry has been opened at Betws Garmon and a new copper mine is about to be opened at Nantmor. ... if the local authorities with their local knowledge and influence could help in getting two or three mines started the company should be able to pay its debenture interest.' By the end of 1924 the company owed £8,493 13s 9d.

In June 1924 the county council's surveyor reported that the roads at Bryn y Felin and Nantmor had not been adopted and required additional work. He had been in contact with McAlpine, did the work, and on 6 December 1924 reported that McAlpine, not the railway company, had paid £179 for it.

Stewart committed suicide on 6 February 1924. He had been in financial difficulty for some time and in December 1922 had staved off his creditors briefly by persuading the recipient of his political donation to return it. The possibility that Lloyd George might have been a party to the donation was mentioned at a post-mortem creditors' meeting, resulting in a denial being issued to the Press Association. Stewart's deficiency was in the order of £600,000 and in newspaper reports he was described as a conman. A question asked about transactions in Welsh railway shares at the meeting was not answered in the report published in *The Times* on 5 July. On 23 December 1923, Stewart had purchased £25,000 ordinary WHR shares for 5s (total) that he sold to Jack for £14,000 on 31 January 1924, a substantial mark-up. On that date he also sold Jack a further £1,695 of ordinary shares for £970. The questioner might also have been alluding to Stewart's FR shareholding, which he also transferred to Jack before he died.

The WHR had agreed to take over responsibility for the NWNGR loan from Stewart with effect from 31 December 1923 although the formalities were not completed until 27 June 1924, the bank opening a loan account in the company's name and approving the payment of £9,500 from it to the account that Stewart had held at its Llanrwst branch. The bank retained the same value in WHR debentures. These transactions give the impression that perhaps Stewart had already decided how he was going to resolve his affairs. By 1933 the loan account had accrued £4,798 9s 10d in unpaid interest.

Tourist traffic in 1924 was badly affected by a wet summer. The interest due from 1 July was not paid and it was 8 September 1924 before the ministry enquired about it. On 11 October the directors had what can be imagined as a heated meeting with the investing authorities to discuss the situation. Nicholls was asked for proposals for withdrawing the passenger service during the winter and he submitted his report on 14 November.

He observed that with average goods receipts of £82 per week since 22 September, when the winter timetable commenced, the railway would not be paying its way if it had to

survive on its freight, even if the debenture interest were removed from the equation. Notwithstanding that, he proposed a daily goods service between Dinas and Bryngwyn, and between Portmadoc and Croesor Junction, a twice-weekly service between Dinas and Beddgelert, and a once-weekly service between Portmadoc and Nantmor, practically Beddgelert, as there was no loop at Nantmor.

Such a service would require two engines in steam and two train crews but would reduce staffing by one stationmaster, two cleaners and six permanent way gangers, said Nicholls, reducing weekly operating costs to £156 from £210; these figures include £67 debenture interest, surely an indication of the burden placed on the WHR by its capital structure. Nicholls also noted that the Portmadoc operation was not a full week's (48 hours) work, suggesting that the men be deployed on the FR in between their WHR duties, for which service the FR would pay. The sum concerned was less than £4 per week.

Concerning the overdue interest, Huson replied to the ministry on 11 November 1924, enclosing a cheque for £500 0s 8d, but in respect of the second half of 1923, which, despite its inclusion in a table of capital expenses prepared earlier in the year had not been issued. Did the local authorities have to ask for their payment, too? Huson wrote that the company was not in a position to make the 1 July payment 'as the traffic receipts are barely adequate to cover the expenses ...' The ministry was to inform the Treasury that it saw no benefit in exercising its right, because it had more than £10,000 in debentures, to appoint a receiver. In this submission, dated 31 December 1924, the ministry claimed that the company's capital account was overdrawn by £6,000 and had been £4,000 overdrawn to the bank on 31 December 1923. The company's annual reports show that the capital account was £6,012 overdrawn in 1923 and that £4,000 was due to the bank in 1922 and 1923; as both items were cleared in 1924 it seems likely that the outstanding funding was responsible for the apparent deficiencies. That year, £3,979 was applied to the capital account.

The WHR was not, incidentally, alone in being unable to meet its financial obligations to the government – the North Devon & Cornwall Junction Light Railway, the other railway that benefited from the unemployment relief scheme, also defaulted on its interest payments; it had a £120,000 loan.

Nicholls' report was implemented with effect from 15 December 1924. Despite his comments about the railway not paying its way with a goods service, goods revenue was considerably more than passenger revenue. The table shows that during the first five years the revenue loss actually increased when the passenger service was more successful. It is notable also that the goods revenue showed very little change after 1922, when only the NWNGR section was operated.

Year	Passenger receipts £	Goods receipts £	Revenue loss £
1922	277	3,790	651
1923	2,462	3,635	1,573
1924	1,914	3,916	2,331
1925	1,089	3,987	742
1926	568	3,388	787

During 1925 the ministry seemed to be increasingly frustrated with the company over its administration. Three requests for a certificate of deduction of income tax being ignored, on 6 March a civil servant visited Davies's London office where he was told that as the money had not been passed to the Inland Revenue it was not possible to issue the certificate, a situation confirmed in writing on 18 March; the revenue informed the ministry, on

20 June 1925, that not only would it accept a certificate that the company 'intended' to pay the income tax, but that it also thought that the ministry should not use its power to appoint a receiver. On 11 May 1925, the ministry had sought an explanation for a £1,557 discrepancy between the certified construction accounts and the figure shown in the company's accounts; Huson's response on 29 October 1925, after a reminder, was that the figure in the accounts was an error.

The company did make some capital expenditure during 1925: £124 6s 8d for a Baldwin petrol loco, £25 on wagons and £37 16s for a trolley. The loco item is a mystery because the WHR did not buy a Baldwin petrol loco in 1925. The FR did, spending £249. Boyd (see bibliography) states that the FR's loco cost £373 but the source of this information is not known. But the WHR

figure is one third of £373 – as the figures in both railways' reports total £377 6s 8d perhaps the cost was shared. There were no changes to the number of either locomotives or wagons in the 1925 returns but in 1926 the railway had one more open wagon than it did the year before. Known for many years as 'the Baldwin tractor', now as *Moelwyn*, this locomotive worked in the Portmadoc area, probably as far as Croesor Junction.

Beddgelert station was sometimes a tempting playground for local children when they thought the trains had finished. On 22 August 1925 the 7.10pm from Portmadoc was in a collision with a platelayers' trolley at the station end of the Goat tunnel. Two boys, Ifan Anwyl Williams of Nantmor, and Griffith Jones Hughes of Beddgelert, had been on the trolley; the former's face was injured and he was taken to hospital, the latter ran off

On a dull day in 1936, Nantmor looked quite neglected. *J. E. Cull*

through the tunnel. The trolley had been left in the siding near the water tank. Stationmaster H. D. Jones, whose report to Robert Evans at Portmadoc is the source of this information, said that he had told the boys to leave the station two days before.

The winter service introduced on 21 September 1925 saw the Croesor shunt retimed to occur between 12.15pm and 1.30pm. If the shunting was unfinished it was to be completed between the arrival of the 12.45 ex-Dinas, due at Portmadoc (1923) at 3.2pm, and the 5.10pm departure to Beddgelert. Bryngwyn traffic was to be worked in a manner that ensured no overtime was incurred.

Jack resigned from the FR board on 9 November 1925, citing medical advice, the same reason that he had given for standing down as FR company chairman a year before. Possibly his resignation from the WHR board, also in November 1925, was for the same reason. It might have been a consequence of the Dolgarrog dam collapse, for which the Aluminium Corporation accepted responsibility, 16 people had died, which had occurred on 2 November. He was not replaced on the board and Davies became chairman. When Jack resigned from the Aluminium Corporation board in 1927 he was said to be close to having a nervous breakdown.

Having approved the WHR for passenger traffic for a temporary six-month period in 1923, Mount returned and re-inspected the line on 6 October 1926. He saw that ballasting was still incomplete near Rhyd Ddu and Nantmor, but subject to its being completed and some other minor works being carried out he recommended that both the WHR between Rhyd Ddu and Portmadoc and the Festiniog's junction railways be approved for passenger traffic. He approved the works on the Britannia bridge as well, despite their not being as he recommended, and noted that the Croesor line to the harbour had been removed, eliminating the triangular layout.

Mount took the opportunity to inspect track alterations made at Croesor Junction, Beddgelert and Waenfawr. At the former a loop had been installed to the south of the junction, breaking up the section between Beddgelert and Portmadoc. With train control by staff-and-ticket the loop was unmanned. A cabin, actually a grounded former FR quarrymen's carriage, was provided in which were kept the staff box, tickets and a telephone. The Croesor line had been connected to the main line but following discussion with Stephens it was to be connected to the loop.

At Beddgelert, an 86ft coal siding had been connected to the loop at the south end of the station. A locked scotch had been provided to protect the running line but Mount required it to be replaced with an interlocked trap point.

The Waenfawr installation Mount inspected was a siding connection to the Dudley Park Granite Quarry. He required the single-bladed trap point installed to be changed to a double-

77830   ABERGLASLYN PASS, WELSH HIGHLAND RAILWAY

Russell heads for Portmadoc through Nantmor cutting.
Frith/Author's collection

Top: **The competition: a loaded charabanc stops for a photograph at Pont Aberglaslyn.** *Commercial postcard/ Author's collection*

Right: **On a quiet summer's day the train was stopped for a photograph to be taken in the Aberglaslyn Pass.** *Commercial postcard/Author's collection*

Below: **Seen from the other side of the river, an FR England loco is about to enter the middle tunnel.** *Frith/Author's collection*

bladed mechanism and gave his approval to it. Travelling through Tryfan Junction he suggested that a trap point be installed by the stop board on the Bryngwyn branch to protect traffic approaching from Waenfawr. Subject to undertakings that outstanding works would be completed, he finally approved the WHR and the FR junction railways for use by passenger trains. Stephens gave the required undertakings on 21 January 1927.

When the surveyor's department sub-committee had inspected the Dudley Park crossing site on 16 March 1926 the quarry manager E. Edmunds said that the crossing would be used by trains of between four and 14 wagons 'about three times daily'. No locomotives were to be used. The product was 'prepared' road stone.

By the time of Mount's delayed re-inspection a winter service of one return train from Dinas was in operation. Running from 20 September, any slate wagons found at Croesor Junction were to be conveyed to Portmadoc, the train being designated mixed.

In January 1927, Tourists Hotels Ltd, owner of the Goat Hotel and in liquidation, had partially succeeded in an action brought against the railway for breach of contract. In purchasing land from the company the WHR had entered into a covenant to provide an access road to land the hotels company wished to sell as housing plots; the company's liquidator claimed for loss of profit on 48 plots priced to sell at £5,450, £5,130 over the land's agricultural value, and for £1,000 for loss of patronage caused by the railway. An order for £1,000 damages was made against the WHR; perhaps the award could be interpreted as the railway winning the first claim but losing the second.

Tourist Hotels' liquidator had already been warned by the county council that a successful claim would result in the WHR being placed in liquidation. It can be no surprise, therefore, that when the investing authorities met on 12 February 1927 they resolved to take the necessary steps to appoint a receiver and manager, recommending Stephens for the position. Making a successful claim for the unpaid debenture interest they were then able to petition for the appointment. Amongst the debts listed was the county council's claim for £630 2s 9d in respect of repairs to the bridges. The GWR claimed £934 17s 1d for 'exchanged traffic (and other accounts in dispute)'. The FR was owed £1,036 2s 5d. Mr Justice Eve, who heard the petition, made the order on 4 March 1927, saying 'the service was not a very regular one. After one had waited a considerable time one might be told there would be no train and one would have to walk' – the railway's reputation did it no favours. The investing authorities agreed to pay up to £10 per £3,000 invested to cover the costs incurred. In 1935 Deudraeth was to refuse to pay its account, thinking it was for new expenditure. An application to release funds to the debenture holders became stalled by the inability of the GWR and Haworth & Walsh, the Cwm Cloch owners, to prove their claims; six years later there was still no sign of progress.

Stephens was known for the brusque manner with which he communicated, usually from his Tonbridge office, with staff. A softer side was revealed when he loaned £50 to cover the staff wages due on 3 March 1927. Occurring in the interval between the receivership application and Stephens's appointment as receiver from 4 March, the bank had indicated that it would not honour the railway's cheque. The matter came to light when the investing authorities angrily demanded an explanation for his claim for reimbursement.

The *Manchester Guardian*'s 'Miscellany' columnist, on 25 March 1927, apparently misunderstood the receivership proceedings, saying of the railway that it 'has exasperated many, but it shall not disappear without one kind word.' He told the story of how on a cold January morning, a woman was the only passenger at Beddgelert for the Dinas train. The carriages were not heated and she chose 1st class accommodation for the extra warmth that the cushions might give. Just before the train was due to start she removed a hot water bottle from her case and 'instructed' the driver to fill it for her. He did so, telling her to request a refill when it was cold. If true, the incident occurred in 1924. A few days later Stephens informed the paper that the railway was still operating.

'This is a dead loss, probably the result of the action of the Caernarvon CC in asking for the appointment of a receiver and manager. This department foresaw this expense and warned the county council of the likely effect of it', wrote a ministry official incensed at the £1,395 in legal charges incurred in 1927. He made his remarks after comparing the 1926 and 1927 accounts on 17 July 1928. He also commented on £600 in directors' fees, 'voted by shareholders'; they might have been voted but there is no guarantee that they were paid. The accumulated losses on the revenue account were £22,741 at the end of 1928. One consequence of the receivership was that debenture interest ceased to be debited to the accounts, although that did not stop the ministry from staking its claim in respect of the years following.

The GWR had tried to advance its entitlement to payment for use of the Portmadoc crossing by submitting its claim, at Stephens' request, to court. Its affidavit was dated 29 March 1928 and the WHR's rebuttal was dated 27 October 1930.

The watchers watched. A view from the train at Bryn y Felin. *FR Archives*

WELSH HIGHLAND RAILWAY, AT BEDDGELERT

Above: **Moel Tryfan** at Bryn y Felin in 1923. The abandoned PBSSR formation can be seen on the right-hand riverbank. Two other photographs of the same train are reproduced on page 54.
Valentine/Author's collection

Right: An enlargement from a picture postcard shows the river bridge in the centre of Beddgelert at the bottom, the Goat Hotel above it to the left, and the station to the right. Cwm Cloch farmhouse is above the station; to its right, obscured by bushes, is the abandoned PBSSR cutting with the railway formation just above.
Salmon/Author's collection

There was some debate over the legal status of the crossing, the GWR claiming priority because the Aberystwyth & Welsh Coast Railway Act of 1861 pre-dated the Croesor Tramway's construction, but, the WHR responded, the AWCR at Portmadoc was not built according to the 1861 Act but according to the AWCR's New Lines Act of 1862, passing to the north of the rock called Ynyscerrigduon instead of the south. The standard gauge line between Portmadoc and Afon Wen was of confusing legality because, due to a parliamentary oversight, in 1862 both the AWCR and the Carnarvonshire Railway had been given powers to build it. The Croesor & Portmadoc Railway Act of 1865 permitted the CPR to use AWCR land for the purpose of the crossing and the CPR's book of reference did not show the AWCR as having any interest in the land concerned because, claimed the WHR, it was owned by

Roberts. The WHR asserted that the additional works concerned were purely for the GWR's own benefit and that it should not be responsible for their costs.

In January 1930, the GWR had submitted a bill for the crossing's running expenses for the six months ending 31 December 1929 which was disputed, Evans writing to Milne, by then the GWR's general manager, on 13 February 1930. He pointed out that the WHR now only used the crossing twice a week, that the signals being charged for were in position before the WHR and were, therefore, not a valid expense.

Evans's comment on the reduced use of the crossing was made during the winter, when there were no passenger trains, but from 1930 trains from Beddgelert terminated on that side of the crossing; passengers were escorted across the GWR. Whether the WHR reduced its use of the crossing in an attempt

Above: **A busy day at Beddgelert in 1934. Miriam Jones, the 'schoolgirl station mistress' wearing Welsh dress, stands with the loco crew on the left. Following an interview with Evan R. Davies she was appointed because she spoke English. The coal merchant has at least two wagonloads of coal in stock.** *Author's collection*

to mitigate the GWR charges or because the GWR became uncooperative because of the unpaid bills is not clear. There is photographic evidence that the crossing was used by passenger trains during the FR lease period. By the time of the winding-up a debt to the GWR of £237 had been accepted but it appears that the GWR had failed to substantiate the claim it made in 1923/4. It did not get the £237 either, of course.

Drivers' returns for the late 1920s/early 1930s give an insight into railway operations. On 16 March 1928 *Russell*, with driver William Hugh Williams in charge, worked 15 wagons of coal and five of manure, and a brake van, from Dinas to Bryngwyn, taking 50 minutes for the journey; one wagon of manure was left at Tryfan Junction and two at Rhostryfan. The crew having spent 45 minutes working the incline and 20 minutes shunting, the loco returned to Dinas with 17 wagons of slate and the brake van, collecting an empty slate wagon from Tryfan Junction en route.

Driver Hugh Roberts and stoker Gwyn Roberts were in action with the Baldwin on 12 June 1930, with a Bryngwyn working of empty coaches, purpose unknown. Ten minutes were spent shunting at Rhostryfan and at Bryngwyn, 45 minutes working the incline. Arriving at Dinas at 12.20pm the rest of the day was spent lifting *Moel Tryfan* to adjust its springs.

On 12 May 1931, the same team worked a goods train, load unspecified, hauled by *Moel Tryfan*, to Rhostryfan, then to Beddgelert before returning to Dinas. The 29-mile journey took 4 hours 20 minutes including 50 minutes shunting at Rhostryfan and Beddgelert. Two days later they spent the day, from 8.30am until 4pm, cleaning *Russell*, the Baldwin and *Moel Tryfan*.

Some idea of the state of the railway may be gained from the directors' returns that have survived for 1929. Data from specimen weeks, not entirely random, has been tabulated (*see below*).

Traffic staff included a guard, based at Dinas. In 1928 a member of traffic staff had been based at Beddgelert, at least until September. Slate carried via Portmadoc was mostly Croesor production. A goods mileage of 36 might represent three trips to Bryngwyn and a trip to Croesor Junction; the drivers booked five miles to the former.

Extracts from director's returns – traffic – 1929

Date	Traffic staff	Loco staff	PW staff	Coal used	Passengers carried	Goods carried (tons)	Slate carried – Dinas (tons)	Slate carried – Portmadoc (tons)	Passenger mileage	Goods mileage	Shunting mileage
12.1	3	2	5	36cwt	-	47	81	67	84	36	46
20.4	3	2	4	51cwt	4	71	89	51	114	36	47
1.6	3	2	4	50cwt	27	60	197	79	132	45	49
17.8	3	2	4	80cwt	483	64	139	59	220	36	49
7.12	2	2	2	30cwt	2	37	45	41	100	27	30

Extracts from director's returns – revenue – 1929

Date	Passenger revenue	Goods revenue	Loaders	Croesor haulage	Wages	Profit/loss	Revenue (year to date)	Loss (year to date)
12.1	11s 11d	£17 17s 2d	£5 18s 5d	£5 2s	£25 7s 2d	(£26 18s 2d)	£59 9s 10d	(£53 1s 8d)
20.4	4s 6d	£10 12s 6d	£6 1s 7d	£4 1s	£21 19s 10d	(£7 2s 1d)	£598 6s 11d	(£396 15s 3d)
1.6	£1 8s 5d	£13 3s 5d	£11 3s	£6	£24 6s 11d	(£2 7s 2d)	£821 6s 9d	£468 6s
17.8	£49 17s 3d	£14 12 8d	£8 17s 5d	£4 13s	£24 18s 3d	£37 7s 10d	£1,437 15s 3d	(£375 19s 2d)
7.12	2s	£7 18s 6d	£3 15 10d	£3 13s 6d	£17 12s	£23 3s 6d	£2,101 19s 3d	(£483 11s 2d)

The week ending 1 June represented the year's peak for slate carriage and the week ending 17 August the peak for passenger carriage, 403 of those passengers being booked via Dinas. The financial consequences of these weeks were as shown above.

It is notable that, except in August, the goods traffic was much more productive in terms of mileage operated than the passenger traffic. In the winter the railway would have been better to have given the passengers offering the fare the use of a bus.

The slate loaders at Dinas were self-employed on piece work for the slate they transhipped. In November 1930, D. O. Jones, the factotum there, was in correspondence with Stephens over their situation. There were normally two men working as a team but to deal with 20 wagons a day, 200 tons a week, another pair was needed, paid for by the regular loaders, even if there was insufficient work to keep them fully occupied. If the work fell away and they were laid off they could expect no dole, for they were outside the remit of the Employment Insurance Act.

Glaslyn RDC was in financial difficulties by 1930, its clerk asking the ministry for assistance in having its loan repaid. The rejection of the investing authorities' appeal, on 18 March 1930, to the GWR and LMSR for either of them to take over the WHR was followed by an appeal for additional financial assistance from the ministry on 29 July 1930 which was also rejected. Even wielding the spectre of 600 jobs lost if the quarries closed for want of transport facilities had no effect. The ministry did, however, meet the GWR and LMSR to discuss the WHR on 9 February 1931. Neither of the railway companies were interested in acquiring ownership but they were prepared to consider working the line on a cost basis providing it was possible to obtain a guarantee of the working expenses.

Ordinary passenger services on both the FR and WHR were withdrawn from 22 September 1930. The *Manchester Guardian* had noted that passenger numbers on both railways had declined with the growing popularity of bus services. It had been a poor year for the WHR, with the 1,343 passengers carried generating only £58 income; overall the railway had made a loss of £474.

The investing authorities set up an advisory committee to investigate the means by which railway operating costs could be reduced, reporting on 17 January 1931. On the Croesor section Moses Kellow was contracted to provide haulage at 1s 6d per ton; whilst both Rhosydd and Park & Croesor quarries were closed due to a depression in trade, it was hoped that Rhosydd would reopen. In that event it was suggested the WHR arrange its own haulage as 'we have reason to believe some of the neighbouring farmers would undertake the work at 1s per ton.'

Of nine quarries that had shipped slate via the WHR, Alexandra, Moel Tryfan and Cilgwyn were not working and stocks, expected to be exhausted in February 1931, were being shipped via Carnarvon; Park and Rhosydd were shipping to Penmaenmawr, presumably via Portmadoc and Afon Wen; Glan yr afon, Garreg Fawr and Victoria were closed, and Clogwyn y Gwyn shipped via both Dinas and Portmadoc.

It was suggested that operations be restricted to the NWNGR section temporarily, permitting staffing to be reduced to (Dinas) agent, driver, fireman and ganger, until 31 March. The positions of delivery agent and checker, at Portmadoc, and audit accountant could be abolished, the latter function to be carried out by the receiver. On the commercial front, the transhipment charge should be reduced to 8d per ton, the average for the district.

The extent of any reaction to these proposals is not known. In March the advisory committee recommended that the railway should re-open for tourists in July, operating in conjunction with the FR and the main line railways; that one of the locos be 'put in proper working order' for the passenger traffic; that fresh sleepers be laid where required and that buildings should be repaired where necessary. These proposals were adopted by the investing authorities on 24 April 1931, when they rejected a proposal by W. Hugheston Roberts, Portmadoc, and G. Parry Jones, Deudraeth, to close the railway. Henceforth the passenger service would be restricted to the holiday season of July, August and September.

On 17 March Stephens was reported to be unable to undertake his duties so the authorities resolved that his assistant, J. A. Iggulden, be appointed in his stead.

There was a sign of changing times when the investing authorities met on 24 April 1931. Cars had been noticed parked in the yard at Rhyd Ddu; Iggulden was asked to investigate the financial arrangements.

By the time the passenger service had ended on 3 October 1931 there was no traffic from the Bryngwyn or the Croesor quarries and the railway was effectively closed. On 15 October Iggulden proposed the appointment of a watchman and suggested retaining the services of the Dinas agent for a few weeks to complete the returns and accounts. On 5 November the authorities agreed to an experiment of employing four men for two days per week to run a goods service until 31 December. This probably continued as it was not mentioned again until 27 October 1933, when the service was reduced to one train per week. Although it had been a better year for passenger traffic, increasing to 2,459 passengers, goods traffic had declined and the loss increased to £742.

Nothing that had been done for the railway had worked out – £1,259 deposited against the Carnarvon extension and invested in government stocks was worth only £700 in October 1931, when a court order was obtained to release it to the revenue account. Without it there was no money to pay the wages and the 1931 season had only been possible because the county council made a loan of £250 to pay wages, buy coal and to repair a loco.

Stephens died on 23 October 1931, the settlement of his affairs with the railway being protracted and not resolved until 1946; in 1933 it was established that his estate was due £691, including arrears of salary. Carnarvon accountant Richard Thomas Griffith took over from Iggulden as receiver; he was also clerk to Gwyrfai RDC, one of the investing authorities. He was unused to the duties of a receiver and bought a book, *Keep on Receiving*, for guidance. When D. G. Jones, the county treasurer, disallowed this and other expenses, including the cost of a trip to Tonbridge to take over the receivership and his professional bond insurance, he complained: 'I never asked to be appointed ...'

On 23 March 1932 Iggulden wrote to the county council that there were insufficient funds for the railway to renew its third party insurance policy at £35. By return the council offered to advance the £35 but by then Iggulden had a coal bill, £12, and the locomotive boiler renewal premium, £6, to pay. Another of Stephens' assistants, W. H. Austen, became his successor as engineer and locomotive superintendent.

The 1932 passenger service attracted 4,327 passengers, generating £254. A reduction in train mileage reduced expenses but the railway still lost £278. Although the figures for 1933, 6,445 passenger generating £484, were much better the railway still made a loss. Meeting on 27 July, Griffith told the investing authorities that passenger traffic receipts were comparable to the same period in 1932. After discussion, the authorities deferred 'consideration of closing down the railway'.

The company's accumulated loss was £24,201, averaging £2,000 per annum. Such a restricted service was not convenient for the railway, either. On 27 June 1932 an engineman took a loco from Dinas to Boston Lodge, returning thence by bus, fare 1s 6d, and on 30 July driver Roberts took one of *Moel Tryfan's* steam pipes to Boston Lodge, again at a cost of 1s 6d, train fare this time – might he have travelled via the LMS?

Operationally the railway ended 1933 with a surplus of £30 but it was not enough. After consultation with the investing authorities the railway's closure was announced to take effect from 1 January 1934.

Continuous attempts were made, including approaches to the ministry and the Commissioner for Crown Lands, Cilgwyn's landlord, to encourage the quarries to send their output via the WHR. On 19 January 1934 the county council held a meeting with O. W. Owen, the manager of the Caernarvonshire Crown Slate Quarries Company, operators of Cilgwyn, Braich, Moel Tryfan and Alexandra quarries since 2 August 1932. The company had been allocated up to £18,000 of government funds to employ the unemployed to clear overburden after rockfalls and in expectation that the working quarries would pay royalties to the crown estate. The councils thought that the company should support another recipient of public funding.

Cilgwyn output could be diverted to Penygroes by road with considerable savings in both time and cost; between April and December 3,156 tons of slate had been shipped to Penygroes at a cost of £430; via the WHR the same volume would have cost more than £1,735. The railway was the most cost-effective means of shipment from Moel Tryfan however, 764 tons sent via Dinas in 1933 having cost 2s 6d per ton, and the company expected to link the Alexandra Quarry, not then in production, to Moel Tryfan by road and then send its output by WHR also. Unfortunately, the slate industry was set for another of its periodic depressions.

The news regarding the quarries caused the ministry to establish what the position might be if the company was liquidated. It therefore asked the county council, on 8 February 1934, for a copy of the 1933 accounts, an estimate of the likely realisations of assets, and details of the company's creditors.

Griffith itemised the expenditure. The LMSR supplied sleepers on two occasions (£23 6s 8d) and coal was obtained from Llay (five times, £68 16s 11d) and Bersham collieries (twice, £23 12s 1d). The county council was paid a total of £7 0s 7d for three bridge repairs and E. Jones & Son was paid £2 7s for a bridge beam. The Hunslet Engine Co was paid £6 15s for 'engine repairs'. E. Jones & Son also supplied fencing posts (£4 6s 2d), while W. Price supplied netting and staples (£2 2s 6d).

Outstanding debts included the county council (bridge repairs, £630 2s 9d), George Cohen Sons & Co (trolley, £22 10s), the FR (goods supplied, £1,119 19s 8d) and McAlpine (implements, £167 15s 3d). Hunslet was owed for pony truck tyres supplied for *Russell* in 1930.The judgement debt to Tourist Hotels Ltd, now £1,146 15s 5d, was also still outstanding.

The only property that Griffith thought was worth anything was the station houses at Dinas, £120, Quellyn, £50, and Rhyd Ddu, £25. The plot of land at Carnarvon bought by the PBSSR, valued at £3,500 in 1920, was now valued at a mere £100. He thought that the rolling stock and tools would fetch £45 but did not value the track because he thought it would cost more to lift it than it was worth.

When this information was circulated at the ministry it attracted some comments: 'It is quite clear that the assets held scarcely meet the cost of winding up and the debentures held by the ministry are of no value, this further information only confirms the hopelessness of the position ...'

Responding to a good 1933 season on its own line the FR decided to try to run the WHR directly. On 10 May 1934, Davies informed the county council that the FR would take over and run the WHR for one year without rent, or a nominal £1 if required, then to take a lease for a minimum of 21 years with an option to renew for 21 years on payment of 10% of the gross receipts. His letter followed a meeting that he and Austen had had with council officers the same day. He pointed out that

On 11 August 1934 the Baldwin and *Russell* were in charge of the trains. One of the Hudson toastrack carriages is in the Baldwin's train but the passengers' dress suggests that they were not experiencing the best August weather.
FR Archives

Right: **An innovation on the WHR, perhaps its only innovation, was the conversion of one of the carriages to serve refreshments in 1927.** *Welsh Highland Heritage*

Below: **Russell was altered to fit the FR loading gauge in the winter of 1924. Changes to its chimney, dome and cab roof can be seen in this photograph. At the expense of the locomotive's appearance, the scheme failed. The semi-open 'Gladstone' car is next to the loco.** *Welsh Highland Heritage*

'there is little hope of increasing the average revenue derived from passenger running ... unless a better service is given ...' During the calendar year to May 1935 revenue from freight traffic over 12 months had been, at £446 12s 9d, almost the same as that from four months' passenger traffic, £464 18s 9d.

Much work needed to be done to get the rolling stock and track into fit condition by 1 July, the start of the summer season. Walter Cradoc Davies, Davies's brother and successor as FR company chairman, was to estimate that the FR spent more than £1,700.

At the ministry a civil servant noted that 10% was a smaller proportion than paid in other cases 'but it would ... be difficult to get any more out of the Festiniog company in view of the very small volume of traffic ... it is difficult to say what the alternative, i.e. refusal, would result in. The receiver and manager's credit must be nearly exhausted and when it is the line will presumably be closed down.' At a meeting with a ministry official Davies said that he believed the line could be made to pay if worked in conjunction with the FR 'by a management experienced in the working of light railways of this nature.' As the FR had effectively been running the WHR since 1922 this was rather a strange claim to make. Davies went on to say that he looked to a considerable development of tourist traffic, and that he would be disappointed if in the course of a few years the receipts were not at least doubled.

He was pressed to give more than 10% but pointed out that the railway was in poor condition and in need of investment.

When asked to consider an earlier break for a rent review he argued that the FR must be allowed to reap the rewards of its investment. The officer felt that Davies 'clearly knows the strength of his position and appears to have secured the support of the local authorities.' In the short term the deal might not benefit the stockholders, he thought, but it afforded 'the best prospect of keeping the line open and thus of securing in some measure the objects for which it was built, so that the money spent on it ... may not be entirely wasted.' It was realised that, if the line closed, there was no prospect that the realisation of the assets would provide anything for the investing authorities.

A meeting to discuss the proposals took place between the authorities and Davies in London on 30 May 1934. Davies's refusal to accept responsibility for maintaining the road surfaces on the overbridges proved a sticking point until the ministry representative suggested that the county council adopted the roads, expenditure on class 1 and 2 roads qualifying for a ministry grant. The authorities agreed to the lease and when the county council met the next day it agreed to accept responsibility for the maintenance of the bridges.

When the 42-year lease was brought into effect from 1 July it contained some changes from Davies's original proposals. The FR was to pay £1 for the first half-year, at which point it could back out. For the following 13 years the rent would be 10% of the gross income, reflecting intended expenditure to bring the railway up to scratch. For the next 7½ years the rent was to be 10% of the gross income plus 5% of any gross income exceeding £2,000; thereafter it was to be reviewed. The lease detailed all the WHR's assets, including two broken clocks at Beddgelert.

Had WHR traffic picked up as expected the lease might have been a reasonable deal, although it was still unlikely to earn enough to pay the debenture interest. For the FR it was a disaster, committing it to pay rent even if the WHR made no operating profit. With hindsight there should have been a further opportunity for the FR to withdraw but that would have required a rent review that Davies was anxious to avoid. Was there any alternative apart from closure? If the stock and track had been in better condition a lease covering the holiday season renewable on an annual basis and rent based on profit might

Above: **At the start of the lease in 1934 the FR repainted all the stock. *Russell*, seen arriving at Beddgelert under schoolboy supervision, was painted green, as in this photograph.** *FR Archives*

have been feasible, but Davies was determined that the FR should recoup the cost of making the WHR operable. A more fundamental solution would have been to restrict the passenger service to Portmadoc and Beddgelert or Rhyd Ddu and to forget about using the WHR for circular tours.

While the negotiations were in progress correspondence between Davies, Griffith and Evans touched on the relationship between the two railways. Griffith complained about a lack of cooperation between the railways but Evans replied that the FR did help the WHR, encouraging bookings at Blaenau Ffestiniog and escorting passengers to the WHR station. He said that the complaint originated with D. O. Jones at Dinas and that he found WHR personnel at Portmadoc unhelpful, particularly in not directing arriving passengers to the FR. He pointed out that he had also been of assistance to Griffith on administrative matters and obviously felt aggrieved by the nature of the complaint.

Regrettably, Davies was to die before the year's end, and his co-directors probably did not realise that they had the option of abandoning the WHR at the end of it. The slate traffic in 1934 was satisfactory though, but in 1935, Moel Tryfan and Cilgwyn quarries were to divert their traffic to the LMS at Talysarn or Penygroes to the WHR's detriment, with the gross receipts for the whole year turning out to be less than those of the half-year of 1934.

In August 1934 *The Railway Magazine* published a reader's suggestion that the WHR should be taken over by a 'railway

enthusiast with means' for a negligible sum and popularised, like the Ravenglass & Eskdale Railway, with miniature stock and scale locomotives. This was the first published suggestion that the WHR's focus should be changed radically.

Despite the lease and an enthusiastic report about the alleged popularity of the circular tours in the *Manchester Guardian* on 27 August, 1934 was not a good year for the WHR company. Stephens' executors issued a summons for the monies due to the estate and by October the bank account was overdrawn. The bank told the receiver, Griffith, that it held him personally responsible for the shortfall. Not unnaturally he thought this was unfair and offered to settle by instalments. On the railway the FR repainted the locos and carriages, the latter appearing in different bright colours. It also offered a special through fare from Dinas to Blaenau Ffestiniog. It failed to compete, however, with road competition offering more spectacular routes over the Llanberis Pass and similar roads.

Evan R. Davies was only 63 years old when he died on 2 December 1934. His obituary in *The Times* noted that he was the mayor of Pwllheli for the fourth time and was 'interested in local railway undertakings'. He had been elected to the county council at the age of 21 and became the youngest alderman in England and Wales at the age of 24. A 'lifelong friend' of Lloyd George, he had been attached to his secretariat during the First World War. He had also been an unsuccessful Liberal candidate for Wrexham and North Caernarvonshire constituencies. His estate was proven at £24,267. Walter Cradoc Davies took over as chairman of the FR company and seems to have set himself the task of extricating the FR from the WHR.

At the other end of Beddgelert station, looking towards the Goat Hotel tunnel on 11 August 1934. Behind the footbridge, an aqueduct carries the hotel's water supply across the cutting. *FR Archives*

Right: **The Baldwin taking water at Beddgelert, c1936. The water tower's concrete base was a McAlpine construction. There were others like it at Portmadoc and Snowdon Ranger.**
FR Archives

Below: **Russell** **has an impressive exhaust as it climbs around the Cwm Cloch curves towards Rhyd Ddu. A trolley has been tied to the end of the train, c1933.**
H. W. Comber/FR Archives

Right: **Just to demonstrate that the climb could be made without the exhaust here is** *Russell* **again, seen from the back of the train a little further on, about to enter the deep cutting.** *H. F. Wheeller/FR Archives*

Right: **The photographer's wide-angle lens emphasises the size of the cutting, 45ft at its deepest.** *H.W. Comber/FR Archives*

Below: **'You stand there and I'll take a photograph of you with the engine.'** *Moel Tryfan* **at Rhyd Ddu in 1923.** *Author's collection*

His first move, early in 1935, was to tell the county council that the WHR had been worked at a loss and to ask the authorities to forego the rent. After slate traffic from Moel Tryfan dried up he went to investigate and claimed that he found evidence that the quarry was using WHR wagons to move slate to the Drumhead for onward transportation by road. Since the lease had started the WHR had carried 709 tons of Moel Tryfan slate earning revenue of £87 15s 1d.

In February 1935, Austen submitted a report on WHR repairs and renewals to Evans. The state of the Bryngwyn branch, including the incline, was deplorable, he said, and it was a surprise that stock stayed on the road and that there had not been serious derailments. At least 1,000 replacement sleepers were needed to bring it up to fair condition. Elsewhere, 1,500 sleepers were needed, as well as attention to fencing.

He considered the Baldwin to be in satisfactory condition but *Russell* required a new smokebox and other work at a cost of about £65. *Moel Tryfan* was in really poor condition though, and needed a heavy overhaul. Austen identified frame repairs, cylinder boring, piston renewal, retubing and stay replacement amongst work needed at a cost, including labour, of between £250 and £300. However, he said that with the availability of the Baldwin and if *Russell* was repaired, attention to *Moel Tryfan* could be deferred.

So far as the carriages were concerned an expenditure of £25 would make them fit for the season's operation. The state of the wagon fleet was a different story, for he thought many wagons were beyond repair, and recommended spending £150 to bring 30 of them up to serviceable condition.

Whether *Russell* received its new smokebox has not been determined, but the loco did remain in service. *Moel Tryfan* probably never worked again although work was to be carried out on its boiler in 1937.

Another meeting was held with the Caernarvonshire Crown Slate Quarries Ltd on 12 February 1935, for which the cessation of slate traffic over the WHR seems to have been the trigger. Griffith, the receiver, and W. C. Davies and Evans, from the FR, were present. It had been three weeks since the WHR had carried any Moel Tryfan traffic; J. Riley represented the company. He felt that the purpose of the government grant had been misunderstood: 'We have been rather humbugged, we have had deputations ...' He could save £600 per year shipping via Penygroes and by not having to deal with derailments when wagons were taken to the incline. Some customers collected their slate from the quarry. He denied Davies's claim that Moel Tryfan slate was being taken to the Drumhead in WHR wagons and then taken by road and said that when he had two shifts working at Moel Tryfan, he forecast October, the output would be sent by rail.

At some point the FR had sold the 1923 station building in Portmadoc for £25. J. H. W. Coggins, the auditor, questioned the money going to the FR and not the WHR. On 30 March 1935 Evans explained the background to Austen, saying that he had previously told Coggins, too.

In 1936, FR shareholders were told that expenditure for the previous year included '£100 rent payable under the terms of the lease of the WHR undertaking. The traffic ... did not come up to expectations and the directors are hopeful that the rent, or some part of it, will be waived.'

On 31 December 1936, W. C. Davies met the investing authorities. The FR had run the WHR for 2½ years and wanted to be released from the lease. He said the track was in poor condition when the FR took it over and needed a 'substantial sum of money' spending on it; 1934 produced a loss of £506. In 1935 one train a week sufficed for coal and groceries traffic, covering its cost. That year, receipts were £1,001, producing a loss of £596 including the 10% rent. When the seasonal passenger service ended on 30 September 1936, revenue had been £1,033, against costs of £1,283. A weekly goods train run

Above: **A busy scene at Rhyd Ddu as trains cross in 1923.** ***Prince's*** **tender has been modified to couple to NWNGR stock.**

A new point lever has replaced the NWNGR lever with the integral token-release lock. Despite being renamed 'South Snowdon' in 1922 the old NWNGR nameboard has not been changed. *Author's collection*

Right: ***Moel Tryfan*** **arrives at Rhyd Ddu in 1924. Waiting with the Dinas train is** ***Russell,*** **still in its original condition.** *FR Archives*

Below: **In September 1923** ***James Spooner*** **was photographed at Rhyd Ddu while it was being prepared to return to**

Above: **A stop at Glan yr Afon to photograph a ladies' outing. The end of the siding, and Qwellyn, are visible on the right. The railway must have been short of capacity to justify fetching out the Oakley's private carriage from the FR. As it was based on a slate wagon chassis, the ladies must have been well shaken by the time they got home.** *FR Archives*

after that period had to be taken into account, with a proportion of overheads and the 10% rent added, too. The WHR faced strong bus competition and took twice as long to make the journey.

The FR had made a loss of £105 in 1935, after allowing for the WHR's 10%; without it, both lines would have covered their expenses. From March 1936 the Blaenau Ffestiniog quarrymen were on strike for nine weeks, during which the FR continued operating to clear stocks from the quarries; at the end of the year the FR was £1,000 worse off than it was the previous year. Most FR passengers were from the North Wales coast, travelling via the Conwy Valley, a fair percentage travelled through to Dinas; very few joined the WHR from the LMS at Dinas. The LMS, with its interest in Crosville, shared with the GWR, encouraged its passengers to take the bus at Blaenau Ffestiniog – the FR objected to this and traffic picked up. The WHR also lost FR passengers to the buses at Portmadoc, despite the railway's best efforts. The situation would be worse in 1937 because Crosville had erected additional stands outside the station at Blaenau Ffestiniog.

By the time of this submission the last passenger train had already run, on 26 September 1936. In January 1937, Cynon Evan Davies, the FR's company secretary, had what might have been a chance meeting with an LMS official at Crewe on a Sunday evening. He learned that if the WHR was not to run in 1937, Crosville intended to change the vehicles on Portmadoc–Caernarvon route services used by tourists on the 'five valleys tour' to larger coaches. He felt that the LMSR and Crosville were not interested in promoting joint FR/WHR tickets, preferring to concentrate in increasing their own traffic. The WHR was officially closed, so far as the FR was concerned, for goods traffic from 1 June 1937. During the lease period passenger trains had been restricted to the tourist season of July, August and September each year, whilst goods trains had run as required.

The creation of the WHR can be attributed to two men,

Evan R. Davies and Henry Joseph Jack. Davies had an involvement with 2ft gauge railways in Caernarvonshire since at least 1901 until his death in 1934. He submitted the 1914 LRO application, was a director of the company and was responsible for the FR's lease in 1934. As a friend of David Lloyd George, and his private secretary for a time, he had access to those crucial Whitehall contacts.

Jack had been working at the Aluminium Corporation's Dolgarrog plant since 1909 but appears not to have become interested in railways until after 1918, when that company acquired control of the PBSSR. In 1920, he must have been responsible for Stewart acquiring control of the NWNGR, and becoming its receiver. He was behind the revival of the 1914 LRO application and the acquisition of the FR. Being remembered for his strong personality and as chairman of the county council he was very likely responsible for persuading the smaller councils to support the WHR. Perhaps it was Jack who invented the 'Welsh Highland' soubriquet for the railway.

What were their motives? Jack was a successful businessman; he probably believed the WHR could be successful too; had it been really successful it would have been electrified and a big NWPTC customer. Davies said it would open up the locality to tourism and improve access; for him success would have been increased local authority revenues. They succeeded in getting the railway built without any private funding beyond that used to acquire the NWNGR debentures, and the £10,000 put up by W. H. McAlpine. The two were friends; perhaps their weakness was in not noticing that the world was changing.

Right: **Prince** taking water at Snowdon Ranger in 1923. *Welsh Highland Heritage*

Below: **Russell** passes Salem during the FR lease period. *Welsh Highland Heritage*

Bottom: A poor-quality photograph of **Russell,** but it is the only one known of Rhostryfan, c1933. *H. W. Comber/ FR Archives*

Above: **The landscape around Bryngwyn in 1934 looks very desolate but there was still a small amount of slate traffic to be had.** *R. W. Kidner/Author's collection*

Right: **The sketch plan produced by the Crown Estates showing the quarries that connected to Bryngwyn in 1934.** *NA*

Below: **Dinas carriage shed was a focus for local children.** ***Moel Tryfan* peaks out from its position on the loco disposal road.** *G. Hughes/Welsh Highland Heritage*

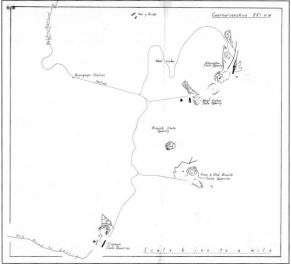

Above: **Unfortunately, loads like this one behind *Russell* were the exception rather than the rule. Dinas, c1933.**
H. W. Comber/FR Archives

Right: **Running for the train at Dinas in 1934.** *Derek Burridge/ Welsh Highland Heritage*

Below: **Moel Tryfan and crew wait for time at Dinas in 1930. Next to the well-loaded passenger carriage is an ex-WD Hudson bogie wagon followed by a NWNGR goods brake van.** *FR Archives*

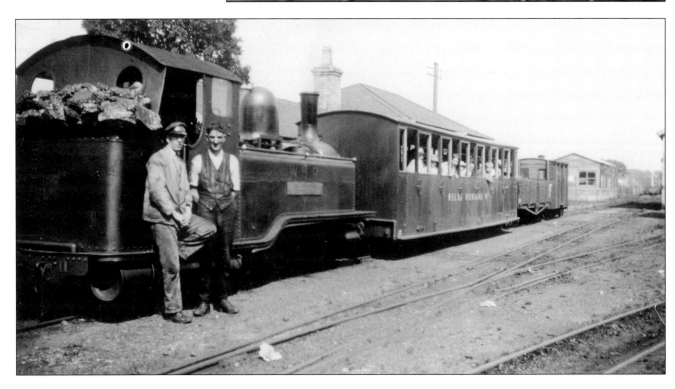

Above: **The end of the line. Passengers wait for a connecting train on the LMS. Behind them the board promotes connections for 'Snowdon, Beddgelert, [blank], Portmadoc and Blaenau Festiniog'.**

Welsh Highland Railway.

Suspension of Passenger Train Service.

On & from December 15th, 1924, and until further notice, the passenger train service on the Welsh Highland Railway, shewn in the Company's Time Tables, dated September 1924, will be discontinued.

Goods and parcels traffic will continue to be dealt with, except that Perishable Traffic will **NOT** in future be accepted for conveyance.

For particulars of goods train service, and times of acceptance and delivery of goods and parcels, see notices exhibited at the **Stations**.

Portmadoc.
1st Dec., 1924.

E. H. R. NICHOLLS,
Manager.

No 89.   Lloyd & Son, Printers, Portmadoc.

5

The Liquidation and Revival Proposals 1937-90

For most companies that would have been it. A few months of legal work, a few meetings, disposal of any assets, a final statement and the whole sorry affair consigned to the history books. However, with the WHR, as has been seen, nothing was straightforward.

The investing authorities asked Davies to submit the FR's case for being released from the lease in writing. They would not, at this stage, agree to the lease being relinquished but would pass Davies's request on to the Treasury and the ministry; if they were agreeable the authorities were prepared to make an application for approval for the receiver not to press for the rent.

Davies's letter was discussed at a meeting of the investing authorities held on 29 April 1937. The authorities had met an officer of the Ministry of Transport's Finance & Statistics Department. It was suggested that the WHR company be wound up, subject to court approval, and the assets realised; the FR should pay a lump sum in addition to the rent due at the time of release. At Carnarvon this course of action was agreed, the sum payable by the FR being set at £500.

Responding to the county council's report of the meeting, Portmadoc UDC agreed that the FR should be released from the lease and that the WHR should be wound up. It also required that it should have the opportunity of purchasing the track between Croesor Junction and Portmadoc to facilitate Park & Croesor and Rhosydd quarries being re-opened, the quarries being inaccessible to road transport. Deudraeth RDC's position was unchanged from 1922/23: 'I beg to state that the council have all along been in favour of doing away with this railway', its letter started. It also wanted access to the Croesor quarries to be protected.

The county council, acting for the debenture holders, formally put forward the proposal that the FR should be released from the lease in exchange for a payment of £500 and outstanding rent to the company, on 22 November 1937. Taking some time, the FR responded on 15 February 1938. The letter was signed by company secretary C. E. Davies, a son of Evan R. Davies, and secretary from 1924 until 1955, a signatory of the 1934 lease and managing director of the Snowdon Mountain Railway since 1930. He reviewed the situation and said that the rent now due was about £210, which the FR was unable to pay or to borrow. He made a counter offer of £600 in full discharge of all claims, payable in three annual instalments, recognising that there was no way of telling if the company would be able to fulfil the obligation being offered.

He went on to ask if the FR could keep *Moel Tryfan*, then lying partially dismantled at Boston Lodge. Davies said it had failed its insurance examination in July 1934 and there was therefore no obligation to return it to working order. In closing Davies laid claim to the railway between 'our Portmadoc station and the GWR main line'. This length was put down at the expense of the FR, he said, asserting the right to remove rails and sleepers along it. The claim, eventually accepted, was wrongly made as the boundary between the FR's junction railway and the WHR was where the route left Madoc Street.

The news that the WHR was not likely to be reopened soon brought a suggestion that it should be adapted for other uses. On 28 July 1937 the *Manchester Guardian* published a letter from Clough Williams Ellis, the developer of Portmeirion, suggesting that the precedent set by the LMS in handing over the Leek & Manifold Light Railway

Above: **Snowdon Street crossing in Portmadoc in 1948. The flour mill loading shelter juts out from the back of the manager's house on the right. The 2009 alignment is to the right of that shown.** *Author's collection*

Right: **Looking towards Portmadoc with the 1923 FR station building and the water tower base on the right.** *Welsh Highland Heritage*

Left: **Pont Croesor, 25 August 1965.** *P. F. Plowman*

Below: **Near Croesor Junction, with the track still in situ, 1947.** *Author's collection*

Below middle: **The Afon Dylif bridge, 1947.** *Author's collection*

Below bottom: **The Afon Nanmor bridge, 1947.** *Author's collection*

trackbed to Staffordshire County Council and its dedication as a public footpath should be noted, for the WHR's 'many miles of well-graded, well-ballasted track would make an admirable bridle path.' His idea was quickly adopted by the Ramblers' Association.

Before moving on, an insight into the relationship between the FR and the WHR can be had from correspondence between Evans, Davies and J. H. W. Coggins, the auditor, in the summer of 1938. Coggins wanted to establish the intra-company indebtedness since 1927, when the WHR entered receivership. The WHR owed £1,281 8s 10d, while the FR owed £224 9s 0d. The WHR debt included £163 7s 4d for the services of the FR's Portmadoc stationmaster for 338 weeks, at 9s 8d per week, from 1 January 1928; Stephens had agreed the amount. On 28 July 1938, Davies wrote to Coggins: 'I don't see that we should tell the Welsh Highland people of the amount due to them for interchange passenger traffic from July 1933 to June 1934. The receiver has doubtless no records as he would appear to have kept inadequate books and is not able to file and pass his accounts to the high court.'

On the same date Coggins told Davies that he had reinstated £81 19s 1d due to the WHR for the period between 4 March 1927 and 31 December 1929 that Stephens had told him to write off 'as a wrangle'. He also drew attention to £82 18s 7d paid to the WHR by Evans for 1931-2 in November 1933, 'much against my wishes.'

By now the GWR appeared to realise the futility of pursuing its claims against the WHR. On 27 July 1938 the investing authorities were told that the GWR was prepared to withdraw its claims subject to the authorities accepting that the soil on which the crossing lay was the GWR's property and the authorities recognising that the GWR's lien on 'certain materials at the Croesor crossing was a valid one' and was not challenged. Presumably 'certain materials' included the manganese crossing which had been installed by the WHR.

At a meeting held on 1 September 1938 the county council, having previously obtained agreement to terms from the other debenture holders, resolved to accept £600 from the FR in full discharge of all claims 'provided the full amount is paid forthwith, or in the alternative, the sum of £300 is paid forthwith, and the remaining £300 to be paid on 30 September 1939, adequate security being given for the payment of the above terms the Festiniog Railway Company to be allowed to retain the steam engine *Moel Tryfan*.' The FR neither made payment nor gave adequate security for it, so therefore, despite subsequent events, never secured legal title to *Moel Tryfan*.

In further correspondence with the council on 2 February 1939 Davies explained that the FR had 'expended a fair sum of money in advertising by way of posters, handbills and guide books, etc' promoting the combined attractions of the WHR and the FR. He went on: 'Our experience, however, has been that the Welsh Highland Railway does not appeal to the public in anything like the same degree as does our own railway. The latter has a length of 13 miles odd and travels an appreciable part of its line through scenery which is not open to the tourist by any other means of transport. In addition its known antiquity and recent centenary are other factors contributing in no small degree to its popularity. The Welsh Highland Railway, on the other hand, with its long length of 22 miles, though passing by or through such well-known beauty spots as the Pass of Aberglaslyn and Beddgelert, has nothing but its novelty to recommend it to the public. The two places last mentioned are equally accessible by road.'

He pointed out that Crosville was a strong competitor and whilst the railway took two hours from Portmadoc to Dinas the bus ran at regular intervals, had greater comfort, ran to the centre of Carnarvon and took half the time. Evans produced an inventory dated 19 April 1939.

Iggulden's correspondence with the council, meanwhile, with respect to both Stephens's estate and his own salary of £50, due to him for his six-month tenure as receiver and manager, was as drawn out as anything else to do with the WHR. On 9 March 1939 he threatened to remove rail to the value of the sum outstanding on Stephens's estate. The county council replied on 6 June saying that 'several enquiries have been received in respect of same' and that the authority's London agent, T. D. Jones, was to obtain the instruction of the court concerning the sale of track materials. Iggulden's claim, like that of Stephens's estate, was not settled until 1946.

No fewer than 14 scrap dealers and others were to declare their interest to the county council between closure and 1941. The Federation of British Industries, whose assistant secretary V. Boyd-Carpenter was clearly a railway enthusiast, took a particular interest, arranging inspections of the line with Evans for itself (i.e. Boyd-Carpenter) and for George Cohen Sons & Co, with Boyd-Carpenter in attendance. On 3 May 1939 Cohen had, following a second inspection, offered £3,815, their best price, for 'track, rolling stock, sleepers, buildings, telegraph poles and wire, etc.'

Following his death Griffith had been replaced as receiver by George Gregory Williams, the county council's treasurer, on 8 February 1939.

Some two years after the last train, the LMS Estates Department decided it would be appropriate to establish the boundaries at Dinas, putting down pegs in addition to the existing boundary posts in July 1939.

Counsel's opinion was sought by the county council on 23 May 1940, W. Gordon Brown QC delivering his opinion on 5 June. It would not be possible to get a Board of Trade winding-up order under Section 7 of the Light Railways Act 1912, he said, because inability to carry on the undertaking arose from financial difficulties, not from the sale of the undertaking. The undertaking, anyway, could not be sold without the authority of Parliament. The railway company could be wound up, he thought, under Section 338 of the Companies Act 1929 providing the FR's lease was determined first. The liquidator could then discontinue working the railway and realise the

Above: **Nantmor cutting, 25 August 1965.** *P. F. Plowman*

Right: **In the Aberglaslyn Pass a wall was made across a tunnel mouth to pound animals and deter walkers. There is evidence of it here, and of it being broken down.** *J. R. Hollick/FR Archives*

assets. An abandonment order would not be necessary before presenting a winding-up petition. He was unable to determine who should best petition for a winding-up order. Finally, he opined that the receiver could not be held personally responsible for any loss sustained by landowners or tenants in respect of abandoned cuttings, nor could he be compelled to repair fencing.

The council responded by commissioning John Lloyd of Ishelen, Carnarfon, to inspect the railway, a function he performed between 22 July and 9 August 1940, charging 69 hours at 1s 8d (8½p), total £5 15s (£5.75) plus travelling expenses of 9s 6d (47½p). He found all stations to be in a very bad state, broken into, windows broken and frames removed. The buildings at Quellyn (Snowdon Ranger) and Rhyd Ddu had been converted to dwellings, although the latter was empty. After the tunnel at Nantmor obstacles had been built across and along the line. The military had built a wall across the line at Plas y Nant as an obstacle.

Lord Stamp, chairman of the LMS, involved himself in WHR affairs on 27 September 1940, when he sent a memo to the secretary of the Ministry of Transport, Sir Leonard Browett. Starting: 'This is nothing to do with the LMS or Whitehall; it is just a bleat from a private citizen! When I was tramping round Snowdon for a week in August I was impressed by the derelict Welsh Highland Railway and the possibility of lifting it for scrap'. He concluded 'I got our district engineer to give me a report on what was involved in the way of recovery and cost and I enclose a copy ...' Browett passed on Stamp's memo and report, asking: 'Is there any possibility of getting at the scrap or must the court procedure continue to grind along its laborious and tardy way?'

Stamp's engineer, C. R. Irving, looked at the FR before estimating that it would cost some £2,325 to dismantle the WHR, making no valuation of the materials involved. Obviously not knowing too much about the WHR's setup he included the Croesor Tramway, but only five of the six river bridges in his calculations.

Locally, Deudraeth RDC raised objections to the WHR being dismantled, repeating its call for the retention of the line to Portmadoc from the Croesor quarries although it had no objection to the line between Croesor Junction and Dinas being sold. The *Liverpool Daily Post*'s 9 November 1940 report included the council's claim that the Rhosydd Quarry had paid £4,000 for track laid on the Croesor Tramway.

In January 1941 the county council's London solicitor, T. D. Jones, wrote reporting on a meeting held with the chief clerk at Chancery Chambers. Officials there had been critical, saying that the company should not have abandoned the undertaking without statutory powers. 'On the other hand it was pointed out that if in fact the Ministry of Supply should formally requisition under the emergency powers the rails then the receiver can afterwards come to the court for the necessary directions on the footing that he is no longer able to carry on the undertaking, the rails having been acquired by the ministry.' This opinion cleared the way for the track disposal, and had actually been mooted in Whitehall during 1940 after the same device had been used on the Southwold and Edgehill Light Railways.

The topic of the WHR's future was raised in the January and February 1941 issues of *Modern Tramway*, when Arthur E. Rimmer suggested that if it could not be used in substitution for road transport to aid the war effort it could perhaps be acquired by voluntary organisations and run by railway enthusiasts. Rimmer is considered, in some quarters, to be the father of WHR preservation and maintained his interest in it until he died in 1999. Further attention was drawn to the railway's plight by a three-part article published in *The Railway Magazine* during the year.

Left: **Cohen's demolition train in the Aberglaslyn Pass, 1941.** *J. R. Bolton/ Welsh Highland Heritage*

Below Right: **Beddgelert station site with the station building and stores hut remaining in situ, 1947.** *Author's collection*

Below: **Camping within sight of Moel Hebog and the WHR trackbed in Beddgelert Forest in the 1950s.** *Frith/Author's collection*

Above: **Pitt's Head, with track still in position but becoming overgrown where the formation was waterlogged under the bridge, 1947.** *J. I. C. Boyd/ Welsh Highland Heritage*

Above right: **Rhyd Ddu in 1939, more than two years after the trains had run.** *Author's collection*

Right: **Snowdon Ranger, rented as a holiday home since 1933.** *Welsh Highland Heritage*

Below: **Waenfawr station building has been said to have been in good order until it was attacked by evacuees during the war.** *Welsh Highland Heritage*

Below right: **Tryfan Junction and the demolition train in 1941.** *J. R. Bolton/Welsh Highland Heritage*

These two publications might have been responsible for an enquiry made by B. V. Kirby MP on behalf of the Ramblers' Association early in 1942. A letter to Kirby from the Ministry of War Transport, 'we have no power', was dated 4 March 1942. The Ramblers' Association's Liverpool & District Federation therefore circulated the county council and others proposing that the freehold should be acquired with a view to its dedication as a public footpath. When, on 3 December 1942, the council supported the Federation's proposal the motion was seconded by William George. Hardly surprisingly there was no cash on offer, so the Federation launched an appeal to raise £2,000 to be handed to the county council as an earnest of 'widespread desire to acquire this unique right of way.' By 16 October 1946 £1,000 had been raised.

Meanwhile, the requisition proposal was formalised by a Ministry of Supply requisition order dated 13 March 1941. The order covered the railway and sidings, except for the Croesor section, all equipment at Dinas, goods wagons, 50 wheel sets, two steam locomotives, and various scrap items lying around the permanent way. A supplementary order issued on 1 August 1941 referred to the carriages and other rolling stock.

The requisitioned assets were sold to George Cohen, Sons & Co Ltd for £12,855; it seems that the Ministry of Supply charged an administration fee of £55, for the WHR only received £12,800. Cohen started on site in August 1941 and worked through until the following year. With bases established at Dinas, Rhyd Ddu and Porthmadog, the company advertised

40,000 sleepers and 1,200 tons of rail as well as 'trucks & chassis' and 'spare heavy wheels & axles' for sale. Most of the rail was still in Cohen's yard after the war and was apparently offered to the Talyllyn Railway c1951. Boyd-Carpenter arranged for locomotive nameplates and worksplates to be deposited at the LNER's railway museum at York.

The county council's solicitor prepared a summons releasing the FR from its lease for presentation to the High Court in September 1941. Of the £600, £200 was to become due immediately the lease was surrendered, the remainder one year after the end of the war or from the date of any armistice, whichever happened first, payable in four annual instalments. The order gave the FR all rights pertaining to the junction railways; Cohen offered £180 for 600yd of track at Portmadoc on 10 July 1942, presumably this section.

The council's winding-up summons was issued on 7 October 1941. When served on the WHR's solicitor, Ninian Rhys Davies, he found that the company had no current directors. Using company law he caused the majority shareholders, including himself and Jack, the latter had called himself Henry Jack Macinnes since 1934/5, to call an extraordinary company meeting. Not unnaturally the non-existent directors failed to respond, giving the requisitioning shareholders the right to call a meeting, which they did for 29 May 1942. At the meeting, attended by Davies, one other and five by proxy, Walter Cradoc Davies, Ralph Freeman and Crossley Colley, were elected directors but took no further interest in WHR affairs beyond accepting the summons.

Railway buildings also came under military scrutiny and on 18 November 1941 Rhostryfan and Rhyd Ddu station buildings were requisitioned. On 6 January 1942 the track between Pont Cae'r Gors and Hafod Ruffydd was requisitioned for the War Department for use as mobile target practice by shooting at slate wagons; the Air Ministry first raised this idea with the FR on 16 November 1939. In 1944, the War Department had a tenancy for accommodation at Beddgelert for £15 per annum but the circumstances are not known.

Another hiatus in the WHR's winding-up occurred in 1942 when, on 16 April, further opinion was obtained from Brown. Generally speaking he thought the wrong approaches were being used to secure both the release of the FR from the lease and a winding-up order for the WHR. However, at a hearing on 3 November the

FR gained approval to agree to surrender the lease – it appeared that there were no powers to force the FR to surrender it. The surrender was formalised by an agreement with the receiver dated 12 August 1943, whereby the FR agreed to pay £550, still by instalments, instead of the original £600, the £50 reduction being compensation for the expenditure incurred by the FR in reconstituting the WHR board in 1941. The first instalment of £150 was paid on 21 August. An undated commentary on the claims filed with the petition remarks on the claim made on behalf of E. R. Davies, Nee, Stephens and Westall, all deceased, for directors' fees. Originally £1,439 19s 3d, it had been reduced to £1,002 9s 3d: 'No trouble was taken to distinguish between the parties ... had there been any prospect of it being paid ... they would no doubt have carefully made out the amounts due to each director.'

When Rhostryfan station was surrendered by the military on 6 January 1941 the council had it inspected to see if a claim for damages could be made. It was soon told that it had been in appalling condition when requisitioned. Military occupation was resumed later, for the War Department was paying £2 10s rental per annum in 1944. On 13 December 1945 LAC 1103869 W. J. Hughes wrote to the county council, in Welsh, from RAF Langham in Norfolk. He said he had been born in the village and wished to convert the station buildings to a bungalow for himself and his wife; after 5½ years in the RAF he had no other hope of getting a house.

Even in wartime the Ordnance Survey wished to keep its mapping updated, on 19 August 1943 asking Portmadoc UDC

Above: **The road was realigned and a new bridge built across the Bryngwyn incline in the 1960s.** *Author's collection*

Left: **There was insufficient room to store all the carriages under cover at Dinas and the surplus were stabled on the running line outside as in this 1939 view.** *A. E. Rimmer/Welsh Highland*

how it could contact the railway to obtain details of the 'extent of railway dismantling.' The council replied that the request should be sent to the county council.

On 26 January 1944 the county council petitioned the High Court for a winding-up order for the WHR. The hearing took place on 7 February when Mr Justice Uthwatt made the order. T. D. Jones reported that there was some considerable argument as to whether the court had power to make the order. The petition stated that the only assets were £12,800 received for the requisitioned stock and equipment, and the £400 due from the FR.

The total deficiency of the WHR at 4 March 1927, when the receiver was appointed, was given as £175,171, of which £150,877 was in respect of land, buildings, permanent way and (unspecified) equipment, written down to £20,000 in 1944. Amongst the unsecured creditors were the FR, owed £1,036, and the NWNGR, owed £1,081. The Kent & East Sussex Light Railway and the North Devon & Cornwall Junction Light Railway, both parts of Stephens's empire, were owed money, as was the Snowdon Mountain Railway. The county council was still owed £630 for repairing the roads over the NWNGR bridges. The Shropshire & Montgomeryshire Light Railway, another part of Stephens' domain, owed the WHR £4.

Of the £90,000 ordinary share capital, issued to secure the NWNGR and PBSSR undertakings, £26,696 was held by Evan R. Davies's estate and £52,891 by Jack. The next largest holdings, each of £1,430, were registered to William D. Penrot and others of Finchley and the executors of C. V. T. Hodgson. The executors of Charles Breese and William George held £750 each, Ralph Freeman and Crossley Colley, £300 each,

Above: **This 1939 view of the loco shed at Dinas is deceptive ...** *Author's collection*

Right: **... for the roof was collapsing on the locos stored within.** *FR Archives*

Aitchison's executors, £25, and Eleanor C. Russell £965. There were 46 shareholders in all.

Debts	£
Unsecured creditors	6,521
Preferential creditors	1,494
Debentures	84,774
Interest to 4/3/27	13,300
Shares	90,000
Total	**196,089**
Assets	**£**
Cash	125
Stock	25
Land, buildings, permanent way, equipment at cost	170,877
Stamp duties	2,316
Debts	768
Estimated to produce (in 1944)	20,918
Rents (annually)	177

These figures are taken from the statement of affairs produced by company secretary Ninian R. Davies and certified by him on 11 May 1944. Alwynne Aubrey Thomas of Llandudno had been appointed liquidator on 20 March 1944 but it was January 1946 before Williams was discharged as receiver and he could take over the estate. With Evan Davies & Co claiming that the company's deeds and other documents were subject to a lien for unpaid costs and the requirement to establish title to the property it was some time before Thomas was able to make any progress. Representatives of the investing authorities formed an overseeing committee of inspection. At some stage the committee agreed that Thomas's remuneration would be 10% on any realisations and 7½% of any distributions. The county council became aware of this arrangement in 1955 and complained that the debenture holders' approval should have been obtained. From time to time Thomas would appoint solicitors and surveyors to advise him.

In his 23 June 1944 observations on the winding up, the official receiver commented: 'It is clear that after payment of the receivership costs and expenses there will be a substantial deficiency on the debentures and there is no prospect of any funds becoming available in the liquidation for the unsecured creditors. The share capital of £90,000 has also been irretrievably lost.' In a statement to court of 9 November the causes of the WHR's failure were given as failure of traffic to expand as expected and the financial structure of the company.

Left: **At Dinas a view from the standard gauge bridge looking towards Afon Wen in the 1950s shows the former NWNGR/WHR yard in the occupation of the Gwynedd Rivers Authority and the buildings replaced. Later enlarged, the yard returned to railway occupation in 1997 and the present rail access is from the standard gauge formation.** *J. Moss/FR Archives*

Middle left: **Tryfan Junction looking towards Waunfawr on 16 April 1960. By the time restoration was started the area was so overgrown that it was possible to pass the ruins of the station building without knowing. One of the contractors working in Beddgelert was to tell the author that as children he and his friends would sit on the building's back wall chatting and loosening stones as they did so.** *Ron Fisher*

Below: **Despite being the largest structure on the NWNGR the Glanyrafon bridge was rarely photographed and views of it are now obstructed by tree growth. This photograph, taken on 16 April 1960, gives an indication of its size.** *Ron Fisher*

Left: **In the 1960s WHR(1964) stored track materials at Beddgelert and Nantmor, as seen at the former on 25 August 1965.** *P. F. Plowman*

Given the nature of the share capital's creation it had been a long time since it had represented anywhere near its face value.

The proceeds of the requisitions had been invested in 2½% National War Bonds. These were redeemed in 1946 and a court order of 12 December approved dispersal of £13,185 as follows, in order of priority: G. G. Williams (receiver's expenses); estate of the late Holman Fred Stephens; R. T. Griffith (receiver's expenses); J. A. Iggulden (for acting as receiver and manager); Minister of War Transport costs; FR Company costs and WHR costs, some £1,800 in total. The remainder was passed to the liquidator.

In October 1946 Thomas received a bill from the LMS for the WHR's share of Dinas signalling costs. After failing to persuade Thomas to transfer land at Dinas in lieu of the debt, the LMS was to cancel it and, on 29 December 1947, give him a deed of release of its interest in the site.

On the trackbed Thomas sold the Nantmor station building for £5 in July 1946. He had bridge beams at Cwm Cloch valued at £10, offering them for sale at £15 to Twiston Davies, the landowner, in September 1948. In October he sold the station buildings at Beddgelert to the village policeman, Tom Williams, for £56; Williams was to buy two girders for £5 in August 1949. The Croesor section rails were sold to W. O. Williams of Llanfair, Harlech, for £8 per ton in November 1948. The remnant of the parliamentary Croesor Tramway and parts of the

Right: **Intended to be the base from which the reconstruction of the WHR would be launched, WHR(1964) gained access to the standard gauge Cambrian Siding at Portmadoc in 1973. This was the scene at Pen y Mount in the autumn of 1974.**

non-statutory tramway were removed by 1950. FR volunteers recovered track from a part of the junction railway in 1960.

The Ramblers' Association's footpath proposal was strongly pursued during the late 1940s/early 1950s. Some county councillors had indicated support for the scheme but when a WHR sub-committee met on 13 January 1948 it declared, having undertaken a two-day tour of inspection, that it could not recommend the proposal to the council in view of the heavy cost and presumed liability for the erection and maintenance of fences. When the association pursued the matter with the Ministry of Town & Country Planning the council responded, inter alia, on 18 January 1949 that it had 'decided to inquire whether certain sections ... can be purchased for road improvements, such as eliminating bad corners, 'S' bends and hump-backed bridges', not the last time that such a suggestion might be made.

As this period coincided with the promotion of the first national parks, the association came to hope that the National Parks Commission would register the trackbed as a long-distance route under Section 51 of the 1949 National Parks and Access to the Countryside Act. The commission, however, felt that traversing the route did not, on its own, qualify as an 'extensive journey' as defined in Section 51(1) because it would take only a day or two to walk.

The Ministry of Transport tended to badger Thomas for news of the liquidation in the late 1940s, especially as he was not always quick to reply; on 11 April 1949 he managed a long report. He had sold removable chattels to the value of about £1,600 and was getting valuations for land at Caernarfon and at Dinas station. He had found it impossible to establish the extent of the WHR's land holdings due to poor record keeping in the past, deeds were incomplete, plans were missing and descriptions were vague and impossible to key to maps. He proposed selling the land at auction with possessory title, saying 'unless we do this the liquidation will drag on indefinitely.' It did anyway, but he obviously did not understand that he actually had no power to sell the trackbed.

The beams at Pont Croesor were sold to the North Wales Rivers Catchment Board for £50 in May 1951. In November 1951 a Colonel Goodchild of Beddgelert told Thomas that he was prepared to pay £250 for land, possibly including the station buildings (the record is not explicit), at Rhyd Ddu; Thomas had had the land valued at £150. In October 1952, Goodchild was to withdraw his interest as the (unspecified) council had told him that most of the land was required for a road diversion, road widening and a car park. Gwyrfai RDC then complained to Thomas that it should have had first refusal on the site; Thomas offered it to the council for £250 provided

Goodchild was 'compensated for his expenditure in protecting the property from further damage.'

In 1952, Thomas was reporting progress, separately, to the ministry and the county council, saying that he had been careful to maintain a right of way in case he was able to make a sale to the Ramblers' Association, yet when he sold the NWNGR shed site at Dinas and Rhyd Ddu station in 1954/5 the trackbed was included in the sales. Beddgelert Parish Council had declared an interest in the station site there but apart from Waunfawr and Snowdon Ranger he thought it would be difficult to sell the trackbed if he didn't get a buyer for all of it. In October, Thomas was asked to negotiate with DW Investment Holdings Ltd but the purpose of this company's interest is unknown.

The investing authorities received some good news later in 1952 when Thomas made a distribution of 2s in the £. Further distributions of 1s 3d and 1s in the £ were to be made in 1954 and 1962.

In 1953, Thomas approached the Snowdonia Park Joint Advisory Committee to see if it would buy the trackbed. The committee had no powers to purchase on its own account so put the matter to the National Parks Commission. On 12 November it resolved that the counties of Denbigh, Caernarvon and Merioneth should work together to submit proposals for the establishment of a long-distance route including both the WHR and the FR, then crossing southern Snowdonia with a view to continuing through mid-Wales to the proposed Brecon Beacons National Park and thence to St David's in the Pembroke National Park, and from Dinas to Conwy and St Asaph. On hearing that the park authority had been established in October Thomas made a direct offer to it.

The trough that carried water over the railway from the Goat Hotel reservoir to the hotel was renewed at a cost of £185, plus 6% administration charge levied by the county council which carried out the work, early in 1953; the hotel contributed £25. In June 1953, Thomas met members of the Festiniog Railway Society who wanted to see if they could take over the WHR company, not the assets, as a way of gaining control of the FR.

By 1955, Thomas thought he was making progress and was close to completing the liquidation. The county council had bought Dinas station site for £2,350 on 25 May 1954. On 4 November 1954 he had agreed to sell the station buildings and yard at Rhyd Ddu for use as a car park, also to the county council, for £125, although on 10 August 1955 the district valuer revalued it to £210 14s 4d. The sale went through sometime after Thomas made a statutory declaration in July. On 2 September 1955 he sold the Dinas depot site, complete with trackbed through the road tunnel, to the Gwynedd River Board for £972 9s. By 6 December he had sold a further, unspecified, plot for £60.

When Gwyrfai RDC complained about unauthorised car parking at Rhyd Ddu in September 1958 Thomas informed it, of course, that the land was owned by the county council. In December 1958 the Cread Mountaineering Club was given permission to park on railway land at Rhyd Ddu 'without creating any tenancy rights and subject to termination at any time.'

Events moved slowly and in August 1959 the county council was advised that the National Parks Commission had no plans for a long-distance route in Snowdonia. However, in saying that there had been no intention to consider a Snowdonia route for two years, the commission had agreed that the council's request, 'that this particular route should be given priority' would be an item on the agenda for a meeting in September.

The council was also informed that there were adequate rights to create footpaths without resorting to purchase and any purchase made under existing general powers would not attract Exchequer assistance even if ultimately the long-distance route was to use it.

Thomas had actually offered the trackbed to the county council in 1958. He must have begun to tire of the WHR, for in 1960/1 he had been considering handing over the trackbed to the Crown as unsaleable but almost as soon as he had formed the thought the situation changed. In February 1961 he had received 'two distinct declarations of interest' but the only one that he logged in his diary was made by Robert 'Bob' G. Honychurch, a Shrewsbury businessman. A report on his proposal was published in the *Manchester Guardian* on 10 April. A dialogue was established between Honychurch and Thomas and on 16 July Thomas attended an informal meeting held in Shrewsbury where he explained that he would accept £750 'for quick sale of trackbed.' Thomas's advisers had told him to accept whatever he could get because a sale by auction would cost more than it would raise. The 19 supporters who attended the meeting agreed that the Welsh Highland Railway Society should be formed and appointed officers to act until a general meeting could be called.

Honychurch was not the only interested party, for on 9 May 1961 an organisation called Minitrains had offered £40 per acre to buy the section between Beddgelert station and the Nantmor tunnel mouth for a 15in gauge overhead electric tramway, 'for which the equipment is already in stock.' Thomas rejected this approach out of hand, as the price offered was unacceptable due to Honychurch's enquiry.

The society submitted planning applications to restore the railway to Merionethshire and Caernarvonshire County Councils in August 1961. The first issue of the society's journal, dated September 1961, informed members that initially operations would be centred on Beddgelert, with trains running to Nantmor or Hafod y Llyn, whichever was more convenient. If operating the first section was profitable then the line would be extended.

Another meeting, held at Crewe station in October, led to a formal offer to purchase the trackbed subject to obtaining planning permission. In December, Merionethshire gave planning permission for the two miles of railway in that county but Caernarvonshire rejected the application for four reasons: portions of the trackbed affected proposed road improvements; rebuilding would prejudice plans for a long-distance footpath; steam trains would intrude in a peaceful area of the park and might start fires in Beddgelert forest; and if the revival failed the current situation would be worsened. Despite this setback Honychurch maintained contact with Thomas over the proposed sale. On 13 August 1963 Thomas informed the BoT companies' liquidation branch that he had obtained the creditors' approval to sell the trackbed for £750.

Earlier in 1963 the society's membership secretary told an enquirer that the county council had given planning permission

'in principle' subject to agreement concerning car parking at Beddgelert and resolving issues concerning proposed road improvements; two steam locos had been acquired, diesel locos would only be used on works and construction trains, and rail was being purchased. Possible sources of material in France and South Africa had been 'thoroughly investigated' and rejected. In the meantime, lacking access to any part of the trackbed the society established a depot on former Shropshire & Montgomeryshire Light Railway property at Kinnerley, Shropshire, in 1963. The society was incorporated as Welsh Highland Light Railway (1964) Limited [WHR(1964)] in January 1964, a proposal to register a company in 1961 not having been fulfilled. Negotiations with Thomas failed due to his death on 6 July 1964, before contracts could be exchanged.

With Thomas's death responsibility for the WHR's assets transferred to the office of the Official Receiver (OR), based in London. The OR was required to act in the interests of the debenture holders in securing the best price for the assets, of which the trackbed itself was the most significant. The elected representatives of the investing authorities had difficulty in understanding that as debenture holders their first priority was also to obtain the best return on their capital investment, not in seeking to obtain odd bits of land for other purposes. The best price was always going to be received for the entire trackbed, rather than for isolated sections.

So far as the trackbed was concerned, the OR's objective was to ensure that it would pass to a body with sufficient resources to take on the liabilities, so that it did not return to him via another bankruptcy. Because the WHR was a statutory undertaking disposal of the land could only take place with either an abandonment order under the 1962 Transport Act or a transfer order under the 1896 Light Railways Act, although this was not always understood. Negotiations became complex and protracted and progress suffered from a lack of consistent local authority policy, a cautious OR, and the fleeting interest of outsiders.

The dispersals that Thomas had made in anticipation of an early sale of the trackbed left the OR in a difficult position, for he had less than £200 with which to administer the estate and the receivership. When it became necessary to obtain legal advice he had to seek approval and funding from the investing authorities. Had this not been necessary he might have been in a position to make better progress.

Whilst WHR(1964) established links with the OR and the local authorities, outside interest in the WHR was not diminished. Transit Properties Ltd (incorporating Minirail Ltd) of Frampton Cotterell, Bristol, offered £25 an acre for the land between Rhyd Ddu and Nantmor on 24 August 1965, an offer that was repeated on 12 November 1969. One of Transit Properties' directors was L. M. Anderson, who had made the Minitrains bid in 1961.

A Colin Heard of Yeovil offered £1,250 for the section between Beddgelert and Nantmor on 14 March 1966. WHR(1964) offered £2,500 for the entire route, an amount that was doubled by a J. R. Green of Bexhill, Sussex, in May 1967. Green was a retired businessman and reputed millionaire. He offered to let WHR(1964) be involved in running the railway rebuilt under his control.

The OR took Green's bid seriously and decided legal advice was called for, so on 28 November 1967 asked the debenture holders for funds. A meeting was held in Caernarfon on 20 March 1968 to consider the request. Due to the absence of the OR no decision was made. The Ministry of Transport's representative observed that the local authorities did not present a united front, with some concerned about the motives of a prospective purchaser, whilst others welcomed the idea, citing the benefits of the FR. He also noted that most of the

Top: **Three-quarters of a mile of railway was built by WHR(1964) between Portmadoc and Pen y Mount and, after an LRO was obtained, a train service was started on 2 August 1980. The Ruston & Hornsby diesel locomotive** *Kinnerley* **is seen running round its train at Portmadoc in the autumn of that year. Subsequently a shop and café were built on the site beyond the headshunt.**

Middle: **A steam service was launched using the newly restored Peckett 0-4-2T** *Karen* **on 1/2 May 1983 and was photographed leaving Portmadoc before an admiring audience during that weekend.**

Right: **After many years of trying, the FR managed to sell the 1923 station site in the 1980s. It was being prepared for development when seen on 26 March 1994.**

local authority representatives failed to understand that their priority was to secure the best deal for the debenture holders and complained about the OR's desire to sell the land as a single unit, selling piecemeal would serve only the local authority interests. He said that the county council was delaying in order to inform Green of its anxieties and to explore the possibility of making a joint offer.

Another meeting, held on 24 April 1968, was attended by the OR, H. C. Gill. Green was not prepared to contribute to the cost of obtaining counsel's opinion but had increased his bid to £5,500 so the debenture holders would not lose out if he were successful. The county surveyor said any delay in establishing rights of access to the trackbed would cost £250,000, as it 'was obstructing the realignment of a main road in the area and a bridge costing that amount would need to be constructed', but quite how he achieved this logic is unclear. The meeting's chairman suggested that Green sought to buy the land in order to hold the councils to ransom over the sections they wanted.

Receiving counsel's opinion that the OR had no power to sell without either an abandonment order or a transfer order, a draft contract was prepared. Green, however, was served with a receiving order in May 1968. Although he successfully appealed against it he ceased to be proactive. The OR appears to have been frustrated by delays in Green's responses to letters and his failure to instruct solicitors in any event, and in January 1969 he was unofficially dropped in favour of WHR(1964) which had matched his offer. Green did visit the OR on 17 February 1969 but to no avail. Nothing was heard from him again.

Another meeting of the debenture holders had been held at Caernarfon on 3 February 1969. The OR was represented and three members of WHR(1964) and two representatives of Development Securities Ltd, a McAlpine company, were also present. One of the latter was Richard Hilton, who had previously worked for the FR and who had been associated with WHR(1964) until 1967. The local authorities identified about one-eighth of the trackbed that they wanted for various schemes and the WHR(1964) members said they were prepared to enter into a joint purchase with the county council that took account of this.

Thereafter, whenever any inquiries were made about the availability of the trackbed, the standard reply was that the OR was dealing with a prospective purchaser. This was the response that Tony Hills, now the proprietor of the Brecon Mountain Railway, received on 24 August 1972, after he had inquired on behalf of Hills & Bailey Ltd of Llanberis, saying that they wished to re-open all or part of the railway for tourists.

WHR(1964) must have been confident when its solicitor Stanley Keyse took part in an informal meeting to discuss the WHR at the Ministry of Transport on 17 July 1970. Two ministry officers were accompanied by an OR representative, the OR's solicitor and the railway inspector, Major Peter Olver. Keyse said that WHR(1964) was prepared to buy the whole line and dispose of those sections surplus to its requirements; an abandonment order would be required in respect of the latter. Reconstruction would start at Portmadoc and the line would be re-opened in stages. The type of service to be operated had not been decided. The ministry could not approve a draft LRO but would give advice on a proposed order.

By 1971 WHR(1964) had offered £5,750 which was recommended for acceptance by the OR. However, the county council was not prepared to give its approval until it had reached agreement with WHR(1964) on the council's land requirements.

The road schemes that threatened the trackbed's integrity came to the fore during 1971. On 12 March, the county surveyor, T. Lloyd Roberts informed WHR(1964)'s chairman that railway land at Waunfawr was needed for a road improvement scheme that was to commence that year. The new road would cross the site on an embankment and the old bridge would be filled in. He was proposing to seek permission from the OR for consent to enter the site. There is no evidence that he did this but had he done so the likelihood is that the OR would have told him that nothing could be done that would hinder the reinstatement of the railway. In another letter, Roberts told WHR(1964) that giving the railway a tunnel through the embankment would cost £250,000, which it would have to pay for.

If it had acquired the trackbed at this time it was WHR(1964)'s intention to apply for an amendment order covering the trackbed between the former GWR crossing at Porthmadog and a point approximately one mile beyond Waunfawr. With trains terminating at Waunfawr, it claimed that the extra formation would permit the development of servicing facilities outside the National Park, although the National Park boundary is at Betws Garmon. The company's solicitor informed the ministry that the proposal to fill in the bridge 'could be prejudicial to any scheme for reopening the railway'.

On 6 July 1971, Roberts sent details of 18 road schemes to the Department of the Environment. Under these proposals 10 bridges, including the PBSSR structure at Beddgelert, would have been demolished. The road was to be diverted on to the trackbed between Gwyrfai Terrace and Betws Garmon and between Castell Cidwm and Snowdon Ranger. Between Llwyn Bedw and Gwyrfai Terrace and between Rhyd Ddu and Pitt's Head the road would have been widened on to the railway. Eastern and western bypasses were promised for Beddgelert. Nantmor level crossing was to be widened and at Porthmadog an indication was given of where that town's proposed bypass might cross the line. Of all these schemes only the last has been the subject of any design work and its construction is still several years off as this book is being written.

In Whitehall the ministry had obtained Treasury approval, on 11 June 1971, to have the outstanding WHR debt written off. The stock, effectively the certificates, was sold by tender to R. G. West on 14 December 1985.

A matter of on-going concern throughout this period was the incursions taking place on the trackbed along with claims for adverse possession. On 25 August 1965 G. V. Swann, tenant of Snowdon Ranger station building since 1933, offered to buy the property for £350. He added that if his offer was not accepted he would claim possessory title, saying that he had ceased to pay rent, £10 per annum, in 1948 because he was not certain that the person he was paying it to, Thomas, was entitled to receive it. Resident in Newcastle-under-Lyme, Swann was a solicitor.

Llanwnda Parish Council successfully registered Rhostryfan station site as a village green with the county council but following an objection being made the registration was overturned on 2 January 1973 at an inquiry. The objector was George Morgan, Cae Hen, who had himself incorporated part of the trackbed into his farm near Tryfan Junction and demolished one of the overbridges to improve his access.

In 1973, an exchange took place with landowners at Ynys Ferlas, near Nantmor, when a claim of adverse possession was made. This was resisted, as all such claims were, and concluded with the owner's husband saying he wanted to ensure his wife was compensated if approval was given for the railway to be rebuilt. By 1975 some 30 adjacent property owners had been identified as making claims for adverse possession of sections of the trackbed. For many years WHR(1964) members reported incursions to the OR, with varying degrees of success.

After buying the former Cambrian siding from British Railways in 1973 WHR(1964) moved its equipment from Kinnerley to Porthmadog. Later the BR land opposite the Queen's Hotel was also purchased, as was other land adjacent to Gelert's Farm in 1975. A depot was set up, a three-quarter mile long railway built and a LRO obtained in 1980. The first trains ran on 2 August that year, terminating at Pen y mount, alongside the WHR trackbed. The WHR(1964)'s railway is located on what is commonly known as the Beddgelert Siding, in reference to the partially constructed standard gauge Beddgelert Railway, of which it was a part. However, several old plans, including those deposited with the PBSSR's 1901 bill, refer to the narrow gauge, Croesor Tramway, loop as the Beddgelert Siding and the standard gauge line, when it is named at all, as the Cambrian Siding.

Unknown to WHR(1964), later in 1973 the Department of the Environment informed the OR, in confidence, that 'they considered the proposals then submitted ... as being neither realistic nor viable.' The company had not shown that it was able financially to develop the railway and, to do so on the proposed piecemeal basis, was unsatisfactory. In its view, the area already had a proliferation of similar lines and it did not see that this line offered anything new or unusual which would make it a financial proposition. This view was adopted by the OR although strictly speaking the decision on whether there should be another railway in a locality should rest with the planning authority.

Local government reorganisation in 1974, when Gwynedd County Council took over the responsibilities of the Caernarvonshire County Council, brought with it a hiatus for WHR(1964). Not only could it not establish the relationship that it had enjoyed with the old authority but in November 1974 it read in the *Daily Telegraph* that the new council's Snowdonia National Park Committee was going to acquire the trackbed and convert it into a footpath.

WHR(1964) went on the offensive and told the OR that it had involved the local MP, Dafydd Elis Thomas. WHR(1964) officers had met him on 2 November 1974 when he agreed to represent the company in its dealings with officialdom. On hearing this an officer at the Department of Trade recommended, internally, that the OR had done all that was reasonable or possible and should apply to be released from the receivership and leave it to the debenture holders to sort out the disposal of the trackbed. As the president of the Welsh Assembly, Lord Elis-Thomas has visited the restored WHR on several occasions.

Because of the number of parties declaring an interest in parts of the trackbed or claiming possessory title or other rights in it the OR had, by 1975, obtained counsel's opinion. Once again it was advised that land essential to the company's undertaking could not be sold without first obtaining an abandonment order or a transfer order 'unless the undertaking had failed without hope of revival', a position ruled out by the existence of a preservation society, counsel had helpfully observed. Counsel had also suggested that if the debenture holders agreed to any sale, other parties, including those who might have offered more money, could not object.

In 1978, WHR(1964) succeeded in getting restoration to Pont Croesor, just over 1½ miles, included in the district plan. The railway had been omitted from the draft plan so the matter was raised at a public inquiry, with the county council objecting to its inclusion. The inspector found in the railway's favour though, prompting WHR(1964) to produce a feasibility study the following year.

Over the years the focus of WHR(1964)'s ambitions regarding the trackbed varied according to the whims of the local authorities. The county council, meanwhile, came to adopt the position where it was prepared to acquire the trackbed but its intention to use parts of it for non-railway purposes required an abandonment order, a move that could have constrained any future railway reinstatement.

The OR received an offer for the trackbed from John Ellerton in December 1979, but by June 1980 this had been withdrawn, confirming the OR's opinion, first expressed in 1975, that the county council was the only viable purchaser; it even appointed a surveyor to value the property. Ellerton, who was to take over the Fairbourne Railway in 1984, had been interested in developing a 12¼in gauge railway on a part of the trackbed and had, earlier in 1979, offered to work in conjunction with the WHR(1964). The latter's board responded by refusing to countenance the establishment of another railway on the trackbed, the company considering it had the right of first refusal of purchase of the trackbed and that its position was unassailable.

The WHR(1964)'s planning application for the section between Porthmadog and Rhyd Ddu submitted in May 1981 was rejected, however. The county council formed a WHR sub-committee, on which WHR(1964) was represented, to oversee matters relating to the trackbed. Although it tended to be reactive to events affecting the trackbed the sub-committee did propose that the council buy the assets from the OR for £1, an offer that was submitted in October 1981. The council intended to take responsibility for the liabilities and to lease parts of the trackbed to WHR(1964) as that organisation developed the resources to expand.

Although the OR accepted the council's £1 offer there was still no move to convey the trackbed to it and on 18 May 1982 WHR(1964) submitted its own offer of £5,750. The OR informed the Department of Trade & Industry that WHR(1964) would not comply with the OR's conditions: to pay the OR's costs; to commit to obtaining and paying for an abandonment order; to indemnify the OR against any claims; not to seek compensation from the OR in respect of any successful claims for adverse possession, and to meet all expenses until completion.

At around this time a split developed within WHR(1964), when some members thought that alternative means to secure the trackbed for railway use should be investigated. They managed to acquire the certificates for 82½% of the WHR company shares and for £19,950 of the debentures and formed Trackbed Consolidation Ltd (TCL) as a corporate identity. On 19 November 1983 TCL informed the OR that it was intending to make a formal offer to reconstruct the company, saying that if this proposal failed it would offer £10,000 for the assets, exclusive of legal costs. The OR decided, in January 1984, that 'the only reasonable solution to bring the long protracted matter to finality' was to sell the trackbed to the county council for £1 because it would comply with the conditions. Informed of this on 24 February 1984, two TCL members responded by writing to their MPs complaining about the OR's refusal of their £10,000 offer.

Even though the certificates held by TCL could not be registered to it TCL used its position of beneficial owner to call a WHR company creditors' meeting to put forward a scheme of arrangement, whereby the company could be removed from receivership. TCL offered to pay £3,000 to the OR to cover the costs of winding up the company, £9, 674 (11.41%) to the debenture holders and £326 (5%), to the creditors. The meeting, on 23 July 1984, was adjourned when TCL could not get the required 75% majority in favour. Earlier, in May 1984, five members of TCL who were members and, in some cases, officers of WHR(1964) had had their membership of that company withdrawn after they refused to hand over their debenture and share certificates without compensation, in the belief that WHR(1964) intended to do nothing with them.

Left: **After a substantial fundraising effort and moving the loco to five sites, WHR(1964) completed the restoration to working order of ex-NWNGR/WHR Hunslet 2-6-2T *Russell* and it entered service in works grey livery in 1987. It was painted in NWNGR maroon livery during the following winter and in 1988 participated in the FR's Steam 125 event, running as far as Rhiw Goch. July 1987.**

Above: **On 18 August 1996 WHR(1964) returned the 'Gladstone' car to service in NWNGR livery. On that date it was seen passing the company's Gelert's Farm works being hauled by *Russell*.**

Left: **The company's other steam stalwart has been Bagnall 0-4-2T *Gelert*, imported from the Rustenberg platinum mines in South Africa in 1982 and which entered service in 1991. Passing Gelert's Farm works on 25 October 1997, it looks as though it has been freshly repainted. It was subsequently turned to face Porthmadog and is currently painted dark blue.**

In the autumn of 1998, the FR's England 0-4-0ST *Palmerston* visited the WHR(1964) site for a brief period as seen at Pen y Mount on 25 October 1998.

When the debenture holders' meeting was reconvened in January 1986 TCL's effective holding was increased by having access to any rights attaching to the former Ministry of Transport holding. Due to objections from the county council, Dwyfor and Meirionnydd District Councils, it was still unable to obtain the required majority. Dwyfor had been in favour before the meeting but changed its mind. Had TCL been successful at this stage it could have met its obligations with £5,000 in cash contributed by its members and a £15,000 overdraft arranged with the Midland Bank. Its intention was to act as landlord for WHR(1964) rebuilding the railway.

Progress appeared to be on the horizon when, in January 1988, an LRO application for the Pont Croesor section was made jointly by WHR(1964) and the county council, but events overtook the application and the order was not made. Unbeknown to either applicant the FR had taken an interest in the trackbed, making a secret bid to the OR to buy it for £16,000 in October 1987. The FR at this time was still recovering from the stresses of building its deviation line and completing the restoration of its route to Blaenau Ffestiniog. Its interest in the WHR followed concerns, expressed by employees, about the impact if it was reopened in competition with the FR.

During discussions with the county council that started in September 1988, the FR also requested it's interest must be kept secret; officers were told that the FR was concerned about the effect on its revenues if the WHR was extended beyond Pont Croesor. The FR also told the council that if it was successful in acquiring the trackbed it would be willing to transfer it to the council at no cost in return for an undertaking that it would not be used for railway purposes.

At some point in 1989 the OR asked WHR(1964) for an indemnity against its costs at a proposed hearing to approve the sale to the county council. The company offered £10,000 which the county council agreed to match. An extension appeal fund established by WHR(1964) had raised over £12,000.

The FR revealed itself as the rumoured mystery bidder to the council in December 1989 and informed the WHR(1964) at a meeting held on 4 January 1990. In a statement published later, FR chairman John Routly said that the FR was in a position to take responsibility for the trackbed and anticipated renting a section of it to WHR(1964), extending the lease in the light of experience.

WHR(1964) was determined that co-operation with the county council was the only way to secure its objectives yet hindsight shows that this policy had been subject to many changes in direction and delay. It also seemed to have been intimidated by the scale of the perceived liabilities inherent in ownership of the trackbed. It requested the FR to withdraw its bid, saying that it did not wish to be its tenant.

TCL responded to the publicity by offering, on 29 January 1990, its WHR share and debenture certificates to WHR(1964) to enable that company to play a part in bringing the old company out of receivership. When it was rebuffed it met FR representatives and, realising that their objectives were the same, donated the certificates to the FR Trust, a registered charity.

The FR's credibility was not assisted when copies of its correspondence with the county council were leaked to a WHR(1964) director. It later came to light that a meeting held in the council chamber had been recorded, unknown to the FR contingent. The WHR(1964) press and media campaign was very effective, both locally and within the heritage railway movement. The FR did not respond well to WHR(1964)'s criticisms and was not effective at getting its view across. Its board and senior management, however, were undergoing changes that brought with them a fresh view, that the WHR should be seen as an opportunity, not a threat.

By May 1990, the FR had set its stall out. Not only was it going to restore the WHR in its entirety but it was going to start from Caernarfon and reinstate the connection with the FR at Porthmadog. Doing so would fulfil the ambition of Spooner and others more than 100 years earlier. The justification for FR involvement could have been extracted from Spring's report (p49), complete with the elimination of the interchange at Dinas.

Rebuilding the Welsh Highland Railway
1991-2009

In deciding to start the restored WHR at Caernarfon the FR knew that the town was recognised as having only one attraction, its castle, then attracting some 400,000 visitors a year, with nothing to entice visitors to stay longer than the minimum needed to view it. As a commercial centre it was in decline. The standard gauge trackbed to Afon Wen was, and remains, part of the Lôn Eifion cycleway; as far as Dinas it could easily accommodate both cycles and trains and at Caernarfon the terminus could be very close to the castle. The rationale was that many of the castle's visitors would easily be tempted to take a train ride if they heard or saw it during their visit.

However, committing to rebuild the WHR in its entirety was not the end of the matter. There were considerable hurdles to overcome before reconstruction could be started and trains run again. The controversy continued for several years and it took a court hearing and three public inquiries before complete approval for the transfer of the WHR assets and the reconstruction was obtained by the FR.

A WHR(1964) member, also a member of the FR Society, claimed that the FR's activities were *ultra vires* and threatened to obtain an injunction to stop them. In response the FR Trust established Ffestiniog Railway Holdings Ltd in 1991 to handle the FR's non-FR activities, and transferred the share and debenture certificates to it. The same individual also organised a petition calling on the FR to withdraw its bid and to take no further action concerning the trackbed.

The OR's High Court application for permission to sell the trackbed to the county council for £1 was heard over four days from 11 November 1991. The FR's ownership of the WHR share and debenture certificates was deemed to qualify it to participate in the case. It applied to have certificate transfers validated, leading the way to a scheme of arrangement by which the WHR's assets could be removed from the OR's control, to prevent the sale of the trackbed to the county council, and to allow the OR to sell the trackbed to the FR. As the certificates

had been transferred to the holdings company that organisation was made a party to the application in substitution for the FR.

The judgement was made on 20 December 1991. Justice John Vinelott found the application to register share and debenture transfers 'misconceived' but declared that the FR Trust or some other body, but not the FR, should be able to apply for transfer order. It was therefore not for the court to decide between the competing claims but for the Secretary of State (for Transport).

The county council and WHR(1964) commissioned a feasibility study which reported in 1993 that a revived WHR would be successful. Meanwhile, in July 1992, the county council offered the FR the opportunity of taking on the railway between Caernarfon and Rhyd Ddu, and a £300,000 grant, while keeping the remainder for WHR(1964). The offer was refused.

The FR Trust, jointly with FR Holdings, made an application for a transfer order to take over the remaining assets (and liabilities) of the original company in tandem with an application for a Dinas–Caernarfon LRO in October 1992. The county council/WHR(1964) alliance made similar applications in December and a public inquiry was held at Caernarfon in November/December 1993.

Earlier, on 2 May 1993, an extraordinary general meeting of the FR Society had voted on two resolutions: for the society to dissociate itself from the attempts to acquire the WHR trackbed and for the society to call upon the other elements of the FR group to refrain from making further attempts to acquire the WHR. Several of those who had called the meeting were also directors of WHR(1964). Both resolutions were lost.

The inquiry inspector's report and recommendation, dated 4 March 1994, and the transport minister's decision were published on 20 July 1994. The inspector found that reinstatement of the WHR would be in the public interest and that either party had the capability of undertaking it. He found in favour of WHR(1964)/Gwynedd for five reasons: local authority support would be an advantage in dealing with planning and environmental

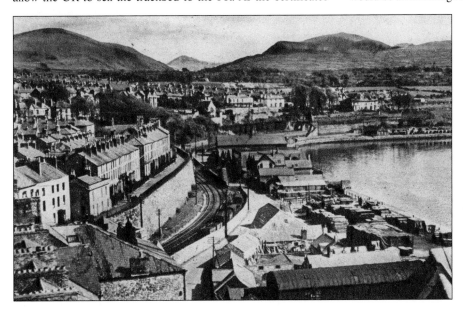

Viewed from the ramparts of Caernarfon Castle the site of the WHR's new terminus can be seen in standard gauge days. *Tuck /Author's collection*

issues; the county council would be able to secure a higher level of grant funding; WHR(1964) facilities at Porthmadog would be an advantage; WHR(1964) would be dedicated to rebuilding the WHR, whereas the FR might be sidetracked by other projects; the FR was controlled by shareholders but the democratic form of WHR(1964) was more likely to encourage volunteers. The recommendation was, however, overruled by the minister. This was undoubtedly a political decision, given that the government of the day had a policy of diverting risk from the public to the private sector wherever possible.

In a statement headed 'We've been robbed', WHR(1964) responded by declaring that it would co-operate with the FR and dedicate its skills and expertise towards the expeditious rebuilding of the WHR.

Above left: **The Millennium Commission's announcement that it was to award a grant to the WHR was made on 2 October 1995. The Commission's representative discusses the award with Alan Pegler (president, FR Company), Gordon Rushton (then general manager, FR Company) and Michael Schumann (FR Trust).**

Above right: **Before work could be started much planning was required. On 15 June 1996, Michael Schumann and Michael Pritchard, of Sharp, Pritchard's, the FR's Parliamentary agent, consider the legalities at Snowdon Ranger.**

Above: **Work was formally started at Dinas on 15 January 1997, when a ceremony was performed by the first loco on site, the Funkey *Castell Caernarfon*, and an excavator.**

Below: **Stacks of track panels were to be seen at Dinas on 1 April 1997, when the platforms were under construction.**

The WHR (Transfer) LRO was made on 4 March 1995. Armed with it the FR negotiated with the OR for the transfer of the WHR's assets, substantially the land. For reasons that are unclear, but perhaps excessive caution on the part of the OR, it was 30 June 1999 before the transfer took place, for the symbolic price of £1. On 17 August the end came for the WHR (Light Railway) Ltd, when official receiver Mark Boyall wrote: 'The winding up is for practical purposes complete. There will be no distribution to creditors.'

Planning permission for the Dinas-Caernarfon section was given on 6 December 1995; the WHR's 1964 chairman sent a letter of support. The following year the county council approved a 999-year lease for £1 per year payable in advance. Fortuitously both the Dinas station and old loco shed sites had become available, their purchase also being agreed in 1996.

Approval of the Caernarfon Railway LRO had been given with the transfer order decision in 1995 but it wasn't until 8 October 1997 that it was made thanks to a campaign of obstructive letter writing. Originally a part of the Nantlle Railway, the history of this part of the line was outlined in Chapter 1. Some relics of the Nantlle route still survive between Caernarfon and Dinas, notably tunnels at Coed Helen and Plas Dinas and the river bridge at Bontnewydd. The standard gauge railway to Afon Wen, the Nantlle Railway's successor, had been closed in 1964.

July 1996 was a busy time for WHR(1964). Some of its members helped to lay track for the WHR locomotives due to arrive from South Africa at the FR's Glan y Pwll depot on 24 July; its change of name to Welsh Highland Railway Ltd was registered on 25 July and it achieved charitable status on 28 July. During the year it reinstated the five TCL members whose membership had been withdrawn in 1984. There was no public announcement about the change of name, not even in the organisation's journal.

The LRO turned out to be the last made in England and Wales. Since 1992 applications for new railways and similar works have been made under the Transport & Works Act. Therefore a Transport & Works Order (TWO) was required for the WHR, the Ministry of Transport having declared that the original powers were no longer valid. An application submitted in April 1997 sought an order to authorise the reconstruction of the WHR from Dinas to connect with the FR at Porthmadog. A very detailed and complex environmental statement accompanied the application, to explain just how the railway was to be built and its likely impact.

The original route was maintained except for deviations at Tryfan Junction, to improve sighting on a minor road, at Rhyd Ddu, to bypass the car park located on the former station site, at Croesor Junction, to improve the alignment, and at Porthmadog where a new alignment was devised to connect to the FR. The section through Porthmadog was defined as a street tramway, a concept that was felt to give more flexibility in the choice of control installations. Although some aspects were to be overruled after the order had been made the completed scheme does include street tramway elements.

Compulsory purchase powers were sought to deal with claims for adverse possession. It was argued that it would be wrong for an individual, or group of individuals, to be able to overturn the wishes of the secretary of state. The application also included a request for deemed planning consent, a legal device that avoided a duplicate application under planning laws; decisions on the appearance of structures were reserved for the local authorities.

When published, the application triggered some remarkable reversals from organisations previously supportive of the railway, including the Snowdonia National Park Authority (SNPA), against the advice of its officers, and the National Trust. Perhaps not too remarkably, some of the objections were very reminiscent of those made to PBSSR/NWPTC applications 90 years earlier. In contrast, members of the Caernarfon Chamber of Commerce displayed posters declaring support in their premises.

A public inquiry was held in Caernarfon, starting on 9 December 1997 and ending on 28 January 1998, but not continuously. Great play was made by some objectors on the suitability of the Aberglaslyn Pass for railway use, with claims made that it would be unsafe, despite the large numbers of pedestrians who had been using it as an unofficial walking route. These claims were to have an unexpected impact on future events.

During the course of the inquiry the FR reached an agreement with several objectors, securing their withdrawal. A key item in the agreement reached with WHR(1964) was that that company would build the railway towards Pont Croesor when the Dinas–Waenfawr section was complete. Agreement was also reached concerning the use of the name, vintage train operation, and for WHR(1964) to develop a WHR heritage centre at its Gelert's Farm site. The issue of the name arose because WHR(1964)'s application to the Patent Office of the words 'Welsh Highland Railway' with a logo as its trademark had been registered on 30 May 1997.

Despite this agreement and a gradual improvement in relations between the FR and WHR(1964) some of the latter's supporters had difficulty in accepting the change in the status quo and maintained a campaign to hinder the FR's efforts; the

Above left: **Laying track within sight of Caernarfon Castle, 21 September 1997. The point was removed when the platform was extended in 2006.**

Above: **The ex-South African diesel locomotive hauled WHR's new carriages to Caernarfon for the first time on 2 October 1997. The ensemble was greeted by the railway inspectors who had arrived to conduct the inspection the following day. The building on the right was built by Caernarfon's most famous Victorian engineers, de Winton & Co.**

Left: **The FR's Alco 2-6-2T *Mountaineer* made the first steam-powered run to Caernarfon, on 4 October 1997. The train was photographed at Coed Helen.**

delay caused to the Caernarfon LRO has been mentioned. FR directors and others connected with it, including this writer, were also targeted on a personal basis.

Towards the end of the inquiry a new organisation emerged to campaign against the railway. Called Gwarchod, Welsh for 'guardians', its objectives were quite wide ranging but it has only been heard to speak against the WHR. It maintained an operation to obstruct the development and to try to discourage partners and prospective partners from associating with the railway. Some organisations were remarkably tolerant in dealing with the complaints and allegations made, even when they were submitted outside published deadlines for consultation, and insisted in responding to them in detail.

Local media also gave the objectors a ready outlet for their complaints, often without offering the opportunity for the FR to respond. It was to be many years before reference to the WHR did not automatically include the description 'controversial'. The developing internet gave the parties an opportunity to express their views and gave the opportunity to disseminate news internationally. The professionalism of an enthusiast website developed by Ben Fisher, a lecturer at Bangor University, led to it being adopted by the FR as its official WHR construction site.

Before the TWO decision was made another relevant public inquiry took place, starting in July 1998, for the SNPA had proposed withdrawing support for the WHR from its structure plan. It emerged that the authority had changed its mind about the railway on the basis of a personal objection made by the chairman of the authority's planning committee. One of the key points made was that the authority's plan was required to be in conformity with Gwynedd Council's plan and the latter supported reinstatement of the WHR.

The SNPA maintained that the special qualities of the park could not be appreciated from a railway carriage, but only by moving slowly through the landscape, by walking or cycling. It is not for the authority, the inspector was to say, to dictate how people should enjoy the Park's special qualities, adding that based on his experience of the FR it is possible to appreciate the landscape in greater comfort and safety from a train. By the time of the inquiry over 5,000 WHR supporters had made their views known to the authority.

The SNPA's report was published first, on 9 March 1999. Of the WHR, the inspector concluded that the 'principle of its reinstatement is in the public interest and does not conflict with national park purposes.'

Right: **After a weekend of trials, which saw hundreds of local people making the return journey between Caerarfon and Dinas for £1 each, the official opening took place on 13 October 1997. Posing with NGG16 class Garratt No 138, were (from left) fireman Nigel Dant, driver Paul Ingham and Welsh Highland Light Railway Co general manager, Roland Doyle.**

Below: **Garratt No 143 arrives at Dinas from Caernarfon on 20 September 1998, the Pullman *Bodysgallen* newly in traffic. Visible in the trees above the loco is Plas Dinas, the ancestral home of the Armstrong-Jones family which the Queen visited in 1963. It is now a hotel.**

Below right: **With work just started on clearing the line between Dinas and Waunfawr ready for reconstruction, the FR trustees and other railway officials walked the route between Waunfawr and Tryfan Junction on 7 October 1999. The day before it had been passable in comfort but there had been several hours of heavy rain overnight, the effect of which can be seen.**

Left: The day before, the soft state of the ground as it was at Gwredog Isaf, near Tryfan Junction, was obvious.

Middle: The Gwredog Isaf bridge was replaced as a mitigation measure, site constraints eliminating the scope for a balanced design. Much use has been made of gabions, stone in wire baskets, to support or restrain ground subject to movement. 15 April 2000.

Bottom: Clearance at Tryfan Junction on 7 October 1999. A few days earlier the remains of the station building had been hidden from view. Contrast with the photograph on page 95.

Consulting engineers were appointed by the FR, under terms agreed by the SNPA, and their report was submitted on 19 May. The FR was anxious to make progress, otherwise the final decision would be devolved to the National Assembly for Wales, then due to come into existence on 1 July, and subject to further delay. The SNPA, though, prevaricated and put off making a decision on the report by commissioning its own consultants to analyse it.

It was to no avail, however, because the final, favourable, decision was announced on 28 June 1999; the order was made two days later, just beating the deadline. Work could only be started in the National Park, though, when the proposed remedial works, including rock stabilisation, shotcreting in two of the three tunnels and raising retaining walls, had been carried out to the SNPA's satisfaction.

As might be expected in WHR affairs, that was not the end of it. The National Farmers' Union for Wales applied to have the order overturned in July. A ruling in favour of the WHR was made on 24 November. With a contract value of £200,000, the Aberglaslyn work was carried out over the winter of 2000/1. Only then could the reinstatement of the WHR start in earnest.

Despite its objection to the TWO, the SNPA dealt with the reserved planning issues in its area in a professional manner. There was a glitch in 2006, however, when the application concerning the appearance of Beddgelert station building was approved with a restriction prohibiting retail sales except for tickets and railway souvenirs. An appeal to the Planning Inspectorate saw the restriction removed in July 2008.

The FR's strategy for developing the WHR was to have the work done to a high standard to limit future maintenance requirements. The criteria established to attract the sophisticated traveller of the 21st century were: speeds of up to 25mph to be the norm to give an acceptable journey time, with locomotives capable of good acceleration and power to cope with gradients of up to 1 in 40; trains of 10 or 12 cars hauled by a single loco; high-quality coaches with all conveniences, catering etc. Sourcing equipment from overseas (South Africa, Poland, Romania, India and France) has been a characteristic of the WHR's development.

To manage the reconstruction the FR Trust set up Welsh Highland Light Railway Ltd in May 1997. This company oversaw the work between Caernarfon and Rhyd Ddu. In September 2004 Welsh Highland Railway Construction Ltd was registered

The TWO decision was announced in two parts, the first on 7 April 1999. The inspector, whose report had been submitted on 21 April 1998, had recommended against making the order, concluding that the scheme did not meet the criteria for development in a national park. The then deputy Prime Minister, John Prescott, however, declared that he was 'minded to make the order' because he 'attached greater weight ... to the economic benefits accruing outside the park, and ... strengthens ... the justification ... in terms of the national public interest.' He required, however, the implications of reconstruction in the Aberglaslyn Pass to be fully understood, which was dependent upon the FR commissioning consultants to examine the pass and proposing a scheme of remedial works, if found necessary, with the Park.

latter appointed the contractors as required. With the start of work on the Rhyd Ddu to Porthmadog section early in 2005, an engineering team was directly employed and from 2006 the senior engineer worked with the permanent way manager to run the project. The two companies mentioned operated from an office at Dinas and are subsidiaries of Ffestiniog Railway Holdings Ltd. They had the responsibility of delivering the WHR to the FR's requirements and specifications.

The relocation of the cycle track and preparation of the trackbed between Dinas and Caernarfon in 1997 was undertaken on a 'design and build' contract by John Mowlem plc, an expensive strategy to ensure that that section of railway was opened before the TWO order public inquiry started. The concept of appointing Mowlem as main contractor was found to be flawed when it was discovered that the railway could not have access to lay track at the weekends, delaying the start of track laying until June. For subsequent contracts either WHLR or WHRC acted as main contractor.

As the project gained momentum and experience, contracts were arranged so that they could be undertaken by smaller, and therefore more local, companies, enabling the local economy to benefit. These are listed in the table below. Some tasks between Dinas and Rhyd Ddu were carried out by direct labour. Generally, the system was to have the undergrowth cleared, followed by fencing and then repairs or renewals of structures. The contractors completed their involvement by laying a bed of ballast and positioning sleeper bundles ready for the track gangs. A lesson was learned following heavy rain just prior to rebuilding between Dinas and Waunfawr was that the formation could be damaged by the passage of contractors' vehicles. As a result, a layer of slate waste was installed on subsequent sections where vehicles were used. Where necessary, a geotextile membrane was installed under the ballast to prevent mud seeping into it.

Welsh Highland Railway Reconstruction 1997-2008 Contractors

Phase 1

Dinas–Caernarfon	John Mowlem plc, Cardiff (design and build)

Phase 2

Dinas-Waunfawr	Achnashean Contractors Ltd, Llandygai (fencing); Mulcair Ltd, Caernarfon (bridges and culverts); Jones Bros Ruthin (civil engineering) Co Ltd (earthworks); Symonds Group Ltd, Colwyn Bay (consulting engineers)

Phase 3 Waunfawr-Rhyd Ddu

Waunfawr–Bettws Garmon, Castell Cidwm–Glan yr Afon, Glan yr Afon– Rhyd Ddu north	WHLR Ltd (contractor); Achnasheen Contractors Ltd (fencing)

to oversee the remainder. TCL set up a supporting organisation, the WHR Society, as an unincorporated body on 7 June 1992. The society was registered as a company limited by guarantee in September 1994 and renamed Cymdeithas Rheilffordd Eryri in 2002, at the same time that it achieved charitable status. TCL continued in existence as the society's trading arm until it was dissolved in 2004. A second supporting organisation, the WHR Heritage Group, was established in 1997.

The constraints of constructing what is essentially a modern railway within the historic alignment meant that the WHR construction companies retained responsibility for designing the alignment. Consultant engineers defined the structural requirements, designed structures and adopted a project management role, overseen and administered by Welsh Highland Light Railway Ltd, from 1997 until 2005, and Welsh Highland Railway Construction Ltd from 2006 until 2009. The consultants and the construction companies analysed the tenders and the

Betws Garmon–Cae Hywel, Cae Hywel–Castell Cidwm, Glan yr Afon bridge, Rhyd Ddu station	Jones Bros (contractor); Posford Duvivier (consultant); Achnashean Contractors Ltd (fencing)

Phase 4

Rhyd Ddu–Porthmadog	NRG Engineering Services Ltd, Llanfairfechan (topographical survey); Achnasheen Contractors Ltd (clearance and fencing); Arup Rail Ltd (consultant, Bryn y Felin-Traeth Mawr); Phasey Construction, Porthmadog (Rhyd Ddu station car park, access path, Rhyd Ddu-Cae'r Gors); Posford Datrys, Caernarfon (Rhyd Ddu station completion management); William Hughes Civil Engineering Ltd, Anglesey (Cwm Cloch–Bryn y Felin); Colin Jones (Rock Engineering) Ltd, Porthmadog (rock stabilisation at Cwm Cloch, Goat Hotel and Aberglaslyn tunnels, Nantmor); D. Davies & Sons Ltd, Porthmadog (Beddgelert platform shelters); Ove Arup & Partners (consultants); Wright Landscapes (clearance and fencing near Pont Croesor); G. H. James Cyf, Trawsfynydd (Rhyd Ddu station, Cae'r Gors–Cwm Cloch, Aberglaslyn Pass–Traeth Mawr); WHR Ltd, Porthmadog (Pen y Mount-Traeth Mawr); Porthmadog Demolition (Cob Records store); Gelli Civil Engineering (ground works, FR station, Porthmadog; Carillion plc (Pen y Mount–FR station, Porthmadog).

There were many other sub-contractors, too.

After responsibility for the WHR was transferred from the OR in 1999 the county council had claimed that the FR was responsible for the cost of bridge repairs carried out since 1934. The claim foundered when the minute recording the 1934 decision to adopt the bridges was sent to an FR director. Gwynedd Council, the unitary authority that replaced Gwynedd County Council, rebuilt the Betws Garmon and Bryn y Felin overbridges in 2002 and 2008 respectively.

Construction between Waunfawr and Rhyd Ddu had barely started when the foot-and-mouth disease outbreak that started in February 2001 brought work to a halt, despite there having been no outbreaks in the locality. After an acceptable risk assessment/method statement was agreed, work resumed in mid-May. The special working practices required the use of disinfectant and disposable suits that cost over £400 a week. This section was inspected on 18 July 2003, the inspection train consisting of a diesel locomotive and a bogie wagon.

The foot-and-mouth outbreak also delayed the start to WHR(1964)'s contribution. Starting on 24 March 2003, company members, and some from WHRS, prepared the trackbed and laid 700 metres of rail from Pen y Mount to a temporary loop at Traeth Mawr, this segment being opened on 23 March 2007. During the winter of 2007/8 the loop was removed and trains operated in push-pull mode during the 2008 season. In March 2008 company members laid the track on the contractor-prepared trackbed between Pen y Mount and the trap points in advance of the NR crossing.

Taking a lesson from the past, the FR decided that the WHR's revival should be fully funded. In October 1995 the Millennium Commission had announced that it would make a £4.3 million grant towards the cost of rebuilding the railway between Caernarfon and Rhyd Ddu. The Welsh Office agreed a £735,600 grant from the European Regional Development Fund to match the commission's contribution to the Caernarfon–Dinas section. The FR's contribution for the remainder of the line to Rhyd Ddu came mostly from some generous supporters. Historic Houses Hotels and 1st Hydro, later Innogy, provided sponsorship and a track fund was set up to encourage public donations.

After the line to Rhyd Ddu was opened in 2003 the FR was faced with raising the money to complete the line in a single operation as the SNPA would not sanction another temporary terminus in the Park. Despite being encouraged to apply for a Millennium Commission top-up grant to complete the railway in 2003, the application was turned down because the commissioners found the proposals 'less attractive'. By this time there appears to have been a souring of the relationship between the FR and the commission; perhaps the controversy attaching to the railway played a part in this. After the WHR award had been made the commission's rules were modified to include a requirement to have relevant permissions in place before submitting an application. Working to budgets set in 1995, the railway had struggled to fund its contribution for the railway to Rhyd Ddu when the true cost of some of the civil engineering work became apparent. Undoubtedly some expenditure in 1997 would not have been made had some of the problems that lay ahead been foreseen. A gift of £1 million over three years from October 1999 helped enormously but some works, like the Rhyd Ddu platform, were still left incomplete. In 2004, the commission refused to transfer the budgeted cost of platform buildings at Snowdon Ranger and Rhyd Ddu and savings made on the Caernarfon facilities of £40,000 to meet construction overspends, because it would have resulted in a 'reduced project'.

When the WHR was opened between Dinas and Waunfawr on 7 August 2000 the incomplete state of the works at Waunfawr station were obvious. Paul Ingham was again the driver, with Kevin Pye as his fireman; the loco was No 143.

Top: **Dinas station building was restored with support from the Welsh Highland Railway Society, Welsh Highland Heritage and Michael Schumann. In December 2000 it was awarded one of the Ian Allan National Railway Heritage Awards. No 138 passes the building on 26 August 2001.**

Middle left: **Construction in the National Park was not allowed to start until the remedial works in the Aberglaslyn Pass had been carried out, a move that required the long tunnel to be illuminated. 10 February 2001.**

Middle right: **WHR(1964) members clearing gorse on the WHR trackbed at Pen y Mount on 14 April 2001.**

Right: **Trains crossing at Dinas on 14 September 2002. On the right, No 138's fireman is leaning out to exchange the tokens for the single line.**

During 2003/4 a £10,750,000 scheme to complete the railway to Porthmadog was devised. The Welsh Assembly Government announced that it would contribute a total of £5,000,000 of European Union Objective 1 funding and its own funds to the WHR in an event at Waunfawr on 8 September 2004. The Assembly Government was apparently impressed by the high level of private donations the WHR attracted and was to calculate that for every £1 it invested in the WHR £8 was returned to the local economy, making the WHR its most successful development project. Other research showed that by 2003 every visitor to the WHR was worth £50 to the local economy.

Having already obtained gifts of £5,100,000 the FR simultaneously launched the 'complete the WHR' appeal in *Steam Railway* magazine to raise the £650,000 shortfall over five years. Within three months the appeal had topped £1,000,000. In 2006 the 'new trains fund' was launched, attracting £300,000 by July 2007. In April 2007 many contributors extended their standing orders, adding nearly £200,000 to the fund. An appeal made to 'persons of high net worth' in October 2007 had the support of HRH the Prince of Wales who also contributed to it. By August 2008, the appeals had contributed £1,800,000 to the WHR. Construction was started in the summer of 2005.

Other sources of funding for the WHR included more than £1 million, in both labour and cash, from the WHR Society and two grants from the Wales Tourist Board, now Visit Wales, £100,000 for locomotives and carriages in October 1996, and £125,000 for carriages in August 2005. The section of trackbed built by WHR(1964) cost £116,000. Barter Books of Northumberland paid for one of the shelters at Beddgelert whilst the other was funded as a memorial.

The Dinas–Caernarfon section was opened by the mayor of Caernarfon on 13 October 1997. The inspection had taken place on 3 October, the certificate to operate had arrived on 9 October and the LRO had been made on 10 October. Over the weekend of 11/12 October a trial service had attracted over 600 passengers who paid £1 per head. Public running started on 14 October.

The service was extended to Waunfawr on 7 August 2000, somewhat later than anticipated. The line had been inspected on 21 July, when the inspector unexpectedly requested a week's ghost running before opening could take place. This was negotiated down to the equivalent of a week's running, 28 return trips over three days, commencing on 3 August. It was initially operated with a 'Planet' diesel attached to each end of a train of wagons, the two locomotives being needed because Waunfawr loop was incomplete.

Garratt No 143 became the first locomotive to steam to Waunfawr since 1937 during the evening of 5 August, when three runs hauling a short passenger test train tailed by 'Planet' *Conwy Castle*, took place. During the evening of 6 August the two final runs used the full rake of carriages running from Caernarfon.

For the first few weeks, while the loop remained incomplete, it was necessary to outstation a diesel locomotive at Waunfawr on a daily basis to shunt the carriages and release the train locomotive.

The loop became available just in time for the official opening on 15 September. On a fine day, local MP Dafydd Wigley performed the honours; in 1999 he had asked two questions in Parliament about the delay in making the TWO. The large crowd included the FR's president, Alan Pegler, who had travelled from London by train despite poor physical health. Objectors to the railway demonstrated at the station and along the lineside.

To accommodate the opening special train the loop at Dinas was used to cross trains for the first time. The invited guests travelled in the 'normal' train set while the 'ordinary' passengers rode in a train of FR vintage stock, most of which had been used on the 'old' WHR.

The interest and demand for riding on the extended railway were such that the operating season was extended from November until 2 January 2001. Passenger numbers were boosted by the several hundred residents who bought an FR/WHR railcard entitling the holder to travel at a quarter of the normal fare. Indeed, a feature of the WHR has become the high proportion of Welsh speakers travelling at weekends. The popularity of the pub next to Waunfawr station was responsible for the 2001 timetable being modified to transfer the lunchtime layover there from Caernarfon.

HRH the Prince of Wales visited the line on 30 July 2003. Although the track to Rhyd Ddu was complete, tamping was not, so a lightweight train consisting of FR heritage stock hauled by the FR's England 0-4-0STT *Prince*, named after a previous Prince of Wales, was arranged. Prince Charles joined the train at Waunfawr after meeting dignitaries, officials and volunteers. From the halt at Snowdon Ranger to Rhyd Ddu he rode on the loco, taking a turn at the regulator. Small groups of

Left: **Track laying between Waunfawr and Rhyd Ddu was started from both ends, at Waunfawr in March 2001 and at Rhyd Ddu in October 2001. On 5 May 2002, members of the Rhyd Ddu gang are using the rail movers to collect more rails at Clogwin y Gwin, with Quellyn and Mynydd Mawr as a backdrop.**

Below: **The 'Simplex' diesel locomotive, *Dolgarrog*, propels rail to the railhead near Snowdon Ranger on 19 April 1903.**

Below right: **As a prelude to opening the line to Rhyd Ddu, on 13 August 2003 the WHR was visited by HRH the Prince of Wales. He joined the train at Waunfawr and from Snowdon Ranger rode on *Prince*, with driver Tony Williams and fireman Jon Whalley, the FR's mechanical engineer, the Prince driving it for a part of the journey. He was photographed disembarking from the loco at Rhyd Ddu.**

anti-railway demonstrators waved banners at places along the line. The public opening took place on 18 August 2003.

Snowdon Ranger was not the first halt on the new WHR. After local residents petitioned, a halt was opened at Bontnewydd, between Dinas and Caernarfon, in May 1999. The halt at Plas y Nant, between Betws Garmon and Snowdon Ranger, was opened on 15 May 2005. This came about because of demand from residents of nearby Salem and the users of the Plas y Nant guest house who also raised the money to pay for it. Beddgelert forest campsite will be served by a halt called Meillionen Forest Campsite to be opened in 2009. In 2007 planning permission was obtained for a halt at Nantmor and another halt is expected to serve the RSPB's osprey observation centre at Pont Croesor.

The FR originally intended to establish a separate company to operate the WHR but the conditions attaching to the Millennium Commission grant meant that it had to take direct responsibility for it. This means that the general manager and the heads of department serve the same function on both railways. To make the link more obvious the carriage livery is the same on both lines. Suggestions that the WHR livery should be changed to distinguish the railways have, so far, not come to pass.

When the railway was operating just between Dinas and Caernarfon the six carriages obtained in 1997/8 were adequate. After the service was extended to Waunfawr the requirement for a second train for peak operation was resolved by transferring less-used stock from the FR. A policy of using smaller FR locos in expectation that they would be cheaper to run was found to be mistaken when maintenance costs increased. In 2002 and 2007/8 more carriages were built to the WHR profile. Building on the FR experience, a trolley buffet service became a successful part of WHR train operation. Two African bogie wagons adapted for use as bicycle carriers were added to the trains from Easter 2004.

A programme of regular WHR events was developed, starting with an enthusiast event first held on 19/20 September 1998 that has developed into the popular 'super power' weekend. Santa trains, complete with a Welsh-speaking Santa, first ran in 2001 and a beer festival, based at Dinas and involving local pubs accessible by train, commenced in May 2005, the latter very much a society initiative.

External recognition of the WHR has come in the form of a special postage stamp issued by Royal Mail on 1 February 2000,

Right: **The public opening of the line to Rhyd Ddu took place on 18 August 2003. The passengers enjoy the summer's day on the platform as the loco of the first train prepares to run round. Only a seven-car length of one platform edge had been completed.**

Below: **The Super Power events give the WHR a chance to show off, as demonstrated by this view of Nos 143 and 138 with a mixed train on the Fridd Isaf curves, near Rhyd Ddu, on 14 September 2003. Snowdon towers above.**

Below right: **Brian Gibbons, the Welsh Assembly Government's deputy minister with responsibility for transport, announced the WAG's £5,000,000 support for completing the WHR to Porthmadog on 8 September 2004. He was photographed, centre, with Gordon Rushton and Michael Schumann at Rhyd Ddu.**

Right: **The view from a WHR(1964) works train looking towards Traeth Mawr on 29 April 2006. Cnicht is immediately ahead, with the Moelwyns to the right.**

Below: **Rhyd Ddu station platform was extended, and a waiting shelter added, during the winter of 2005/6, the sponsors' train being the first to use it on 8 April 2006. However, a tamper failure prevented right-hand running from being introduced until 1 June 2006. The next day, No 143 entered the station, passing the waiting shelter. The water tanks were painted after the zinc galvanising had weathered.**

Bottom: **On 8 July 2006, No 143 was seen approaching Snowdon Ranger crossing with Cwellyn and Mynnedd Mawr forming the backdrop.**

part of an extensive issue to mark the Millennium, and the British Guild of Travel Writers' 'British Tourism Project of the Year' Silver Unicorn award to the railway in 2001.

Since 1997 several changes and additions were made to the operating railway in the light of experience.

1998   Caernarfon water tank commissioned; Dinas station building restored; Dinas carriage shed erected.
2001   Waunfawr water tank and footbridge commissioned.
2002   Dinas carriage shed inspection pit installed.
2004   Improved passenger facilities at Caernarfon.
2005/6 Caernarfon platform extended, Rhyd Ddu platform extended, waiting shelter erected.
2007   Dinas carriage shed extended.
2008   Facilities for emptying on-train toilets installed at Dinas.
2009   Snowdon Ranger waiting shelter installed.

Although Railtrack had withdrawn its objection to the WHR crossing its line at Porthmadog in 1997 it was still necessary to make an agreement with its successor, Network Rail, over the use and maintenance of the crossing. In 2008 it was agreed that the requirements of both parties could be met by treating the FR as a train operating company, albeit with access to a section of track 2ft wide.

Track laying between Beddgelert and Porthmadog was substantially completed on 31 August 2008, when an ad hoc

'golden' clip ceremony took place at Traeth Mawr. The FR trustees were able to travel from Beddgelert to Pont Croesor by train on 1 October. The trackwork at Porthmadog was carried out during the winter and on 28 February 2009 a formal 'golden bolt' ceremony next to the FR station marked the completion of track laying and the connection with the WHR and the FR.

With so many variables within the Rhyd Ddu-Porthmadog section, the FR decided to adopt a cautious approach to the WHR's 2009 timetable, a position which caused problems for WHR(1964) which hoped to run an ambitious service to Pont

Right: To maintain awareness of the scheme to complete the WHR and to encourage contributions to the appeal, *Palmerston* was operated between Rhyd Ddu and Cae'r Gors with goods wagons during the 2006 Super Power weekend. On 9 September it was photographed passing through Pitt's Head bridge for the first time, the first steam here since the stock recovery trains in 1938. The bridge was built by the PBSSR.

Middle: On 23 March 2007 WHR(1964) opened the line between Pen y Mount and Traeth Mawr using the company's own Bagnall 0-4-2T, *Gelert,* and the FR's *Prince,* seen at Traeth Mawr with Cnicht peeking over the top of *Gelert.*

Bottom: One of the benefits offered to appeal fund contributors was an annual inspection of the works in progress, intended to be made by road. Thanks to a sponsor who covered the expenses, this turned into a special train that travelled as close to the head of steel as possible. On 24 March 2007 the train, comprising two diesel locomotives and lightweight rolling stock because tamping was incomplete, reached the upper curves at Cwm Cloch. The track gang was working to the right, lower down.

Croesor. In January 2009 services to Beddgelert were set to start on 7 April and to Hen Hafod, historically Hafod y Llyn, from 21 May. Although the extension to Porthmadog was not expected to take place until later in the year the first rolling stock transfers from the FR to the WHR using the Porthmadog tramway were scheduled to take place in March.

To reach Porthmadog, the construction of 25 miles of 'new' railway using a mix of contractors, paid staff and volunteers in less than 12 years is unprecedented in the UK 'heritage' railway movement. It is a remarkable achievement, all the more significant considering some of the obstacles that have had to be overcome. However, the railway opened in 2009 is not exactly the railway proposed in the 1990s. For example, a fleet of 60 new carriages and enhanced passenger facilities at stations was anticipated at the planning stage. That these have not been achieved is naturally due to finance, or the lack of it. One reason, in the writer's opinion, was certainly the workings of the Millennium Commission grant, based on 1995 prices with no allowance for inflation or contingencies.

Despite these problems, the Welsh Highland Railway is like no other. It has a superb route, is well made and has sound foundations for the future. The words 'preservation' and 'heritage', as in 'preserved railway' or 'heritage railway', can only be applied to it with some difficulty. Only the route and some structures are preserved. Its historical heritage is mainly dependent on dusty documents in archives and fading memories. It is creating its own heritage.

It has taken over 100 years and the efforts of many people to achieve this dream, a narrow gauge railway between Caernarfon and Porthmadog, and the revival has been long and tortuous. The roles played by historical figures, Spooner, Russell, Aitchison, Jack, Davies et al, have long been recognised but the number of significant contributors to the revival must run to dozens if not hundreds, too many to attempt to mention by name. There are, however, a few who should be mentioned, for without them the WHR would not have been revived in its present form. Bob Honeychurch started the whole thing off in 1961. The company that he founded in 1964 might not have achieved its objectives but it did fly the flag for the WHR for many years. Michael Schumann, an FR trustee, funded the FR's representation at the 1991 court hearing, three public inquiries and an appeal, over £1 million; he was also chiefly responsible for devising the WHR's development strategy. Mike Hart is the FR director who persuaded his colleagues that the company should restore the WHR and then worked tirelessly to secure that ambition, particularly leading negotiations with the Millennium Commission, the Welsh Assembly Government and other agencies and individuals to secure funding estimated to total some £28 million. This book is a tribute to them and to all participants and contributors, known and unknown. Without them, there would be no Welsh Highland Railway.

Left: **By 26 April 2007 the rails had reached Beddgelert.**

Below: **Following gauging trials with Garratts K1 and No 143 the latter hauled a train for the FR trustees and officials travelling to Beddgelert on 3 October 2007. A brief stop was made at the Mellionen Forest campsite, where a waiting shelter is to be provided during 2009. Afterwards, the train was hauled from Beddgelert into the Aberglaslyn Pass by a diesel locomotive.**

Bottom: **Most of the WHR's Santa trains in 2007 were hauled by K1, the first Garratt, seen passing Plas Bodaden on 23 December. Next to the loco is one of the 13m-long carriages built at Boston Lodge that had entered service earlier in the year.**

Right: **Beddgelert forms the backdrop for this view of the railway between the Beddgelert cemetery crossing and Bryn y Felin on 4 May 2007. The unused PBSSR bridge abutments still stand in the field.**

Below left: **The embankment at Nantmor required complete reconstruction using a reinforced earth technique. The slate waste that formed the new embankment was being compressed on 31 July 2007. Some of the plastic-covered reinforcing is visible in front of the roller; in the foreground is the stonework of an existing culvert.**

Below right: **Track laying in the Aberglaslyn Pass, on the embankment built by the PBSSR (page 32). This was the scene on 26 August 2007.**

Left: **The view from the back of the train at the same location during a test run made in preparation for the 2008 sponsors' train on 14 March 2008.**

Below: **Returning to Beddgelert, the train crosses the Bryn y Felin bridge. The road bridge behind was rebuilt later in the year.**

Above: **An aerial sortie was made over the WHR on 7 September 2007. In this view of Rhyd Ddu the line to Beddgelert leaves the picture to the left.**

Above: **At Beddgelert: the railway enters the picture at the lower right and leaves it at the top right, having traversed the Cwm Cloch curves and the Goat Hotel tunnel. The station is slightly left of centre.**

Above: **From Gattws Bach, Ynysfor, to just short of Hafod y Llyn Farm, there is slightly more than a mile of WHR trackbed in this photograph. The old alignment at Croesor Junction still stands out behind the new.**

Above: **Before work started at Pont Croesor, the railway runs across the bottom of the picture. A part of the formation of the incomplete Beddgelert Railway enters the picture on the lower left and, crossing the road, swings up towards the Glaslyn in the upper centre.**

Snowdonia at its best. Beddgelert nestles under the mountains and the WHR, with its track recently reinstated, emerges from the Aberglaslyn Pass. 6 October 2007.

Above: **The second sponsors' train passes through Beddgelert station on 5 April 2008.**

Right: **At Hafod y Llyn shunting was carried out to get the locomotives on the right end of the train. Operationally this location will be known as Hen Hafod to avoid confusion with the FR location with the same name.**

Below: **With Cnicht covered in snow on 6 April 2008, Brian Faulkner's Lister was engaged in moving rail near Gattws Bach. A few minutes later the track gang was working in a blizzard.**

Above left: **One of the crucial components of the WHR's reinstatement has to be the connection with the FR, including the Britannia bridge crossing. With the need to keep the road open to traffic the work took four months in 2008. The first rails were in place, waiting for the concrete to be poured on 17 April.**

Above: **In Porthmadog, both the Britannia bridge and Snowdon Street crossing use tram rail. To avoid weakening the installation with bolted fishplates the rails were welded using the Thermit technique, as seen at Snowdon Street on 13 May 2008.**

Left: **The frontage of the Cob Records store, a stone building in the FR's car park, fouled the WHR loading gauge so an extension was built to compensate for demolishing it. The new frontage was nearly complete on 30 June 2006, when a cable duct was being installed outside. Brian Humphreys, the JCB driver, had worked on different contracts throughout the length of the WHR since 1997, either directly or for various contractors. His son worked on contracts in Beddgelert and Porthmadog, too.**

Below: **Upnor Castle with the works train at Pont Croesor on 5 July 2008. The volunteer gang was undertaking preparatory work for the level crossing at the far side of the bridge.**

Above: **A four-day photographic charter in October 2008 gave participants the opportunity to recreate some views from the past using the FR's England locomotives *Prince* and *Palmerston* and some vintage carriages. On 24 October *Prince* hauled the train, with *Palmerston* at the rear, towards Bryn y Felin with Snowdon, Beddgelert and the abandoned PBSSR abutments visible in the background.**

Below: **Palmerston and vintage carriages in the Aberglaslyn Pass on 24 October. The vantage point is a public footpath.**

Right: **Moel Hebog dominates this view of *Palmerston* climbing towards Cae'r Gors on 27 October. The cutting was filled in whilst the railway was abandoned; when it was excavated old timber sleepers were found in situ.**

Locomotives, Rolling Stock and Infrastructure

Locomotives

The first NWNGR locomotives were two 0-6-4T single Fairlies ordered by Roberts from the Vulcan Foundry Ltd and delivered in 1875, named *Moel Tryfan* and *Snowdon Ranger*. In July 1887, Livesey reported that they had been thoroughly overhauled, the wheels of one having been re-tyred and the firebox of the other having been re-stayed and re-tubed with brass tubes. *Moel Tryfan* and *Snowdon Ranger* were rebuilt/repaired by Davies & Metcalf in 1902 and 1903 respectively. The best parts of both were amalgamated into a single locomotive named *Moel Tryfan* in 1917 and the remaining parts scrapped.

Beddgelert was a Hunslet 0-6-4ST of traditional form delivered in July 1878. It was more powerful than the Fairlies and probably designed for working the Bryngwyn branch. For at least a part of its career, *Beddgelert* had a slightly inclined boiler, an appropriate provision for a locomotive that spent most of its time working on a nearly continuous gradient. It was very likely worn out when scrapped in 1906.

As described in Chapter 2, the NWPTC paid for the Hunslet 2-6-2T delivered to the NWNGR in 1906 and named *Russell*. At the time the order was placed the single Fairlies were probably in poor condition, despite having been recently overhauled/rebuilt, and *Beddgelert* was due to be scrapped. It is quite likely that the Fairlies were deemed incapable of handling the Bryngwyn traffic, for *Russell* was more than twice as powerful.

The use of the FR's *Palmerston* during construction of the NWNGR was described in Chapter 1. On the PBSSR contract Krauss is known to have used Bagnall 0-4-0ST *Progress*, built in 1903.

The PBSSR's electric locomotives would have been 90bhp machines capable of taking 100% overload 'for a short while'. Weighing in at 8½ tons on two axles their designed 'normal' speed was 18mph. They should have been capable, according to the PBSSR's engineers, of hauling a 20-ton train up short gradients of 1 in 20 or hauling the same load up a gradient of

1 in 43 regardless of its length. A liquid rheostat would have been used to bring the motor on line. Having a capacity of only 20 tons suggests the PBSSR intended to run a lot of short trains. In 1905 a general arrangement drawing of the locomotives was submitted to the BoT but it has not survived.

In 1908, Hunslet delivered a single Fairlie 0-6-4T to the NWNGR. It was named *Gowrie*, although not immediately, after Aitchison. It was sold to the Ministry of Munitions c1916/7, most likely because the railway was short of funds; being the newest member of the fleet it would have had more value, and was perhaps not as well liked by the loco crews despite being nominally more powerful than the Vulcan Foundry machines. It survived until c1928.

One or more Dick, Kerr 4-wheel petrol electric locomotives built for the War Department Light Railways were tested on the NWNGR in February 1917.

In 1922/3 McAlpine used a Bagnall 0-4-0ST, previously on the Dolgarrog contract, and five 20hp petrol-engined Motor Rail locomotives on the refurbishment and construction contract. They also hired *Palmerston* from the FR for a short time in 1923.

The WHR inherited *Moel Tryfan* and *Russell* in 1922. The NWNGR having been a user of air brakes and the FR a user of vacuum, there were initially problems with through working until the NWNGR stock was converted to vacuum. Similarly, there were problems with couplings, being similar in appearance but incompatible in practice.

Moel Tryfan required retubing before it could be run regularly in 1923. It was cut down to fit the FR's loading gauge later in the year and was used regularly on both railways as No 11 in the combined fleet. It cost £2 15s 6d to insure its boiler in 1923. As already stated it nearly passed to FR ownership following C. E. Davies's request to keep it in 1938. It is not known if Davies believed that *Moel Tryfan* had not worked during the lease period or was merely certain that the investing authorities would not know but there is photographic evidence of it in action during this

Delivered in 1875, the single Fairlies were ideal for the NWNGR, having a light axle-loading that suited the cheap, lightweight track. *Moel Tryfan's* driver was oiling round when the loco was photographed at Dinas. The train is without continuous brakes, so the two Cleminson brake/composite carriages are coupled next to the locomotive. *Author's collection*

Right: **Moel Tryfan at Rhyd Ddu. The air brake compressor probably accounts for the four bolts on the cabside.** *FR Archives*

Middle: **Snowdon Ranger outside the loco shed at Dinas,** *c*1902, **the paintwork looking particularly fine because the engine had not long returned from Davies & Metcalfe where it had been overhauled and a new boiler fitted.** *Author's collection*

Bottom: **The locos were delivered without cab backsheets but they were soon fitted. Pictures showing either of the locos without them are unusual. Snowdon Ranger at Rhyd Ddu.** *FR Archives*

time. In August 1936, just a few weeks before the WHR was closed, its boiler stays received attention at Boston Lodge. No work was done after 20 August and it remained in a semi-dismantled condition during the FR's closure. It was cut up at Portmadoc in 1954 but its bogie wheelsets survive under the FR Hunslet 2-4-0STTs, *Linda* and *Blanche*.

Russell became, certainly to modern eyes, the locomotive most closely associated with the WHR. Before the 1925 season commenced a poor attempt was made to reduce its stature to fit on the FR. Not only was the attempt futile but the locomotive's appearance was diminished also. During the modifications the upper part of the cab backsheet was made removable, to improve crew conditions in hot weather. Allocated the number 12, *Russell* was painted green during the lease era. The locomotive's boiler insurance had cost £3 3s 9d in 1923. In 1941 it was requisitioned and sold, in 1942 going to the Brymbo Steel Co at Hook Norton, Oxfordshire, where it remained until 1948. Then it passed to B. Fayle & Co at Purbeck, where it stayed until was withdrawn with a broken axle in 1953.

The Birmingham Locomotive Club (Industrial Locomotive Information Section), now the Industrial Railway Society, acquired *Russell* for preservation in 1953 and moved it to the Talyllyn Railway as a display item in 1955. In 1965 it was donated to WHR(1964). Restoration, including fitting a new boiler and restoring its NWNGR profile, was completed at Gelert's Farm in 1987. It visited the FR in 1988 and 1989 and in September 2001 returned to the WHR as a major attraction at the gala event that marked the re-opening of the line to Waunfawr. An overhaul was started in 2007 with the target of returning it to service in 2009.

To expand the WHR loco fleet consideration was given to re-acquiring *Gowrie*, then resident in a Darlington scrapyard, in April 1923. This opportunity was not taken up and an ex-WD First World War Baldwin 4-6-0T was obtained instead. Delivered in July 1923, its size restricted it to the WHR except for visits to Boston Lodge for maintenance or overnight lodging. Although allocated the fleet number 13 it retained its WD number, 590, painted on its tank sides. At first painted black, the FR painted it red in 1934. The Welsh enginemen never got the measure of it and it was never named, although its maker's name was treated as a name. Judging by the number of photographs in which it appears the WHR certainly made good use of it. No 590 was requisitioned in 1941 and cut up the following year.

The WHR steam fleet was augmented as required by FR locomotives. It is reported that double Fairlies worked through to Dinas in 1923 but otherwise only the England engines left the FR.

The FR's former WWI armoured 'Simplex' tractor saw use on the WHR from 1923. *Railway Gazette* reported attending a series of tests on the WHR that year, saying that the locomotive 'may be useful for miscellaneous duties or special trips, or for light goods traffic.' The journal noted a lack of familiarity on the driver's part, stating the tractor 'acquitted itself well' during a journey from Dinas to Portmadoc, via Bryngwyn. This locomotive is preserved on the FR as *Mary Ann*.

Six 'inspection trolleys' were bought by the FR in 1925/6, some of which were used on the WHR. In common with other equipment obtained at this time they probably had military origins.

The FR obtained another former military locomotive in 1925, the 1918-built Baldwin tractor, now *Moelwyn* – see page 70. Following a suggestion that it would be suitable for hauling one-coach winter trains on the WHR, it was equipped with vacuum brakes in 1928.

In July 1928 Kerr, Stuart loaned the WHR that company's first diesel locomotive for trials. This was a six-wheeled machine with a four-cylinder 60hp McLaren engine that was started by a 4hp petrol engine. The *Railway Gazette* for 23 November described a demonstration run on a part of the WHR that had taken place on 19 November. The loco hauled two WHR bogie carriages and a brake van up gradients of 1 in 40 'with ease', stopping and restarting without difficulty and, when descending the gradient, demonstrated the degree of control available. It was based on the FR between March and August 1929 and was later exported to the Union Vale sugar estate in Mauritius. It was returned to the FR for preservation and eventual restoration in 1997.

George Cohen used 40hp petrol or diesel locomotives during the demolition in 1941/2. When lifting the Croesor section in 1948/9, W. O. Williams of Harlech used a 20hp petrol-engined Motor Rail that was abandoned on-site when the work was completed.

The first motive power obtained for the revived WHR was a Funkey hydraulic diesel bogie locomotive from the Port Elizabeth Cement Co and delivered to the FR in 1993, in company with a second allocated to the FR. These South African-built locomotives have 350hp Cummins engines that had seen very little use. Delivered, they cost £5,000, plus £6,000 shipping, each. The first was overhauled at Boston Lodge and named *Castell Caernarfon* by Dafydd Wigley MP in Caernarfon in July 1996, being afterwards delivered to Dinas ready for the start of work in 1997, the first item of motive power on the new railway. It saw occasional use during the first construction phase and is used for off-peak services. From 2006 until 2008 it ran with the wheelsets of the FR's Funkey while its own gearboxes were rebuilt following a failure.

Two NGG16 2-6-2+2-6-2 Beyer, Peacock Garratts were obtained from the Alfred County Railway at a cost of £90,000 each overhauled. Numbered 138 and 143, the latter was the last Garratt built in Manchester. Their boiler units arrived at the FR's Glan y Pwll yard on 14 January 1997, their bogies going to Boston Lodge via Minffordd for attention to bearings, bushes and lubrication. Despite work carried out in South Africa both locomotives required further attention to bring them up to UK standards and to a reasonable degree of fuel efficiency. Both locomotives were converted to burn oil but the increase in oil prices is likely to see them converted back to coal.

No 138 was first steamed at Glan y Pwll in time for display at the FR's 1997 gala and transferred to Dinas just prior to the October opening. Its livery was a rich green. Great interest, from enthusiasts and public alike, was taken in the performance of No 138, used on 19 of the 21 operating days in 1997 and during most of 1998. Crews soon developed finesse with it and competed

with each other for lowest fuel consumption. No 138 was repainted in 2001, but the colour specification supplied by sponsor Edison Mission turned out to be incorrect and the locomotive was repainted again. No 138 was named *Millennium* at Waunfawr on 1 March 2002. A 10-year boiler overhaul was started in 2008.

No 143's boiler and both its bogies received attention at Ian Riley's works in Bury; it was erected at Dinas and first steamed there on 18 September 1998, retaining its SAR black livery in view of its historic significance.

A third Garratt, the red-liveried No 140, was offered to the WHR for a nominal £100 by a group of German enthusiasts; it arrived at Glan y Pwll on 7 April 1997 and was moved to Dinas in 2005. A volunteer team connected with the Wylfa nuclear power station on Anglesey works on No 140 when it is relieved from other, more urgent, tasks.

Top: **It is very likely that the Hunslet 0-6-4T *Beddgelert* spent most of its time dealing with Bryngwyn traffic, only appearing on passenger trains when the loads were heavier. At some stage it was turned to run chimney-first towards Dinas. Here, it is standing in front of *Snowdon Ranger*, c1902.** *Author's collection*

Middle: **Hunslet 2-6-2T *Russell* arrived on the NWNGR in 1906, a result of James Russell's dealings with the NWPTC, and allowed the 28-year-old *Beddgelert* to be withdrawn. The photograph was taken in 1909.**
Author's collection

Left: **Russell had been pulled out of the shed for photographs by newcomer Hunslet single Fairlie 0-6-4T *Gowrie*, seen as delivered, without nameplates.** *Author's collection*

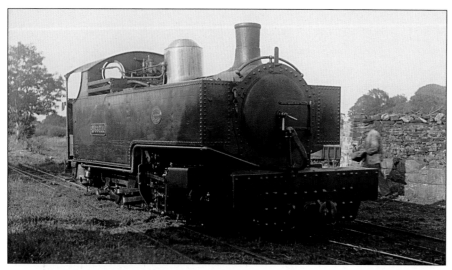

No 87 is one of the first NGG16 Garratts, built by John Cockerill in Belgium in 1936. It arrived at the FR as a fully-funded restoration project for the WHR in February 2006. It is one of five locomotives imported to the UK for a proposed railway in Yorkshire in 1998 and one of three NGG16s sold on to the Exmoor Steam Railway in Devon. Being from a different builder it has visual differences that have been retained to distinguish it from the Beyer, Peacock variety. No 87 entered service as a coal-burning locomotive in 2009.

The first Garratt built, K1, is owned by the Festiniog Railway Trust. Built in 1909 it was re-acquired by Beyer, Peacock from the Tasmanian Government Railway in 1947 and bought by the FR for £1,000 in 1966. Too large for the FR's loading gauge it was displayed at the National Railway Museum from 1979 until 1995. A dedicated team, a sub-group of the WHRS, raised the money, including the cost of a new boiler, and carried out much of the restoration. K1 was launched as an oil burner on 8 September 2006 and was then converted to burn coal at Dinas, entering service on 11 November 2007. Its protracted commissioning was due to difficulties in establishing the cause of overheating bearings. During its first season it proved to be a reliable and economical machine. On 5 September 2008 the Institution of Mechanical Engineers awarded an engineering heritage award to the loco in recognition of its historical engineering significance in a ceremony at Caernarfon.

In 1998, two un-restored South African Franco-Belge NG15 2-8-2s, Nos 133 and 134, were obtained from the promoter of the proposed Yorkshire scheme. There is a lot of interest in seeing these locomotives in action, especially as the leading driving axle is articulated, and there has been much speculation about their likely performance in reverse on the 1-in-40 gradients. Some work was carried out on No 134 at Dinas and in 2008 the WHRS announced that it would take on the locomotive's restoration as a volunteer project.

In 1997 the FR's Alco 2-6-2T *Mountaineer*, then in WD grey livery, was allocated to the WHR as a back up to No 138. On 4 October it became the first loco to steam to Caernarfon. It saw little use and was returned to the FR by the end of the year.

On 13 May 1999, the FR shipped Hunslet 2-4-0STT *Blanche* from Boston Lodge to work lighter trains; it entered service on 7 June. In March 2000 it was exchanged with *Mountaineer*, now in black livery, and which was returned to the FR in September 2001.

A self-propelled experimental flywheel-powered Parry People Mover was tried out on the WHR in 1999. The small, 20-seat vehicle was promoted as a possible solution to the railway's need for railcars if a demand for commuter or off-peak services developed. Following a number of trial trips, the first on 18 March, the vehicle was approved for WHR use on 29 October, entering service three days later. However, it suffered a catastrophic failure on 4 November and was returned to its maker's West Midlands factory.

Rolling stock

In 1874, the NWNGR obtained two bogie brake composites from the Ashbury, Carriage & Iron Co of Manchester. Three Ashbury four-wheel passenger carriages were introduced in 1877. Quarterly instalments of £161 were being made to Ashbury in 1877/8. Three Cleminson patent six-wheel vehicles were supplied by Gloucester Carriage & Wagon Co in 1878.

The Metropolitan Carriage & Wagon Co delivered two bogie carriages in 1891. In 1893/4 Ashbury supplied six more bogie carriages; two enclosed vehicles were followed by two open and two semi-open tourist cars. The 1893 acquisitions were known as 'corridor' cars because of their internal layout. The 1874 vehicles were replaced by the last two obtained by the NWNGR – Pickering brake composites delivered in 1907.

Spring recorded the existence of 13 passenger coaches and a four-wheeled van at Dinas in 1921. He said that the tourist cars had been kept under cover and were in relatively good condition having only seen light summer use. Of the remainder, some required heavy repairs and most needed repainting. The WHR livery was dark green. All the carriages had their height reduced to enable them to work on the FR. The FR charged £6 1s 1d for 'altering carriages' and paid E. R. Owen £4 19s for carriage axles, for WHR stock, in 1923.

Six Hudson vacuum-braked open toastrack coaches obtained by the FR in 1923 were used on both lines. The order was placed in June with delivery requested by 31 July. The contract price was £155 each. By 1929 four had had their bodies removed and were in use as flat wagons.

One of the 1893 'corridor' carriages was converted into a buffet car, first seeing use in this form in the 1928 season.

Above: **In 1934 the FR painted the Baldwin red, as seen here at Beddgelert in 1936.** *S. W. Baker/Welsh Highland Heritage*

Below left: **According to their annual reports the Baldwin tractor was a joint purchase by the FR and WHR in 1925 although it seems unlikely that the WHR paid the FR its contribution. The loco is seen at the flour mill siding in Portmadoc on 11 August 1936.** *W. H. Whitworth/Author's collection*

Below right: **In July 1928, the Stoke-on-Trent locomotive manufacturer Kerr, Stuart supplied its prototype diesel locomotive, No 4415, to the WHR for trials. It was photographed with the Bryngwyn goods train at Dinas. With its roof modified, it was transferred to the FR in March 1929. By 1934 it had been exported to the Union Vale sugar mill in Mauritius and was preserved there after it fell out of use. In 1997, it was acquired for restoration and eventual operation on the WHR and FR; while fund raising takes place it has been placed in store at Minffordd.** *Welsh Highland Heritage*

Right: **The use of the FR's England locomotives on the WHR is represented by this view of *Palmerston* at Tryfan Junction in 1923.** *Author's collection*

Right: **Nos 138 and 140, NGG16 class Garratts at Glan y Pwll, Ffestiniog Railway, on 2 May 1997; No 138 was in steam.**

Above: **September 19, 1998 was the first day that two Garratts were in service on the WHR. Seen at Caernarfon with their steeds, from left, are Andie Shaw, Paul Davies, Tony Williams and Rob Yates. No 143, left, the last Garratt built by Beyer, Peacock, had been steamed for the first time the day before although a few days later it was found to have a cracked superheater header.**

Left: **The first Garratt built, K1, was formally returned to service on 8 September 2006 although restrictions on workshop space at Dinas meant that it was to be 19 October 2007 before problems with overheating bearings were resolved and it entered service on a regular basis. During that period it was also converted from oil to coal firing. The location is Fridd Isaf, near Rhyd Ddu.**

Bottom: **The FR has supplied several locomotives to the WHR since its reopening. On 25 August 2002, *Prince* made a link with the past as it was seen near Gwredog Isaf with vintage carriages. Next to the loco is the Boston Lodge-built Ashbury No 24 which had entered service a few weeks previously.**

The 1934 lease identified the carriage stock thus: three summer open cars – seating capacity 56 each; one corridor coach, capacity 38; one corridor coach, capacity 20 (the buffet car); one inspection saloon coach, capacity 32 (the 'Gladstone' car); two composite carriages, with van compartment, one 1st class compartment, two 3rd class compartments each, capacity – eight 1st class passengers and 16 3rd class passengers.

At the start of the lease period the FR painted the carriages in different colours: green, blue, pink and red, allegedly to make the operation more attractive to the public. FR stock was repainted at the same time.

In 1939, Evans listed two summer opens (56 seats); one corridor (38 seats); one corridor (20 seats); one inspection

Above: **NGG16 No 87 has been rebuilt at Boston Lodge for use on the WHR. Its boiler repair, including complete renewal of its firebox backhead, has been the most complex ever undertaken by the FR. With the boiler turned on its side, the superheater header could be seen on 23 May 2008.**

Below: **Under test, No 87 reached the FR's ground signals at Porthmadog for the first time on 23 January 2009. The grey livery is temporary and due to be replaced by gloss black in due course.**

saloon (32 seats) and two composites, these vehicles being sold or scrapped at Dinas in 1942. One of the 1894-built Ashbury carriages, No 23, had already passed to FR ownership in exchange for three ex-WD bogie coal wagons in 1936. It was overhauled in 1992 and in 1993 appeared in WHR livery, complete with original iron lettering. Before it was transferred to Dinas in 2002 its livery was modified to render it more as it would have appeared in the 1920s.

Ashbury No 26 was sold to a farmer in Groeslon for use as a hen house; it was purchased by the FR in 1959 and returned to service the same year; it was rebodied in 1986. The remains of the buffet car and the restored 'Gladstone' car are in the possession of WHR(1964); the former was recovered from Waunfawr in 1987, the latter from Llanbedr in 1988. They are being restored to form a part of a heritage train. WHR(1964) has also restored Hudson toastrack No 42, the underframe of which was donated by the FR for the purpose. In 1992, Winson Engineering, then based at Penrhyndeudraeth, built a replica Hudson toastrack, No 39, for the FR by adapting a Hudson wagon chassis.

For the revived railway Winson Engineering at Daventry received the £400,000 contract for six carriages in 1997. Winson designed the stock to meet the FR's requirements. The saloons must be the most sophisticated carriages ever put into service on a UK narrow gauge railway. Features include quality timber lining, double-glazing, oil-fired heating, public address, stainless steel-body frames and axle-driven alternators. In summer the heating equipment can be operated as a forced-air ventilation system. The livery is the same as the FR's; internally the seats are covered with hardwearing moquette woven with an FR/WHR motif.

This order comprised a brake/saloon (27 seats) composite with wheelchair access, three open saloons (36 seats), an open (36 seats) and a 'Pullman'. The first five have 12-metre long bodies; the last is one metre longer. Winson also overhauled the South African wagon bogies for the passenger stock, down-rating the springing and adding bolsters and shock absorbers.

The open, No 2020, was delivered to the FR for trials in July 1997, the three saloons, Nos 2040–2, and the brake/saloon, No 2090, following directly to Dinas in October the same year. The open carriage soon proved its popularity. No 2090 can accommodate wheelchair users; its internal layout has been

altered to provide a stowage area for catering consumables; a toilet compartment was installed in 2009. Named *Bodysgallen*, the Pullman-liveried carriage was delivered in September 1998. A premium is charged for its use. The operators of Dinorwic power station, 1st Hydro, sponsored the brake/saloon and Historic Houses Hotels, operators of the Bodysgallen House Hotel near Llandudno, the Pullman. Four of the enclosed vehicles, including the Pullman, have been repainted and have received minor remedial works at Boston Lodge. From 2008 the Pullman has run on Romanian bogies.

No 2020 was returned to the FR for use in a series of gauging trials in 1998. The purpose was to establish the nature of any modifications to the FR's structure gauge that might be needed to accommodate the larger WHR stock when through-running becomes an option. The carriage failed, as expected, to pass through Garnedd Tunnel, but there were other locations where clearances were extremely tight.

Alan Keef Ltd in Herefordshire supplied two semi-open carriages based on the Winson design in 2002. Also delivered that year was a recreation of NWNGR Ashbury No 24, intended for the vintage train used as a second train set in 2002. This vehicle was built at the FR's Boston Lodge works and has the external dimensions of the original vehicle. It was funded by a sponsor with an interest in historic narrow gauge railway vehicles. In 2003 HRH Prince Charles travelled in this carriage. No 13 was returned to the FR in 2008.

Two FR carriages were added to the WHR fleet in 2003. No 100 was an observation car and No 113 a 1st/3rd composite. No 100 was withdrawn at the end of 2005 but, mounted on South African bogies, remained in use as a personnel carrier for the track gangs as No 1000. Nos 100 and 113 were usually worked with Nos 23 and 24 and one of the semi-open carriages.

Three more saloons, Nos 2043–5, were built at Boston Lodge in 2006/7 and entered service during the summer of 2007; 13m long, they have a larger vestibule at one end and increase the railway's wheelchair-carrying capacity. No 113 was returned to the FR in 2008

As an experiment, a carriage was obtained from Romania in April 2007. The body and roller-bearing bogies were modified to the FR's requirements before delivery and internal fitting out was carried out at Boston Lodge. Numbered 2060, it is taller and narrower than the rest of the fleet so it will always stand out. It was ready in 2008 but awaited completion of the through route to Dinas before being delivered. As it was found to be no cheaper than those built from scratch it will remain a one-off.

Romania was the source of some roller-bearing bogies obtained in 2006, when the supply of suitable South African bogies ran out. The first pair entered service under the Pullman car and were found to require suspension modifications.

An order was placed in 2007 for a service car (brake, buffet store and toilet), No 2010, and an observation car, No 2100. The underframes and body frames were made, as composite units, by DWJ Welding in Caernarfon. It is slightly narrower than the other stock to allow for an increase in length to 14m and increasing in the number of 1st class passengers that it can accommodate. On 12 March 2009 the Romanian carriage and the observation car were the first items of stock transferred to the WHR by rail.

A great deal of uncertainty surrounds the NWNGR wagon stock, with no contemporary lists available and the BoT returns being contradictory. In 1886 Russell said that the slate wagons had been supplied by Brown, Marshalls and the 1877/8 receivership accounts record a payment to Brown, Marshalls & Co of £160 17s 4d as the 'instalment due on 1 January on wagons.' In April 1878, Gloucester Wagon Co had been paid £7 7s 6d for wagon repairs. Spring recorded the existence of 90 slate

Top: **In 1877, the NWNGR, under the influence of its engineer, James Cleminson, obtained three carriages with his patent six-wheel flexible underframe. The maker was the Gloucester Wagon Company and the single all-third is shown.** *FR Archives*

Above: **There were two brake/second/third composites, with the brake compartment separating the classes.** *FR Archives*

Below: **Carriage No 8, which became known as the 'Gladstone' car, was built by the Metropolitan Railway Carriage & Wagon Co in Birmingham in 1891.** *FR Archives*

Bottom: **Carriage No 13 was one of two unglazed Ashburys supplied in 1894. This photograph was first published in 1896.** *FR Archives*

Top left: **Pickering No 4 was one of two brake/first/third composites obtained in 1907.** *FR Archives*

Above: **In the WHR fleet No 4 became No 8 and was photographed bearing that number at Dinas on 8 August 1935.** *H. F. Wheeler/ FR Archives*

Left: **With its roof missing, the FR's driver, Tom Davies, has no protection from the elements sitting in one of the Hudson toastrack carriages that had been used on the WHR. The location is Boston Lodge.** *FR Archives*

wagons, 12 open goods wagons, 13 coal wagons, 14 bolster wagons and 20 bolster check wagons in 1921; photographs show other vehicles that do not fit these descriptions. According to its returns, the PBSSR owned four slate wagons. Both railways' stock was transferred to the WHR in 1922.

By 1934, the FR lease identified the following goods stock: 22 2-ton slate wagons 'in fairly good running order', 20 awaiting repairs and 'about' 20 requiring rebuilding; eight coal wagons, capacity 3 tons 10 cwt, 'in fairly good running order, but bodies are in rather bad state of repair, bottoms particularly bad', and two awaiting repairs; three other open wagons of 1 ton capacity; two 2-ton covered vans; a 25ft-long carriage converted into a timber wagon, capacity up to 3 tons; two guards' vans awaiting repair; two petrol platelayers' trolleys, and two 'propelling trolleys'.

Evans's 1939 inventory was quite similar except that he omitted the slate wagons that needed rebuilding. He probably used the lease inventory as a template although there are some differences. He admitted that he did not check all the workshop tools. One of each of the trolleys was kept at Dinas and Rhyd Ddu.

For constructing the revived railway a fleet of South African bogie wagons, both drop-sides and flats, was obtained. Six high-sided 'B' wagons have been restored, two as bicycle wagons. One of the flat wagons has a tool van mounted on it and several were adapted to carry rail. A pair of bogie ballast hopper wagons was bought from South Africa in 2000. To increase capacity, a third ballast wagon was obtained from Romania in 2006, but unlike the South African variants, this vehicle can also deposit ballast in the centre of the track.

A South African goods brake van was donated to the WHR by the Sandstone Heritage Trust in 2003. After a volunteer-led overhaul it entered service on both construction trains and mixed trains and is operated during events.

The former Lodge Hill & Upnor Railway 'combination' car was converted for use as a mess car on construction trains. D. Wickham & Co of Ware built it in 1957 as a brake coach with separate compartments for officers and 'other ranks'. The Welshpool & Llanfair Light Railway obtained it in 1961, when it

was among the first carriages used on that line's re-opening in 1963. It was sold on to the South Tynedale Railway in 1988 and arrived at Dinas after a period with a contractor in November 1998. It makes an appearance as a driving trailer during gala events, when some passenger trains are worked in push-pull mode.

A four-wheel hand-braked flat wagon, formerly an ammunition truck, arrived at Dinas in 2001. The then WHLR/FR chairman Mike Hart donated it and, with his sons, converted it to a flat wagon for carrying construction equipment on isolated sections of track.

Track laying was supported by several diesel locomotives, including two ex-passenger locomotives, *Upnor Castle* and *Conway Castle*, both Hibberd 'Planets', from the FR. Other, smaller, four-wheel diesel locomotives were borrowed from various sources. They were: Hunslet *Harold*, from the FR in 1997; Motor Rail *Dolgarrog*, from Innogy in 2002/3 and 2006/8; Barclay *Taxi 2*, from WHR(1964) in 2003; and Lister 56371, from Brian Faulkner, Gloucestershire, for a few months in 2008.

A former NCB Gullick & Dobson tamping machine, of minimal proportions for use underground, was obtained from the Yorkshire Engine Company in 1997. It was used on Dinas–Caernarfon but was not so useful on the line to Waunfawr; it was sold in 2008. The FR's Matisa tamper was tried on the line to Waunfawr but could not be held on the 1-in-40 gradients. In 2002 a Matisa A05 tamper and lining machine was obtained from rail maintenance company GTRM and used on the line to Rhyd Ddu. This machine had a varied past, having worked on standard gauge and metre gauge track. Experience of these machines showed that something better was required and in 2005 a sophisticated Plasser & Theurer KMX tamper/liner was obtained from a colliery in France. It was regauged from metre gauge at Boston Lodge and moved to the WHR in July 2005. East Anglian area WHRS members adapted the ex-MOD wagon that serves as a tool carrier. Not only did it tamp the line to Porthmadog, achieving as much as 650m in one day, but it was also used to make improvements elsewhere on the WHR.

Left: **An assortment of vans, slate and coal wagons photographed at Dinas. The four-ton coal wagon on the right belonged to the FR.** *Author's collection*

Below: **All six carriages built by Winson Engineering Ltd at Daventry appear in this view of No 138 approaching Tryfan Junction on 27 August 2000. The presence of** *Castell Caernarfon* **at the end of the train indicates that Waunfawr loop was still incomplete.**

Bottom left: **On 30 June 2008, the Romanian carriage, No 2060, stood outside at Boston Lodge waiting for the WHR to be connected so that it could be taken to Dinas by rail.**

Bottom right: **The 14m-long WHR observation carriage under construction at Boston Lodge on 30 June 2008. The completed vehicle has been painted in Pullmn livery.**

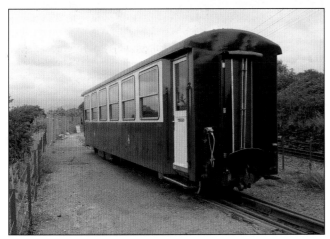

Right: **Repairs to the Plas y Nant river bridge approaching completion on 30 March 2003.**

Below: **The replacement Nantmor road bridge being craned into position on 29 October 2006.**

Infrastructure

Reinstatement of the WHR has been a major civil engineering exercise. Between Dinas and Porthmadog there are over 220 bridges and 120 level crossings and all have required attention.

Between Dinas and Rhyd Ddu the NWNGR overbridges had their foundations underpinned and floors lowered to accommodate the taller rolling stock. Of the NWNGR river bridges, that at Betws Garmon was replaced and the other two repaired and strengthened. The Glanyrafon bridge was repaired in situ and had some strengthening added. The three Warren truss river bridges near Beddgelert were demolished as unsafe in 1999 and were replaced with similar structures designed to take larger loads in 2006/7. In 2006, the railway had replaced the Nantmor road bridge with a similar structure to the original. Pont Croesor was renewed in January 2008. The new bridges were designed by a supporter, a qualified engineer. Learning from the past, he introduced a 1-in-100 gradient into the design to improve drainage and specified both zinc coating and high-quality paint for the steel.

Steel for strengthening NWNGR river bridges was prepared by a Caernarfon company, D. J. Williams & Co, the Brunswick Ironworks. The same company also manufactured the truss bridges, the Nantmor road bridge, Pont Croesor and steelwork required for other structures.

The WHR now has two overbridges that did not exist historically, at Portreuddyn, and has lost one, at Cae Hen, demolished by the landowner and not replaced. The Portreuddyn bridges are mitigation measures introduced for agricultural access purposes. They have been formed of Armco tubes, bringing 21st century design to the WHR's 19th and 20th century structures. The NWNGR arch at Gwredog Isaf was lost when it was re-decked to improve a farmer's access as a mitigation measure; its replacement has become known, not without reason, as 'the ugly bridge'. The bridge at Bryn Gloch caravan park, Betws Garmon, was replaced completely, also as a mitigation measure, with a new bridge designed to accommodate the movement of caravans over it.

Three road bridges over the railway have required attention by the highway authority. At Rhostryfan Road, between Dinas and Tryfan Junction, only the parapets required replacing. At Betws Garmon the bridge was completely rebuilt and the road alignment was improved in 2002. The original bridge contained iron beams cast at the de Winton works in Caernarfon and one of these was retained as a decorative feature. The Bryn y Felin road bridge, near Beddgelert, was rebuilt on the existing alignment in 2008.

Some sites required imaginative solutions. At Cae Moel, where an overbridge crossed both the railway and a stream, diversion of the stream facilitated underpinning the structure and lowering its floor. At Nantmor, where an embankment was substandard as regards both construction and dimensions, the site was cleared to rock and rebuilt using a reinforced earth technique.

To deal with the crossings in Porthmadog, the contract was awarded to a company with streetworks and Network Rail (NR) experience, Carillion plc. It extended from Pen y Mount to the FR station and included the NR crossing, two tramway-type road crossings, underground bridges over a sewer, the modification of the Britannia bridge and, for the Welsh Assembly Government's Highways Agency, the repair of a landslip near the bridge. Work started under Porthmadog-based supervision in August 2007. An unexpected consequence of the Carillion appointment was that the foreman was the man who had occupied the same position for Mowlem at Dinas in 1997.

The numerous culverts were dealt with by means of reinforced concrete with many parapets, abutments and headwalls faced with stone. Securing adequate drainage was a big issue, with some locations requiring substantial structures to withstand anticipated flows.

At a number of sites utilities installed during the closure have been relocated, significantly water mains at Betws Garmon and in the Aberglaslyn Pass and electrical supply line at Betws Garmon and near Cae'r Gors. It may not be unconnected that considerable lengths of roadside walling have been repaired between Betws Garmon and Beddgelert since the railway development started.

Some 50 miles of fencing was required, mostly post and wire with some variation to suit the neighbouring landowners' requirements. At Beddgelert and in the Aberglaslyn Pass traditional fencing was installed.

The NWNGR was originally laid with 35lb flat bottom rail in 24ft lengths, spiked to sleepers. On 2 March 1882 the company reported that 'the charge for maintenance of the permanent way has been abnormally low and as parts of the line where the gradients are the most severe and the traffic the heaviest require renewal ... £100 has been reserved for the purchase of steel rails ...' For the financial year expenditure on permanent way materials increased to £197 2s 4d, suggesting that the renewals were started straight away. In September 1886 the railway bought 95 tons of steel rail and 2½ tons of fishplates at a cost of £397 7s 11d. The rail was in 30ft lengths, weighing 41½lb per yard. In the first half of 1887, 30 tons of rail and 2,000 sleepers were laid, completing three miles of renewals.

The Croesor Tramway mainly used 15ft lengths of 20lb rail laid in cast-iron chairs. At some stage the main line, at least, was relaid with the 'old' 41lb rail that Mount saw in 1923.

For the reconstructed WHR the first supplies of track materials had been previously used on the South African Donnybrook Railway, a 2ft gauge line that had been re-laid with new materials just before it was closed due to a landslip; delivery to Dinas began in September 1996. The rail was 30kg/m (60lb) flat-bottom material in 18m lengths, laid on termite-proof steel

sleepers. In 2001, new rail of the same section was obtained, also from South Africa, it having been calculated that the additional cost of new material was offset by the reduced handling required during tracklaying. New rail was obtained from Poland for the Rhyd Ddu–Porthmadog section in 2006.

The 18-metre (approx) lengths of rail were laid on steel sleepers except under the NWNGR section bridges, where check rails and timber sleepers were used. For Dinas–Caernarfon 80 lengths were supplied in panels. The remainder of the first order was not shipped in matching pairs as requested, requiring four days of preparatory sorting for each day's track laying. Experience probably accounted for the reduced preparatory time spent when the same rail was used between Dinas and Waunfawr. The fixings were used in different combinations to allow for gauge widening on curves. These needed considerable sorting: each sleeper needs one of each of four different types of clip; bolts were both metric and imperial and supplied in two different sizes. Most of the Polish rail has been laid with steel sleepers obtained from India and fixed with steel spring clips. Between Rhyd Ddu and Porthmadog several sites, including Beddgelert station, have seen the use of timber sleepers, where the rail is laid on baseplates, most of them specially cast.

To strengthen the track on what is expected to be a difficult section to operate, heavier fishplates were installed on the sharper curves between Beddgelert and Rhyd Ddu during the winter of 2008/2009..

For the crossings of the A487, the Britannia Bridge, and Snowdon Street in Porthmadog, grooved tramrail, obtained from Austria, was Thermit-welded together in continuous lengths, fitted with a flexible boot and laid in reinforced

Left: **The Afon Dylif bridge was installed on 1 February 2007.**

Below left: **Advantage was taken of a pre-arranged possession to install the Network Rail crossing, the largest component being positioned on 1 November 2006.**

Below: **Another 18m towards Caernarfon. The track gantry in action at Hendy crossing on 25 August 1997.**

Above: 'Planet' diesel locomotive *Upnor Castle* in the engineers' siding at Rhyd Ddu during 2006. Behind the locomotive are two South African ballast hopper wagons and the South African brake van which is used in construction trains. The Matisa A05 tamper is in the background.

Middle: The KMX tamper at Rhyd Ddu on 18 July 2006, shortly after it had been regauged at Boston Lodge.

Bottom: An assortment of works stock at Beddgelert on 9 September 2007. Behind the South African ballast wagons is the Romanian wagon with centre and side dropping facility. With *Conwy Castle* is another South African wagon and the bogie tool van, adapted from an ex-MoD vehicle.

concrete. Some of the rail, coded Ri52-13, was delivered pre-curved, requiring very little manipulation on-site. The boot allows a small amount of flexibility in the installation. Special closure rails were made to effect the transition between the tram rail and the plain rail.

The Network Rail crossing was installed on 1 November 2006. Manufactured by Corus, the crossing is made of 113lb rail with 30ft 80lb transition sections to connect to the WHR's 60lb rail. Trap points have been located on the WHR either side of the crossing. In operation, the crossing will be supervised by a WHR crossing keeper house in a replica of the Cambrian Railways crossing box provided by the WHR Heritage Group.

Most track laying was done by hand. A pair of un-powered rail movers, capable of moving a pair of rails with the minimum of effort, was designed and built at Dinas and successfully employed in 1997; more were built for further extensions. To deal with the track panels a track-laying machine was commissioned from Winson Engineering. Certified as a crane and equipped with an air-powered lifting gantry, it needed a certain amount of tweaking before the gang got the measure of it. When employed between Pant Farm and Coed Helen it probably attracted more interest from local observers than any other activity. The machine was dismantled in 2006.

Between Dinas and Caernarfon track laying was carried out by a mix of paid staff and volunteers. Subsequently all track laying, including its supervision, was undertaken by volunteers. From Rhyd Ddu two gangs were established, working alternate weekends and developing a friendly rivalry to set records or to achieve particular landmarks. There was also a Tuesday gang and several week-long sessions. Volunteers were not restricted to WHRS members, the male sex or the young. Some had worked on the FR's deviation, some were from other railways, from overseas, Some team-building programmes and some were in their 70s, all incentivised by the idea of being a part of the WHR's reinstatement.

Taking advantage of the South African vacuum-braked bogie wagons all works trains have continuous brakes, this practice relieving the railway of the need to install trap points except for one at Beddgelert.

Train crossing at Dinas was made possible by the installation of train-operated trail-able point operators, brought into use simultaneously with the opening to Waunfawr. One had been on trial at the Waunfawr end of Dinas loop for about 18 months previously. Similar devices are used on national railways but Mike Hart devised and built the first WHR versions with modifications to suit 2ft gauge use. A weight holds the point shut, while a specially designed hydraulic damper allows the blades to shut slowly when a train trails through. An electric switch detects when the blades are shut, lighting a detector lamp visible to drivers of trains approaching in the facing direction. Similar mechanisms have been installed at Waunfawr, Rhyd Ddu and Beddgelert. The latter was the first location to have its signalling installed before opening.

The standard length for WHR station platforms is 200 metres, to accommodate trains of up to 15 carriages. Except for Dinas, the intermediate stations have island platforms. Halt platforms are 30 metres long.

The layout at Caernarfon is considered to be temporary until development plans for the locality are finalised. The platform was designed for six-car trains but by 2005 this had become an operating bottleneck and the track was realigned to allow the platform to be extended, a development that did away with the separate siding that served the water tower. Portable buildings accommodate the station facilities. It is anticipated that the station will eventually need two 200m long platforms and an engine release road.

The platforms at Dinas are located on the site of the former standard gauge station to take advantage of the extra clearance available under the former standard gauge road bridge. Two parallel storage sidings alongside the platforms could become bay platform roads if a demand for a Caernarfon shuttle service develops. The goods shed was made weatherproof and has been used for loco storage, maintenance and displays and stalls during events. A locomotive display shed is proposed for the site.

The south yard at Dinas, which includes the former NWNGR site, extended while owned by the rivers authority, had come into Environment Agency ownership. An existing shed, on the site of the NWNGR carriage shed, has been extended and furnished with a pit and wheel drop. Used as a running shed, it can accommodate two Garratts. Another shed, located on the site of the NWNGR loco shed, has been equipped as a workshop.

Waunfawr platform contains the foundations for a station building, to be a larger version of the original if demand requires it. The footbridge is a steel structure, timber clad to give the appearance of a traditional railway structure that links the platform to a car park and a camp site. A water tower is located at the Porthmadog end of the station.

The rock removed to create Rhyd Ddu station was used to widen the formation at Plas y Nant, the extra land needed having been purchased in 1997. Rhyd Ddu has an island platform, a waiting shelter, water towers to serve locos travelling in either direction and an engineer's siding. As at Waunfawr, provision has been made for a station building. A waiting shelter was installed in 2006.

Beddgelert has a loop and a siding that is partially aligned with the 1923 inspection pit. A trap point allows trains from Porthmadog to terminate here. The platform is designed as a promenade so that visitors can enjoy the surrounding scenery and has two waiting shelters. A new water tower serves both platforms and provision has been made for a building.

The last site to receive attention will be the Cob, with widening required to accommodate the WHR at the FR's Porthmadog station. In December 2004 the area was included in the Lleyn & Sarnau Special Area of Conservation under the terms of the EC Habitats Directive and required a marine construction licence, and a fresh environmental statement, before work could be started. The licence was not issued until 20 February 2008 so the work is expected to be carried out over the winter of 2009-10. During 2009 WHR trains will be shunted at the FR station to allow the loco to run round.

The FR is responsible for running the trains, and many of the operating volunteers, engine crew and guards perform the same functions on that railway. The FR Rulebook has a WHR appendix and WHR references appear in the FR's weekly notices. Caernarfon–Dinas is operated using one train working (OTW) previously known as one engine-in-steam. Dinas-Waunfawr was OTW until 2003; both it and Waunfawr–Rhyd Ddu are now worked as staff-and-ticket sections. Beddgelert-Porthmadog operations will be started as a single staff-and-ticket section. At Dinas a shunt token is used when movements are required between the loco depot and the remainder of the site, and vice versa. In 2009 trains can cross at Dinas, Waunfawr, Rhyd Ddu and Beddgelert. In the future, loops could be installed at Plas y Nant, then Hafod and Pont Croesar. A supply of electric train staff machines sufficient to meet the WHR's requirements was obtained from Ireland in 2008.

Appendix 1

Tonnage of slate carried by the North Wales Narrow Gauge Railways 1883-84

Quarry	Year	To Carnarvon Quay (t cwt)	Inland by rail (t cwt)	Year	To Carnarvon Quay (t cwt)	Inland by rail (t cwt)
Alexander Slate Co	1883	2,324 3	3,404 6	1884	1,919 17	2,094 5
Braich	1883	1,022 13	1,456 17	1884	1,059 14	1,533 9
Brynyfferan	1883	41 6	9 15	1884	231 9	32 0
Moel Tryfan Slate & Slab Co	1883	838 3	1,105 5	1884	1,187 6	1,322 3
Vron Slate Co	1883	407 0	615 2	1884	1,069 5	590 19
Bronyfod Slate Co	1883			1884	34 9	60 17
Glanrafon	1883	721 7	694 1	1884	1,383 5	631 18
Bwllchynddenlior Slate Co	1883	11 9		1884		30 15
Hafod y [Wern?] Slate Co	1883			1884	124 8	
Clogwyn y Gwyn	1883	82 11		1884		
Plas y Nant	1883		76 11	1884		
Bettws Garmon	1883	55 17	71 1	1884		
Total		**5,504 9**	**6,432 18**		**7,009 13**	**6,296 3**

Data presented to Parliament June 1885

Appendix 2

North Wales Narrow Gauge Railways Revenue 1877-1918

	1877	1878	1879	1880	1881	1882	1883	1884	1885	1886	1887
Passenger train traffic	£495	£1,250	£759	£1,048	£1,037	£1,001	£967	£1,138	£1,210	£1,157	£1,280
Goods train traffic	£1,277	£2,537	£1,899	£2,437	£2,602	£2,752	£3,049	£3,166	£3,340	£3,381	£3,876
Revenue expenditure	£1,273	£2,688	£3,792	£3,029	£2,676	£2,584	£2,838	£2,811	£2,973	£2,931	£3,410
Net receipts	£4	-£151	-£1,893	-£592	-£74	£168	£211	£355	£367	£450	£466
Ratio expenditure/receipts	100%	104%	200%	124%	103%	94%	93%	89%	89%	87%	88%

	1888	1889	1890	1891	1892	1893	1894	1895	1896	1897
Passenger train traffic	£1,354	£1,387	£1,461	£1,358	£1,589	£2,317	£2,374	£2,537	£2,452	£2,164
Good train traffic	£3,499	£3,561	£3,521	£3,374	£3,497	£4,232	£4,410	£4,785	£4,991	£4,781
Revenue Expenditure	£3,029	£3,111	£3,097	£3,095	£3,147	£3,730	£3,955	£4,283	£4,287	£4,106
Net receipts	£470	£450	£427	£279	£348	£502	£455	£502	£704	£616
Ratio expenditure/receipts	87%	87%	88%	92%	90%	88%	90%	90%	86%	87%

	1898	1899	1900	1901	1902	1903	1904	1905	1906	1907
Passenger train traffic	£1,983	£1,732	£1,583	£1,530	£1,327	£1,098	£1,291	£1,303	£1,188	£1,216
Good train traffic	£4,599	£4,231	£3,955	£3,825	£4,027	£3,390	£3,625	£3,763	£3,549	£3,792
Revenue Expenditure	£3,628	£3,332	£3,369	£3,262	£3,457	£2,971	£2,925	£3,280	£3,017	£3,257
Net receipts	£971	£899	£586	£563	£570	£419	£700	£483	£532	£535
Ratio expenditure/receipts	79%	79%	85%	85%	86%	88%	81%	87%	85%	86%

	1908	1909	1910	1911	1912	1913	1914	1915	1916	1917	1918
Passenger train traffic	£1,348	£983	£923	£919	£582	£649	£336	£234	£104	£11	
Good train traffic	£3,683	£3,335	£2,862	£2,687	£2,415	£2,189	£1,184	£1,316	£1,862	£1,630	£2,148
Revenue Expenditure	£3,217	£3,158	£2,872	£2,852	£2,195	£2,394	£2,052	£1,948	£2,041	£1,827	£2,388
Net receipts	£466	£177	-£10	-£165	£220	-£205	-£868	-£632	-£179	-£197	-£240
Ratio expenditure/receipts	87%	95%			91%						

Appendix 3

North Wales Narrow Gauge Railways Traffic 1877-1915

	1877	1878	1879	1880	1881	1882	1883	1884	1885	1886	1887
Passengers carried											
First class	359	598	540	531	462	496	433	409	431	362	282
Second class		1,712	435	848	953	1,204	1,073	1,076	1,012	1,139	719
Third class	18,518	47,294	26,905	31,859	30,042	29,074	29,210	32,266	32,577	33,114	33,944
Total	**18,877**	**49,604**	**27,880**	**33,238**	**31,457**	**30,774**	**30,716**	**33,751**	**34,020**	**34,615**	**34,945**
Season tickets	1		2	20	23	9	47	71	102	101	152
Goods, mineral and livestock traffic											
Merchandise	304	809	504	611	698	1,054	647	720	594	670	1,118
Coal, coke and patent fuel											
Minerals	5,416	9,736	8,707	10,809	13,306	13,847	15,598	16,573	17,544	18,803	21,752
Train miles											
Passenger	9,388										
Goods	953										
Mixed		27,118	23,479	27,953	28,341	31,405	28,621	31,456	31,703	31,102	30,912
Total	**10,341**										

	1888	1889	1890	1891	1892	1893	1894	1895	1896	1897	1898
Passengers carried											
First class	325	385	400	331	473	643	642	699	726	716	659
Second class	810	877	911	554	515	415					
Third class	34,501	37,752	36,362	27,606	38,550	54,162	51,305	55,072	52,069	49,700	45,626
Total	**35,636**	**39,014**	**37,673**	**28,491**	**39,558**	**55,220**	**51,947**	**55,771**	**52,795**	**50,425**	**46,285**
Season tickets	193	190	214	198	220	328	351	331	362	312	309
Goods, mineral and livestock traffic											
Merchandise	1,053	973	739	726	842	756	1,087	1,352	1,271	1,363	1,448
Coal, coke and patent fuel											
Minerals	17,597	17,763	17,179	15,677	16,112	17,055	17,093	18,210	21,626	23,057	23,020
Train miles											
Passenger											
Goods											
Mixed	30,685	30,697	30,466	30,573	30,747	31,645	33,206	32,637		32,228	30,636
Total											

	1899	1900	1901	1902	1903	1904	1905	1906	1907	1908
Passengers carried										
First class	494	572	585	660	491	582	805	489	497	347
Second class										
Third class	53,688	35,878	37,917	37,891	37,233	42,853	51,451	48,713	44,141	41,394
Total	**54,182**	**36,450**	**38,502**	**38,551**	**37,724**	**43,435**	**52,256**	**49,202**	**44,638**	**41,741**
Season tickets	285	263	417	7	15	9	8	8	24	25
Goods, mineral and livestock traffic										
Merchandise	1,328	1,169	1,168	1,160	1,060	1,873	1,754	885	799	532
Coal, coke and patent fuel										
Minerals	21,791	20,519	20,436	25,234	20,328	17,950	18,030	18,126	18,235	17,724

continued overleaf

	1899	1900	1901	1902	1903	1904	1905	1906	1907	1908
Train miles										
Passenger										
Goods										
Mixed	32,714	31,363	29,314	28,631	27,569	28,011	31,632	28,798	30,072	31,565
Total										

	1909	1910	1911	1912	1913	1914	1915
Passengers carried							
First class	343	245	285	174	226		
Second class							
Third class	43,632	40,549	40,351	23,419	23,309		
Total	**43,975**	**40,794**	**40,636**	**23,593**	**23,625**		
Season tickets	3	1	1	1	2		
Goods, mineral and livestock traffic							
Merchandise	553	535	797	827	1,784		
Coal, coke and patent fuel				4,353			
Minerals	18,253	16,915	14,364	14,422	7,017		
Train miles							
Passenger							
Goods							
Mixed	31,907	27,423	27,471	18,516	19,800	17,026	13,805
Total							

Appendix 4

Croesor & Portmadoc Railway Traffic and Receipts 1904-19

	1904	1905	1906	1907	1908	1909	1910	1911	1912	1913	1919	1920	1921
Goods traffic													
Merchandise (tons)	698	311	308		259	530	314	359	230	244	906	161	256
Minerals (tons)	9,035	8,005	6,553	7,195	7,299	7,841	7,290	7,637	7,112	6,287		1,510	1,730
Goods, mineral and livestock traffic (miles)						2,772	2,772	2,772	2,772	2,772	2,772	1,173	1,311
Revenue receipts													
Merchandise	£50	£39	£116		£204	£157	£109	£122	£112	£22			
Minerals	£455	£382	£377	£497	£369	£376	£358	£378	£346	£304			
Total goods train receipts	**£505**	**£421**	**£493**		**£573**	**£533**	**£467**	**£500**	**£458**	**£326**			
Miscellaneous	£208	£141	£34	£29	£34	£100	£59	£68	£65	£189			
Total gross receipts	**£713**	**£562**	**£527**	**£526**	**£607**	**£633**	**£526**	**£568**	**£523**	**£515**			
Revenue expenditure													
Maintenance of way and works	£83	£64	£78	£69	£60	£63	£62	£72	£51	£56			
Cost of horse power	£242	£203	£172	£176	£185	£195	£181	£191	£175	£154			
Maintenance of wagons	£10	£10	£11	£10	£10	£9	£13			£3			
Traffic expenses	£73	£71	£60	£60	£51	£53	£55	£56	£52	£52			
General charges	£209	£251	£256	£253	£256	£182	£37	£20	£18	£78			
Rates	£15	£30	£26	£22	£26	£24	£24	£24	£42	£86			
Compensation paid to employees				£2	£3		£1	£1	£1				
Miscellaneous		£29							£1				
Total expenditure	**£632**	**£658**	**£603**	**£592**	**£591**	**£526**	**£373**	**£364**	**£340**	**£429**			
Total receipts	**£713**	**£562**	**£527**	**£526**	**£607**	**£633**	**£526**	**£568**	**£523**	**£515**			
Net receipts	**£81**	**-£96**	**-£76**	**-£66**	**£16**	**£107**	**£153**	**£204**	**£183**	**£86**			
Ratio expenditure/receipts	89%				97%	83%	71%	64%	65%				
Rolling stock													
Wagons		4	4	4	4	4	4	4	4	4			

Appendix 5

Welsh Highland Railway Traffic and Receipts 1922-33

	1922	1923	1924	1925	1926	1927
Revenue expenditure						
Maintenance of way and works	£496	£1,180	£1,618	£1,045	£936	£1,498
Maintenance of rolling stock	£133	£139	£55	£13	£64	£26
Maintenance of wagons	£221	£218	£128	£21	£28	£94
Locomotive maintenance	£157	£367	£135	£119	£121	£172
Loco running expenses	£973	£2,483	£2,879	£1,636	£1,200	£1,367
Traffic expenses	£1,734	£1,795	£1,737	£1,661	£1,779	£1,778
General charges	£763	£1,222	£1,306	£1,026	£309	£879
Parliamentary and legal expenses				£51	£107	£1,395
Compensation – passengers						
Ditto – workmen			£43	£42	£38	
Damage and loss of goods, property &c			£47	£32		£82
Rates	£191	£185	£193	£119	£110	£131
Railway freight rebates fund – rate relief						
National insurance – health, pensions	£63	£66	£65	£54	£51	£52
Ditto – unemployment						
Total traffic expenditure	**£4,616**	**£7,650**	**£8,206**	**£5,819**	**£4,743**	**£7,474**
Revenue receipts						
Passengers						
First class	£1	£45	£23	£9	£11	£9
Third class	£227	£2,417	£1,891	£1,076	£550	£610
Total	**£228**	**£2,462**	**£1,914**	**£1,085**	**£561**	**£619**
Third class				£4	£7	£3
Total				£4	£7	£3
Total receipts from passengers	**£228**	**£2,462**	**£1,914**	**£1,089**	**£568**	**£622**
Parcels under 2cwt and excess luggage	£19	£46	£96	£49	£48	£63
Other merchandise by passenger trains		£9	£4	£1		£1
Mails and parcel post						
Total passenger train receipts	**£475**	**£2,517**	**£2,014**	**£1,139**	**£616**	**£686**
Goods train traffic						
Merchandise	£427	£386	£328	£278	£234	£314
Minerals	£2,233	£2,074	£2,427	£2,631	£2,395	£2,286
Coal, coke and patent fuel	£984	£962	£1,072	£1,020	£708	£879
Total goods train receipts	£3,644	£3,422	£3,827	£3,929	£3,337	£3,479
Total traffic receipts	£3,890	£5,939	£5,841	£5,068	£3,953	£4,165
Miscellaneous	£127	£138	£34	£9	£3	£5
Total	**£4,017**	**£6,077**	**£5,875**	**£5,077**	**£3,956**	**£4,170**
Net receipts	-£599	-£1,573	-£2,331	-£742	-£787	-£3,304
Rents from land and houses	£79	£89	£72	£63	£66	£61
Transfer fees	£1					
General interest (net)				£4	£25	£25
Total net income	**-£519**	**-£1,484**	**-£2,259**	**-£675**	**-£696**	**-£3,218**
Balance brought forward		-£571	-£2,055	-£8,493	-£13,443	-£18,437
Chief rents, wayleaves etc	£52		£53	£36	£59	£50
General interest			£37			
Interest and dividends			£4,089	£4,239	£4,239	£4,239
Balance carried forward	-£571	-£2,055	-£8,493	-£13,443	-£18,437	-£25,944
Liabilities						
Capital account (credit)			£4,782	£4,570	£4,442	£3,738
Amount due to bankers, temporary loans	£4,000	£4,000				
Unpaid interest and dividends and Interest and dividends payable	£270	£2,497	£4,092	£8,330	£12,569	£16,808
Amounts due to railway companies and RCHS			£818	£1,212	£1,312	£1,616
Accounts payable	£3,383	£4,419	£2,452	£2,535	£2,554	£5,868
Liabilities accrued	£1,364	£1,708	£646	£1,361	£1,247	£1,673
Miscellaneous accounts						£28
Balance available for dividends and general reserve		-£2,055	-£8,494	-£13,443	-£18,437	-£25,944
Total	**£9,017**	**£10,569**	**£4,296**	**£4,565**	**£3,687**	**£3,787**

	1922	1923	1924	1925	1926	1927
Mileage run by engines						
Coaching Steam locomotives	8,245	36,329	44,241	19,845	8,001	8,069
Freight Steam locomotives	6,484	3,589	4,987	5,561	10,375	14,520
Total coaching and freight Steam locomotives	**14,729**	**39,918**	**49,408**	**25,406**	**18,376**	**22,589**
Shunting FreightSteam locomotives	2,121	2,748	6,138	5,900	3,498	4,224
Total engine miles Steam locomotives	**16,850**	**46,666**	**55,546**	**31,306**	**21,874**	**26,813**
Passengers carried						
Carried Ordinary						
First class	24	562	337	112	101	84
Third class	4,959	57,641	50,148	24,541	12,803	12,933
Total exclusive of season ticket holders	**4,983**	**58,203**	**50,485**	**24,653**	**12,904**	**13,017**
Originating Ordinary						
First class		524	285	66	66	47
Third class	633	46,623	36,370	18,028	8,991	8,368
Total exclusive of season ticket holders	**633**	**47,147**	**36,655**	**18,094**	**9,057**	**8,415**
Goods, mineral and livestock traffic						
Conveyed						
Merchandise	1,442	2,513	2,453	705	565	762
Minerals	10,068	10,761	12,601	13,462	12,660	11,741
Coal	4,252	3,903	4,694	4,548	3,067	3,897
Total	**15,762**	**17,177**	**19,748**	**18,715**	**16,292**	**16,400**
Originating						
Merchandise		478	420	247	227	282
Minerals		10,761	12,601	13,462	12,646	11,712
Coal					9	119
Total		**11,239**	**13,021**	**13,709**	**12,882**	**12,113**

	1928	1929	1930	1931	1932	1933
Revenue expenditure						
Maintenance of way and works	£801	£472	£375	£254	£164	
Maintenance of rolling stock	£229	£26	£103	£190	£78	
Maintenance of wagons						
Locomotive maintenance						
Loco running expenses	£606	£509	£324	£267	£270	
Traffic expenses	£1,415	£1,133	£870	£419	£218	
General charges	£184	£220	£254	£273	£135	
Parliamentary and legal expenses	£54	£10	£82	£56	£10	
Compensation – passengers	£2					
Ditto – workmen	£17		£3	£2		
Damage and loss of goods, property &c	£45	£65	£43	£35	£53	
Rates	£165	£25	£35	£23	£26	
Railway freight rebates fund – rate relief		£5	£83	£36		
National insurance – health, pensions	£24	£18	£18	£15	£13	
Ditto – unemployment	£20	£15	£12	£13	£12	
Total traffic expenditure	**£3,562**	**£2,500**	**£2,202**	**£1,583**	**£979**	
Revenue receipts						
Passengers						
First class	£4	£4		£1	£1	
Third class	£427	£392	£58	£212	£253	
Total	**£431**	**£396**	**£58**	**£213**	**£254**	
Third class						
Total						
Total receipts from passengers	**£431**	**£396**	**£58**	**£213**	**£254**	
Parcels and other merchandise						
Parcels under 2cwt and excess luggage	£50	£15	£38	£28	£28	
Other merchandise by passenger trains	£1	£5	£14	£11	£12	
Mails and parcel post		£18	-£4	£5	£2	
Total passenger train receipts	**£482**	**£434**	**£106**	**£257**	**£296**	

	1928	1929	1930	1931	1932	1933
Goods train traffic						
Merchandise	£193	£152	£121	£95	£70	
Minerals	£1,830	£1,350	£1,050	£234	£126	
Coal, coke and patent fuel	£707	£504	£433	£231	£197	
Total goods train receipts	**£2,730**	**£2,006**	**£1,604**	**£560**	**£393**	
Total traffic receipts	**£3,212**	**£2,440**	**£1,710**	**£773**	**£688**	
Miscellaneous	£11	£8	£18	£24	£12	
Total	**£3,223**	**£2,448**	**£1,728**	**£797**	**£701**	
Net revenue and appropriation						
Net receipts	-£339	-£52	-£474	-£742	-£278	
Rents from land and houses	£69	£61	£54	£44	£43	
Transfer fees						
General interest (net)	£25	£25	£25	£20	£24	
Total net income	-£245	£34	-£395	-£678	-£211	
Balance brought forward	-£22,436	-£22,741	-£22,757	-£23,204	-£23,938	
Chief rents, wayleaves etc	£60	£50	£52	£55	£51	
General interest					-£263	
Interest and dividends						
Balance carried forward	-£22,741	-£22,757	-£23,204	-£23,938	-£24,150	
Liabilities						
Capital account (credit)	£3,676	£1,751	£1,751	£1,751	£1,754	
Amount due to bankers, temporary loans				£250		
Unpaid interest and dividends and Interest and dividends payable	£13,300	£13,300	£13,300	£13,300	£13,300	
Amounts due to railway companies and RCHS	£2,052	£1,381	£1,425	£1,526	£1,783	
Accounts payable	£6,098	£5,845	£81	£5,974	£6,094	
Liabilities accrued	£1,760	£1,831	£2,054	£2,271	£2,911	
Miscellaneous accounts				£17	£28	
Balance available for dividends and general reserve	-£22,742	-£22,758	-£23,205	-£25,089	-£25,871	
Total	**£4,144**	**£1,350**	**£1,281**	**£1,152**	**£1,152**	
Mileage run by engines						
Coaching Steam locomotives	6,345	3,322	1,473	2,410	1,890	
Freight Steam locomotives	6,344	5,231	5,253	3,238	2,450	
Total coaching and freight Steam locomotives	**12,689**	**8,553**	**6,726**	**5,648**	**4,340**	
Shunting Freight Steam locomotives	2,885	2,274	1,663	806	800	
Total engine miles Steam locomotives	**15,574**	**10,827**	**8,389**	**5,454**	**5,140**	
Passengers carried						
Carried Ordinary						
First class	23	27		7	3	
Third class	7,404	5,069	1,343	2,459	4,324	6,445
Total exclusive of season ticket holders	**7,427**	**5,096**	**1,343**	**2,466**	**4,327**	
Originating Ordinary						
First class	5	3		7	3	
Third class	3,508	1,517	656	2,459	4,324	
Total exclusive of season ticket holders	**3,513**	**1,520**	**656**	**2,466**	**4,327**	
Goods, mineral and livestock traffic						
Conveyed						
Merchandise	412	334	218	116	67	
Minerals	10,132	8,160	6,682	1,623	1,935	
Coal	3,153	2,303	1,844	1,956	796	
Total	**13,697**	**10,797**	**8,744**	**3,704**	**2,798**	
Originating						
Merchandise	184	193	78	29	1	
Minerals	10,132	8,135	6,679	1,590	1,935	
Coal	26	30	14	43	44	
Total	**10,342**	**8,358**	**6,771**	**1,662**	**1,980**	

Bibliography

Bishop, Michael; 'The Bruce Peebles affair and the birth of Russell'; *Welsh Highland Heritage*, No 29

Bishop, Michael; 'Lloyd George thought not ...'; *Welsh Highland Heritage*, No 36

Boyd, J. I. C.; *Festiniog Railway*; Oakwood Press, revised edition 1975

Boyd, J. I. C.; *Narrow Gauge Railways in North Caernarvonshire Vol 1 West*; Oakwood Press, 1981

Boyd, J. I. C.; *Narrow Gauge Railways in South Caernarvonshire*; Oakwood Press, 1988/9 (2 vols)

Bradley, V. J.; *Industrial Locomotives of North Wales*; Industrial Railway Society, 1992

David, Trefor; *Tickets of the North Wales Narrow Gauge Railways*; Welsh Highland Railway Heritage Group, 1999

Ellis, C. Hamilton & Lee, Charles E.B; 'The Welsh Highland Railway'; *Railway Magazine*; June, July, October 1941

Hopkins, John; Extracts from Journals – 1958-1990 [statements and comments relating to the WHR published by WHRL, the FR Society and the WHR Society]; unpublished manuscript, 1999

Hopkins, John; *Rheilffordd Eryri The Welsh Highland Railway 1991 to 2003*; Author, 4th edition 2003

Hopwood, H.L.; 'The North Wales Narrow Gauge Railway'; *The Railway Magazine*; July, 1917

Johnson, Peter; 'The Welsh Highland Railway – a narrow gauge epic', *Steam Railway*; January 1998

Johnson, Peter; *Portrait of the Welsh Highland Railway*; Ian Allan, 1999, revised 2000

Johnson, Peter; 'The Welsh Highland Railway: the way ahead', *Steam Railway*, No 250 (October 2000)

Johnson, Peter; 'Welsh Highland …the final instalment'*; Steam Railway*, No 301 (September 2004)

Johnson, Peter; 'Welsh Highland Railway – downhill all the way!'; *Steam Railway*, Nos 327/8 (September/October 2006)

Johnson, Peter; *An Illustrated History of the Festiniog Railway*; Oxford Publishing Co, 2007

Jones, Eric & Gwyn, David; *Dolgarrog – an industrial history*; Gwynedd Archives, 1989

Jones, Gwynfor Pierce & Richards, Alun John; *Cwm Gwyrfai – the quarries of the North Wales Narrow Gauge and the Welsh Highland Railways*; Gwasg Garreg Gwalch, 2004

Keylock, John; *The Welsh Highland Railway – a Historical Guide Part 1 – Caernarfon to Rhyd Ddu*; Welsh Highland Railway Heritage Group, 2005

Keylock, John; *The Welsh Highland Railway – a Historical Guide Part 2 – Rhyd Ddu to Porthmadog*; Welsh Highland Railway Heritage Group, 2008

Liddell, Peter; *The Buffet Car*; Welsh Highland Railway Heritage Group, 2007

Lystor, Derek & Keylock, John; *Tickets of the Welsh Highland Railway 1922-1936*; Welsh Highland Railway Heritage Group, 2007

Millard, Keith & Booth, Peter; *Welsh Highland Railway Rolling Stock Drawings*; 7mm Narrow Gauge Association

Moir, Sydney M. & Crittenden, H.T; *Namib Narrow Gauge*; Janus Publishing, 2nd edition 1982

Official Souvenir to the Snowdon & Welsh Highland Railways; British Publishing Co, no date

Richards, Alun John; *The Gazetteer of Slate Quarrying in Wales*; Gwasg Carreg Gwalch, revised edition, 2007

Rheilffordd Eryri The Welsh Highland Railway; Festiniog Railway Co, (1994)

Snowdon and Welsh Highland Holiday Book; Snowdon Mountain Tramroad & Hotels, 1923

Thomas, Dewi W.; *Hydro-electricity in North West Wales*; National Power plc, 1997

Vignes, Edouard (English translation by D. A. Boreham); *A Technical Study of the Festiniog & Other Narrow-Gauge Railways*; 1878, P. E. Waters & Associates, 1986

'The Welsh Highland Railway'; *The Railway Magazine*, December 1923

'The Welsh Highland Railway – the Ffestiniog Railway's proposals'; Festiniog Railway Co, 1992

Websites
http://whr.bangor.ac.uk – the official construction site
http://www.welshhighlandrailway.net – the operating site

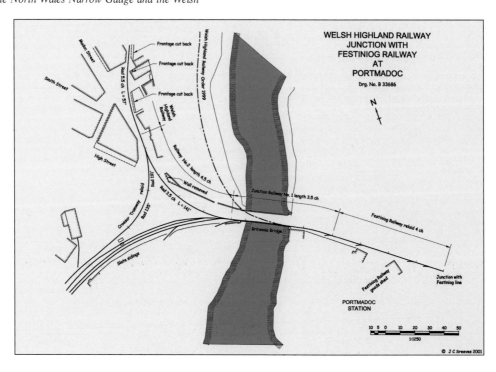

Index

Abandonment Order
Beddgelert Railway 11
WHR 91, 97, 100
Aberglaslyn Pass 24, 29, 31, 33, 35, 36, 38, 45, 55, 61, 72, 89, 105, 120, 132
AWCR 10, 11, 12, 74
Acts of Parliament
AWCR 1861 10, 11, 74
AWCR (New Lines) 1862 74
Beddgelert Railway 1865 10, 14, 15
Beddgelert Railway 1866 10, 11
Carnarvon & Llanberis Railway Extension 1865 9
Carnarvonshire Railway 1862 9, 74
Carnarvonshire Railway (Nantlle Railway Transfer) 1867 11-2, 27
Croesor & Portmadoc Railway 1865 10, 12, 74
Gorsedda (sic) Junction and Portmadoc Railways 1872 33
Light Railways 1896/1912 36, 45, 53, 90, 97, 100
Nantlle Railway 1825 9
North Wales Electric Power 1904 34
NWNGR 1872 11-13
NWNGR (Lease) 1873 14
NWNGR 1876 14, 17
NWNGR (Extensions &c) 1885 19, 25, 27-8
NWNGR 1890 29-30
Portmadoc, Croesor and Beddgelert Tram Railway 1879 23-4
PBSSR 1901 23, 24, 32-3, 35, 37, 53, 59, 83, 100
PBSSR 1904 28, 34, 37
Railways 1921 42, 49, 56
Regulation of railways 1889 28-30, 40-1
Ruthin & Cerrig y Druidion Railway 1876/1884 15
Advertising 30
Afon Glaslyn 9, 33, 35, 57, 58, 117
Aitchison, Gowrie Colquhoun 30, 34, 36, 38, 39, 40-1, 42, 43, 53, 94, 114
Alfred County Railway 123
Aluminium Corporation 40, 43, 46, 47, 49, 60, 63, 67, 69, 71, 83
Austen, W.H. 77, 81
Beddgelert 9-13, 23, 24, 27, 29-33, 35-37, 42, 45, 48, 50, 54, 56-58, 74, 96-7, 99, 111, 113, 115-118, 134
Beddgelert Forest 91, 97
Beddgelert Railway 10, 14, 15, 31, 100, 117
Beddgelert Siding 10, 34, 37
Bettws & Festiniog Railway 11
Bettws Garmon 9, 37, 69, 99, 109, 132
Bettws y Coed 12, 15, 35, 53
Birmingham Locomotive Club 122
Blaenau Ffestiniog 9, 48, 62, 83, 102
Board of Trade 6, 11, 16, 23, 28, 30, 35-38, 40-1, 45, 47, 99
Borth y Gest 10, 32
Branch Nominees 63
Breese, Major Charles 32, 50-1, 63, 94
Bridges
Afon Dylif 55, 89, 132, 133
Afon Nanmor 55, 89, 132
Britannia 10, 58, 60, 62, 67, 71, 119
Bryn y Felin 55, 58, 73, 116, 120, 132
Glanyrafon 21, 23, 95, 132
Nantmor 55, 132
Plas y Nant 132
British Railways 99, 100
British Transport Commission 51
Brown, Marshalls & Co 19
Bryngwyn 6, 12, 36
Bryn y Felin 13, 31, 109
Cae Moel 108, 132
Cae'r Gors 114, 120, 133
Caernarfon 6, 53, 83, 96-7, 99, 102-3, 106, 108, 111, 113, 127
Caernarfon Castle 6, 41, 42, 103, 105
Caernarvonshire Crown Slate Quarries Co 77, 81
Cambrian News 60, 62
Cambrian Railways 10-2, 23, 32-4, 43, 45, 50, 58

Cambrian siding 32, 99-100
Carnarvon 6, 9, 27, 32, 34-36, 38, 40-5, 48, 49, 50-2, 57-8, 77, 90
Carnarvon, Beddgelert & Port Madoc & Pen y Groes and Pwllheli & Nantlle District Railways 9, 11
Carnarvon & Denbigh Herald 60, 65
Carnarvon Harbour Trust 38, 40, 44, 53, 57
Carnarvonshire County Council 6, 7, 35, 44, 46-9, 57, 63, 73, 77, 81, 88-9, 92-3, 95-7, 99, 100
Carnarvonshire Railway 6, 9, 11-2, 74
Car parking 76, 96, 97
Cleminson, James 23
Coal merchant 55, 75
Coggins, J. H. W. 81, 89
Cohen, George, Sons & Co 77, 90, 92-3, 123
Colley, Crossley 69, 93, 94
Construction (1997-2009) 104-5, 107-9, 111, 119, 130, 132-5
Contractors 108, 132
Controversy 102, 103-4, 105-6, 109, 111
Crick, A. G. 62
Cread Mountaineering Club 96-7
Croesor 9, 10, 43
Croesor & Portmadoc Railway 10, 11, 12, 13, 54
Croesor Junction 47, 88, 91, 105
Croesor Tramway 6, 7, 9-11, 15-6, 23, 31-33, 35, 43, 45, 48-9, 55, 59, 63, 64, 74, 76, 91, 95
Crosville Motor Services 83, 90
Crown Estates 16, 28, 77, 85
Cwm Bychan 38
Cwm Dyli 33, 45
Cwm Cloch 29, 56, 58, 73-4, 80-1, 95, 114, 117
Daily Telegraph 100
Darbishire, William Arthur 27, 36
Davies, Cynon E. 83, 88-9, 90, 93
Davies, Evan & Co 63, 69, 94
Davies, Evan R. 33, 44-7, 50-1, 53, 57-60, 69, 71, 75, 77-9, 83, 93-4, 114
Davies, Ninian Rhys 94
Davies, Richard 31, 35
Davies, Walter Cradoc 52, 57, 78-81, 88, 93
Deudraeth RDC 35, 50, 52, 55, 63, 76, 88, 91
de Winton & Co 36, 105
Dinas 6, 9, 34, 37, 50-1, 57, 62, 83, 102, 104, 106, 108, 110, 113, 123
Dolgarrog 33, 43, 47, 63, 71, 83
Druitt, Major E. 30, 31
Dwyfor District Council 102
Edgehill Light Railway 91
Electric Conversion Syndicate 34
Electricity generation 25, 32, 33
Electrification 32-8
Ellis, Clough Williams 88
Enthusiast events 112, 114
Evans, Robert 63, 71, 74, 79, 81, 89
Eve, Mr Justice 73
Excess Insurance Co 37
Fairlie, Robert 14
Festiniog Railway 6, 7, 9-11, 13, 15-6, 23, 27, 32-34, 40, 41, 43, 49-51, 57-8, 60, 62-3, 67, 69-70, 79, 81, 83, 91, 93, 96, 99, 123
Blaenau Festiniog 65, 79
Boston Lodge 7, 15, 58, 124, 128, 131
Glan y Pwll 123, 127
Inspection 61
Junction railways 60-2, 64, 71, 88, 93, 95
Minffordd 34
Portmadoc 67
Rolling stock 60, 70, 83
Tan y Bwlch 62
WHR restoration 104-120
1923 station 58-9, 61, 66, 71, 81, 88, 98
Festiniog Railway Co 7, 46-7, 62, 71, 73, 75, 77-8, 81, 88-90, 93-4, 101-2, 104-7, 114
Festiniog Railway Society 96, 103
Festiniog Railway Trust 7, 102-3, 106, 113-4
Ffestiniog Railway (Holdings) Ltd 103, 108
Foot & Mouth disease 109
Footpath 89, 91, 92, 95-7, 100

Fox, Douglas, & Partners 35, 36, 38, 53-4, 57-60, 62-3, 67
Fox, Sir Douglas 34
Fox, Francis 38
Freeman, Ralph 57, 59, 93, 94
Funding 109-112, 114
Gaumont News 56
George, David Lloyd 7, 33, 36, 38, 44, 69, 83
George, William 30, 32, 44, 50, 56, 59, 92, 94
Glaslyn Foundry 56, 65
Glaslyn RDC 44, 47, 50, 52, 56, 63, 76
Goat Hotel 25, 29, 31, 34-5, 38, 55, 57, 60-1, 65, 73-4, 96
Gorseddau Railway 10-12, 31-3, 59
Grant, Baron Albert 13, 27
Grant Brothers 13, 14, 17, 27
Green, J. R. 97, 99
Great Western Railway 7, 48, 53, 58-9, 62-4, 73-6, 89
Crossing 7, 60-1, 64-5, 66-7, 73-5, 88, 99
Griffith, Richard Thomas 76-7, 79, 81, 90
Gwarchod 106
Gwredog Isaf 107, 127
Gwynedd Archives 6, 7
Gwynedd Council 106, 109
Gwynedd County Council 100, 102-4, 109
Gwynedd Rivers Authority 95-6
Gwyrfai RDC 44, 50, 52, 56-7, 63, 96
Gwyrfai Terrace 99
Gwyrfai Valley 9, 108
Hafod Ruffydd 37, 93
Hafod y Llan (Snowdon) Slate Co 10, 11, 13
Hafod y Llan farm 65, 117
Hafod y Llyn 97
Halts 11-3, 115
Harper Bothers & Co 33-8
Hart, Michael C. 114, 130
Haworth & Walsh 73
Hen Hafod 118
High Court 93, 103
Historic Houses Hotels 109, 129
Honychurch, R.G. 97, 114
Hughes, John Sylvester 33, 40
Hunslet Engine Co 77
Hurcomb, Cyril 51, 52, 58
Huson, William Richard 58, 67, 69, 70
Hutchinson, General Charles Scrope 29
Iggulden, J. A. 76, 77, 90
Inland Revenue 69-70
Inquiry 32, 35-6, 49-50, 56-9, 103, 105, 106
Inspection 105, 111
Investing authorities 56, 60, 67, 73, 76-8, 81, 88-9, 94, 97, 100
Inspection 105, 111
Jack, Henry Joseph 46-8, 50-3, 57-60, 71, 83, 93, 114
Jones, D. G. 76-7
Jones, D. O. 76, 79
Jones, Major E. Bowen 54, 63
Jones, Miriam 75
Jones, T.D. 7, 90, 91, 94
Kellow, Moses 63, 76
Kent & East Sussex Light Railway 94
Kinnerley 97
Law Debenture Society 38-9
Leek & Manifold Light Railway 88
LeFevre 7, 11,
Light Railway Commission 31, 32, 35-6, 38, 44, 52, 58, 60
Light Railway Orders
Caernarfon Railway 1997 104, 105, 106
The Beddgelert Siding 1980 100
Festiniog Railway (Light Railway) 1923 58, 60
NWNGR (Beddgelert Light Railway Extension) 1900 29, 31-5, 37
NWNGR 1905 35
PBSSR (Beddgelert Light Railway Extension) 1906 34-7, 53
PBSSR (Light Railway Extension at Carnarvon) 1908 36-7, 53
PBSSR 36-7, 40
WHR 1922 47, 49-50, 52-3, 56
WHR Amendment 1923 56, 58
The WHR (Transfer) 1995 103-4

Light Railway Order applications
Penmachno, Corwen & Bettws Light Railway 35
Pont Croesor 102
Portmadoc, Beddgelert & Rhyd Ddu Railway 31
Portmadoc, Beddgelert & Snowdon Light Railway 31
PBSSR (Light Railway) & NWNGR (Light Railways) Revival and Transfer of Powers 44, 47, 53, 83
Pwllheli & Nevin Light Railway 32
Pwllheli, Nevin & Porth Dinlleyn Light Railway 32
Pwllheli, Nevin & Porth Dinlleyn Railway 1903 32
Snowdon & Bettws y Coed Light Railway 28, 34-6, 38
Light Railways Investigation Committee 42-3
Liverpool Daily Post 91
Livesey, R. H. 21, 23-4, 27-8
Llanwnda 12, 15-6, 99
Llyn Dinas 10, 33
Llyn Eigiau 33
Llyn Gwynant 11, 32-3, 53
Llyn Llydaw 33
Locomotives
Alco 2-6-2T *Mountaineer* (57156/1916) 105, 125
Avonside Engine Co 0-4-4-0T *James Spooner* (Avonside 1872) 57, 66, 82
Bagnall 0-4-2T *Gelert* (3050/1953) 101, 114
Baldwin 4-6-0PT 590 (45172/1917) 59, 63-5, 68, 73, 75, 80-1, 122, 124-6
Baldwin tractor 4wDM (49604/1918) 70, 122, 126
Beyer, Peacock 0-4-4-0 K1 (5292/1909) 115, 127
Beyer, Peacock 2-6-2+2-6-2 NGG16
No 138 (7865/1958) 106, 110, 112, 127
No 140 (7865/1958) 123-4, 127
No 143 (7868/1958) 109-13, 115-6, 118, 127, 131
Cockerill 2-6-2+2-6-2 NGG16
No 87 (3267/1937) 124, 128
Dick, Kerr 4wPE 46, 121
England 0-4-0STT *Palmerston* (1863) 7, 15-6, 114, 120, 121
England 0-4-0STT *Prince* (1864) 59, 62, 82, 84, 111-2, 114, 120, 127
England 0-4-0STT *Princess* (1864) 59, 62, 65
England 0-4-0STT *Welsh Pony* (234/1867) 68
England 0-4-0STT *Little Giant* (235/1867) 59
FR 0-4-4-0T *Livingston Thompson* (1885) 60
FR 0-4-4-0T *Merddin Emrys* (1879) 60, 124
Franco-Belge 2-8-0 NG 15
No 133 (2685/1952) 124
No 134 (2684/1952) 124-5
Funkey 4w-4wDH *Castell Caernarfon* 104-5, 116, 123
Ganz electric locomotives 36, 39-40, 121
Hunslet 0-6-4ST *Beddgelert* (206/1878) 18, 20, 121
Hunslet 2-4-0STT *Blanche* (589/1993) 122, 125
Hunslet 2-6-2T *Russell* (901/1906) 6, 39, 47, 58, 63, 65, 67, 71, 75, 77-8, 80-2, 84, 86, 101, 121-2, 124
Hunslet 0-6-4T *Gowrie* (979/1908) 26, 42-3, 121-2, 125
Hunslet 4w *Harold* (7195/1974) 130
Kerr, Stuart 6wDM (4415/1928) 123, 126
Lister 4wDM (56371/1970) 118
Motor Rail 4wDM *Dolgarrog* (22154/1962) 111
Peckett 0-4-2T *Karen* (2024/1942) 98
Planet 4wDM *Upnor Castle* (3687/1954) 111, 114, 130, 134
Planet 4wDM *Conway Castle* (3831/1958) 111, 114, 130

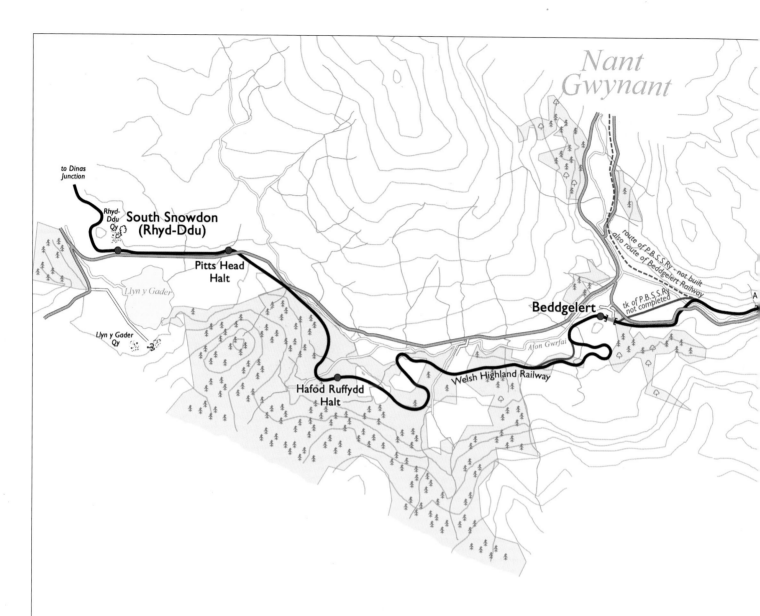

Nant Gwynant

to Dinas Junction

Rhyd-Ddu Qy

South Snowdon (Rhyd-Ddu)

Pitts Head Halt

Llyn y Gader

Llyn y Gader Qy

Hafod Ruffydd Halt

route of P.B.S.S.Ry - not built
also route of Beddgelert Railway

tk of P.B.S.S.Ry not completed

Beddgelert

Afon Gwrfai

Welsh Highland Railway

A

The Welsh Highland Railway
(Light Railway) Co in 1922

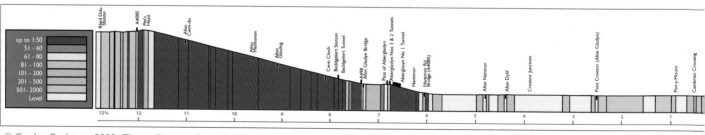

up to 1:50
51 - 60
61 - 80
81 - 100
101 - 200
201 - 500
501- 2000
Level

Rhyd Ddu Station

A4085 Pitt's Head

Afon Cwm-du

Afon Meillionen

Afon Glochg

Cwm Cloch
Beddgelert Tunnel
Beddgelert Station

A498 Afon Glaslyn Bridge

Pass of Aberglaslyn
Aberglaslyn Nos 3 & 2 Tunnels

Aberglaslyn No 1 Tunnel

Nanmor

Nanmor Rd Bridge (A4085)

Afon Nanmor

Afon Dylif

Croesor Junction

Pont Croesor (Afon Glaslyn)

Pen-y-Mount

Cambrian Crossing

12¾   12   11   10   9   8   7   6   5   4   3   2   1